A Bridge to the Mainland

VERONICA KNIGHT

Copyright © 2021 Veronica Knight.

All rights reserved. No part of this book may be reproduced, stored, or transmitted by any means—whether auditory, graphic, mechanical, or electronic—without written permission of both publisher and author, except in the case of brief excerpts used in critical articles and reviews. Unauthorized reproduction of any part of this work is illegal and is punishable by law.

ISBN: 978-1-948928-05-2 (sc)
ISBN: 978-1-948928-23-6 (hc)
ISBN: 978-1-948928-26-7 (e)

Because of the dynamic nature of the Internet, any web addresses or links contained in this book may have changed since publication and may no longer be valid. The views expressed in this work are solely those of the author and do not necessarily reflect the views of the publisher, and the publisher hereby disclaims any responsibility for them.

CONTENTS

Acknowledgments vii
Foreword ix
A Bridge to the Mainland...xi

Chapter 1   My Background...1
Chapter 2   Moving Away to The Far South.....................8
Chapter 3   House in The Woods....................................20
Chapter 4   Summers at My Grandparents 28
Chapter 5   Going Back Home 33
Chapter 6   Becoming a Woman 40
Chapter 7   Trouble at Home... 46
Chapter 8   The Year My World Changed 52
Chapter 9   Meeting Brent..57
Chapter 10 Dad's Missing...62
Chapter 11 Goodbye Brent 69
Chapter 12 Betty is Gone..80
Chapter 13 Hiding Behind My Toe 88
Chapter 14 Visiting with Dad..94
Chapter 15 Becoming A Mother 107
Chapter 16 My Secret Doctor 126
Chapter 17 Goodbye Gram 151
Chapter 18 Escaping The House 161

Chapter 19 My Hospital Escape 171
Chapter 20 Coming Out 213
Chapter 21 The Shark is Gone 248
Chapter 22 Facing Reality 268
Chapter 23 Finding the Mainland 283

I dedicate this book to *Dr. Arielle Kogan*. When I was lost, confused, and scared, she knew just what to say for my world to come together again. I will be eternally grateful to Arielle Words are inadequate to express my appreciation and love for her.

To the editors of the book

These two friends, Sherry and Martha,
have my love and gratitude.
They encouraged me and helped me get
this book out when I could not.

ACKNOWLEDGMENTS

FOR MY DEAR, kind, and thoughtful husband, I love you with my very being. I appreciate your kindness, thoughtfulness, your generosity, but most of all, for the love you have shown me throughout the years. When we met, you said we were going to grow old together. Well, honey, we have, and I have been honored to be your wife. I love the way you love me and have faith and trust in me. Thank you for encouraging me to write this book and thank you for your patience all these years. I knew you the night I met you, and you have not disappointed me.

FOREWORD

I FIRST MET VERONICA in 1975 while working at a large southern medical center on the inpatient psychiatry unit. Veronica was admitted to our service, exhibiting severe headaches, depression, and a dependency on prescribed opioid medications. At the time of her admission, it was astonishing that she was functioning at such a high level socially as well as professionally given the frequency and high dosage of medications she was consuming.

For two months, I worked daily with Veronica on an individual basis under the supervision of the attending psychiatrist. She experienced multiple personal sufferings during her initial treatment period. We have continued to work together on an outpatient basis and then on an ad-hoc basis for the last forty-plus years.

Veronica learned to adjust and accept unamendable and oftentimes trying demands on her life without compromise to her own values. She made difficult life decisions that oftentimes seemed to threaten the very same values she held so close.

This is a book about a woman who experienced childhood trauma, domestic violence and abuse, substance dependence, and depression. She lost her home, family, children, and herself for a period of time. More importantly, it is a book about a woman of tremendous strength, courage, determination, love, and resilience. It is a story of hope for other women who find themselves in a situation that feels hopeless. This woman has not only survived but she also has thrived since she found her true self and took control of her life.

Recently, I had the opportunity to visit with Veronica, review a draft of her book, and discuss our shared experiences. I found the memories and facts set forth in the draft consistent with my own recollection of the events.

I recommend this book not only for its literary merits but also as an example of how life struggles are oftentimes not unidimensional or short term. This book provides an opportunity to see how one person gained success by making a lifelong commitment to understanding herself, giving herself and others grace and compassion and owning her own ability and power to engage in a different, more meaningful, and happy existence.

I am deeply grateful for all the knowledge and wisdom that Veronica has afforded me by allowing me to accompany her on her life's journey. She has enabled me to help countless other women in their journeys as well.

Dr. Arielle Kogan, PhD, LCSW

Virginia

A BRIDGE TO THE MAINLAND

By Veronica Knight

I LOOKED OUT THE airplane window and down to the ground below. Everything looked so neat, like a large quilt. I witnessed patches of land, property so evenly blocked off in squares, and other shapes. Roads, straight and narrow with purpose. Yet, I thought how deceiving this is in so many ways. Most lives lack such order. People run here and there, trying to find contentment. Many individuals live in confusion and search for something, not knowing what. But, just as the roads lead somewhere, so do our lives, and we are at the controls. Our lives have a purpose, a direction, and a reason. I believe this trip is taking me where my life, from the time I was born, was being led. I feel one of my purposes in life, was to write this book, in an attempt to reach others, who have not been as fortunate as I, in receiving help. At the end of this trip, I will be stepping back into my past, staying in a town near where I was raised, in order to write my story.

Many people have feelings that they are not aware of, as was in my case. These feelings may manifest themselves physically. While I was at a major medical facility, many patients came in with physical complaints, many serious, only to find out they stemmed from emotional problems. Suppressed feelings cause depression. Only one who has experienced severe depression can verify the depths to which one's soul can plunge, even to the point of being unable to function physically or mentally. Unless people recognize their feelings, and understand them, they are helpless.

It is my hope that by sharing my experiences with you, in story form, you may also feel the fear, hurt, anger and rejection, joy and finally "insight" I felt. If this should be, then you may have been touched by your sub-conscience, which is the very powerful and knowing element of you. The sub-conscience controls our behavior and us, as I was forced to find out. Perhaps you will find yourself somewhere in these pages. By recognizing the uncomfortable feelings within yourself, you will be encouraged to make those changes in your life that will serve to make living more comfortable. Many individuals feel trapped in their lives and don't know what direction to take. Some do not have the courage to change. These people are not only trapped in their life situations, but are trapped within themselves, unable to express how they really feel.

My sincere hope is that in some way, by my sharing my story, a factual account of my life, it may enlighten yours and give you the courage and confidence to make a change for the better, in the areas that you want to improve.

I have changed the names of places and characters in my book, in order to preclude any uncomfortable situations.

Suddenly, I was startled, as a commanding voice said,

"Fasten your seat belts please. We will be landing shortly." I took a deep breath...

At the end of this trip, I will be stepping back into my past. I will be staying at a small motel across from the medical center where I was a patient for 8 weeks a few years ago. Just twenty miles away, is the town I grew up in and where the nightmare occurred.

As I stepped from the airplane, it seemed strange to be back where so much had happened in the state where I was raised from the age of eight. I am now thirty-nine. I left two years ago. So much has changed.

I returned to the town where, with the help of a psychoanalyst and many others, at a well-known hospital, I found out about myself and received life-saving help. I received treatment for two years as an inpatient and as an outpatient. It was truly a blessing for me that the hospital was interested in my case and took me on as a "case history patient." I could have never afforded the care and help I received. It was suggested, by some of the doctors, that perhaps I could share my treatment with others, those patients who were not as fortunate as I, in receiving this priceless care. It has taken me many, many years to complete this book, but finally it is happening.

I thoughtfully walked from the plane thinking my son Tony is in this town too. The reality of it washed up into my face like a gush of cold wind. Even on that warm night tears stung my face. He was so close and yet I could not reach him. Just down the street, he lay in a children's hospital, crippled from a traffic accident that happened almost a year ago. It was almost too much to take in, the reality of it all.

Has it really been four years since I was a patient here? Has it been two years since I last saw my two older sons, mother, sister and close friends? I left town so hurriedly back then I was only able to take my youngest son and a few belongings.

Stepping out of the plane from one world into another, I was afraid. I told myself, there is unfinished business here. This is what I need to do in order to be free of the past. It seemed the past would not leave me, even in my dreams. It was always there. I wanted to be rid of the bad feelings and I had to see Tony, no matter what. He was my son. I loved him dearly and I missed him more than I could ever possibly explain. Nothing was going to stop me from seeing him, this time. I took a deep breath and walked with determination towards the waiting room, suddenly strong and confident.

My eyes searched for the friend who was to pick me up. I saw her familiar face from across the room and it was welcomed. We hugged and kissed. Holly's son and mine had been friends since they were toddlers and we were neighbors. The boys were now fourteen years old. She too, had lost her son to her ex-husband. We understood each other's feelings very well. Holly helped me with my suitcases and we proceeded to the place where I was to stay. No one was to know that I was here, just 30 miles away from my hometown. It wasn't safe for me. I was determined to mostly stay in my room, working on my book and just visit with my therapist and my doctor. They had encouraged me to write this book and I needed them now to help me verify some of my writings. Also, there is much information at this hospital and in this town that I want to include in my story, especially concerning my son, Tony being a very important part. I hoped to help Tony in some way, as I felt so helpless since his accident.

My son Tony, not knowing why his father and I had divorced, was angry with me for divorcing his father and wouldn't talk to me. He was just a child. I could not tell him the real reason. I didn't want to talk badly about his father. His Dad was very important to him. I was the "bad guy."

What made it so hard now was Tony's accident. He was playing at the railroad tracks with two of his friends. They were playing a game of jumping on the freight train when it showed down coming through town. They would ride the train for a distance and then jump off. This time it was going faster than usual and when Tony jumped on the train, he slipped, but his shirt caught on a part of the train. The train dragged Tony for a distance, until his shirt ripped off and he fell. Just writing this I can only imagine the horror of what he experienced. He had a concussion, a broken neck and a severed spinal cord. It was a miracle he had lived and did not have any brain damage.

Up to this moment, my ex-husband's actions have prevented me from having any direct contact with my son or visiting him in the hospital. I have been very concerned about Tony and what he was thinking or feeling, as he tells no one. He must think I don't care to come. He doesn't know that his father threatened to take his brother from me, if I came. I'll get into more of this later in the book.

I knew from past experience, how important it was for him to have both parents that were concerned and that he was aware that he was loved, and cared for. I was put in a position that I had to choose between two sons. How can a mother do that? To me, it was impossible. I needed to be with Tony as he was hurt and I needed to protect the young son that I had with me. I was warned not to go to the hospital to see him or I would be sorry. I'll explain more of this later also. This was my worst nightmare ever - not being with my son. I felt like I was being torn in two.

As we drove from the airport, so much raced through my head. Holly assured me again that she wouldn't tell anyone that I was here, as she knew I was going to try to see Tony. She understood. She too had run away from her abusive husband. Unfortunately, he found her.

I knew my ex-husband had been looking for me too, in hopes of taking my youngest son away from me. He had always told me if I ever left him, I would not get the children and he would stop at nothing to get them. I had waited eighteen years before I had the courage to leave him. What he had promised came true with the exception of my youngest Roy who was now twelve years old. I just felt it best not to tell anyone of my being close to my hometown, for the time being, until I was ready to leave. I needed this private time to concentrate on the book alone.

My plan was that just before returning home out West, I would attempt to contact my son's doctor. My greatest hope was to see Tony. I had to handle it very carefully. Above all, Ronald must not know I was here. How was it possible to safely accomplish all I wanted to do? Still afraid of him and what he was capable of, I reminded myself to take one step at a time. I prayed for guidance. I had missed Tony so. Deep down I felt he wanted to see me too, although he had never said he did. I was his mother. Didn't that mean something?

Holly and I pulled up in front of the motel. The 'No Vacancy' sign was out. I held my breath hoping the old gentleman I spoke to had indeed kept my room. There were not but two motels within walking distance to the hospital where I would be visiting every day, so I was relieved to find that a room had been held for me. I unlocked the door to the room and gave a little laugh and said,

"You know Holly, I stayed here in this motel twenty one years ago on my honeymoon. "Oh no," she said, won't that bother you staying here."?

I smiled and said, "not at all, it seems to me as though it never was. Isn't that strange? I don't feel like the same person I was back then, and you know, really, I'm not."

I was so young and inexperienced. I had just turned eighteen and felt so grown up, when really I knew nothing about life.

"Can you believe I was a virgin after three years of going with Ronald?" It seemed so important to me that I waited.

"I remember feelings, even back then, I wasn't sure I wanted to marry him, but he loved me and I wanted to leave home so much. I thought marriage was my only way out. I didn't know there were other options, and that I was stepping into something much worse. Truly, I had nothing to compare it to. Ronald was as inexperienced as I."

Holly just looked at me.

I smiled and said, "Well not quite as much as I."

I knew her feelings on that, as she had told me often in the past. "You know," I continued. "Even as the years went by, I didn't realize I was so deeply depressed. I had felt so obligated to marry him. I didn't know all the reasons why until I came here to the hospital. Here I learned to have the courage to leave."

Suddenly, I realized I was rambling on and said in a much lighter note, "No, it doesn't bother me to stay here."

Holly hugged me in that reserved manner of hers. I appreciated her friendship so much, as I did my other close friends. They were the ones who stood by me when my own family did not.

The motel was badly in need of repairs. The sidewalk was cracked and paint peeling off the walls. I looked at the small, cramped, dark room I would be spending my time in for the next three weeks. The old furniture smelled musty, but the room looked clean. The furnishings consisted of a double bed with a green bedspread, two end tables, a chair and a television set. A small bathroom led off the bedroom. I did not need much room to write. I was glad the room was small. It seemed cozier. I liked the idea that I would be alone with my thoughts for a while, that I might write them as I intended. I needed this alone time. My son, Roy had stayed back home with Cliff where he was safe. I appreciated the relationship they had. Cliff cared very much for Roy and took good care of him in my absence. I had married a good man.

I would be seeing Dr. D. and Arielle everyday to discuss what I was writing about my experiences while there at the hospital, and what had transpired over the last few years since I left town. That was part of the agreement in them seeing me as a case history. I learned from them, but they also learned more about my experience, which helped them with others in similar situations. I had kept in touch with Arielle over the phone the past few years and I really missed her. I felt very fortunate to have their help as well as their interest in me. To this day, I thank God for sending me to them. I know without a doubt He had a hand in this. He knew I needed help here on earth. I had never written a book before.

I said goodbye to Holly and promised to call her before I left. I was sleepy on the airplane and could not wait until I was at the motel. I could go to bed and sleep. Now, I am filled with so much anxiety, rest is impossible. Unpacking, I caught myself sitting on the bed from time to time, thinking, where do I start? I had never written a book before, but felt I could. I felt frustrated because I wanted to begin right away. Tonight. I told myself, now Veronica, don't be so impatient with yourself. Give yourself a chance to adjust. Adjust is a word I am familiar with. I walked outside and down to the small office. The light was still on, so I knew the elderly man was still up. When he answered the door, I asked him if he would hook up the switchboard again so I could make a long distance call. I ran back to the room and dialed my home number. The phone rang once, then twice.

"Hello" my son, Roy said. He sounded so near. Not 3,000 miles away.

"Hello, honey. How are you doing," I asked.

"Fine mom. Thanks for the gift and note. I found it when I came home from school."

He sounded so grown up and so dear to me.

"Be good and help Cliff all you can. He needs your help now, okay?" I said.

"Okay, Mom. He is right here waiting to talk with you." Roy said. Cliff came to the phone and said,

"Hi, Hon." Found your note you left in the cabinets. It was good getting it."

I had left them both little love notes in various places that they would find from time to time.

"I want you to take all the time you need and you are not to worry about a thing here. Roy and I will get along just fine." Cliff stated.

I was very grateful for my kind, understanding and patient husband. The last few years have been very rough on us emotionally. So much had happened. It was he that finally said,

"I am calling the airport to get you reservations so you can go and start writing on your book, and I know Tony has been on your mind too. You need to go and take care of these things. It's overdue."

He had never discouraged me but was always encouraging. I just felt it hard to leave him and Roy. I worried about Roy being taken by his father while I was away, but knew I couldn't be with him all the time. I had legal custody of Roy in the state we lived in, but knew that wouldn't stop my ex-husband. He stopped at nothing to get what he wanted since I left him.

When I left Cliff at the airport, I had many mixed emotions and was choking back the tears when I said to him.

"I feel like I am going on a mission." He looked at me and said, "You are,"

After hanging up the phone, I undressed and went to bed, but sleep would not come. I lay there thinking about the life I had back West. How different it was from the life I had in this town. With Cliff and my son, we were comfortable. I didn't have to worry about paying bills or having the necessities of life. I felt comfortable with Cliff emotionally too. I felt secure when he held me and secure that he loved me. He reminded me of my father and grandfather in many ways. He was much older than me, and I realized that he was a father figure in some ways, but our age difference didn't matter to me. He not only offered me a better life than I had before, he was also good to my son. I tried to be a good wife to him as well as a good mother to Roy.

Being here in this town, so many memories began to flood my mind. I didn't want to think of them, but they just kept coming. What hung over our heads constantly was the past and the ugliness we experienced here in our hometown where I returned. We had moved several times out West knowing my ex-husband was looking for Roy and me. I didn't know what to expect from him. He was capable of anything. I didn't want to think anymore.

I turned over and switched on the light beside the bed, deciding to read awhile. I picked up a book someone had given me at church. The titled read "Faith precedes the Miracle." What an appropriate title! How important faith is. To have faith in our Creator and through believing and understanding we can obtain faith within ourselves. I don't know what made me reach for the book before leaving home. It had been on the bookshelf for many months. I didn't seem I have the time to read it. I had it with me now, and read until I felt sleep overcoming me. I felt grateful.

I slept late into the next day and realized looking at the clock; it was too late to call Arielle, my counselor. She would be with patients at the hospital now. Arielle had given me her home number to call her if I felt it was urgent to talk with her or ask a question. I appreciated this and never wanted to take advantage of it, so I didn't use it often over the years. But it gave me a feeling of security knowing I could and she was there.

I dressed and walked over to the hospital. How enormous it seemed. The Medical Center is a beautiful teaching hospital and campus. The university is a well-known medical school throughout the world. I could see there were many more buildings than I remembered two years ago and a new parking garage. How time changes everything. As well as our environments, we too change over the years, our personal feelings, emotions, situations and our lifestyles. Our bodies begin to show age, as our minds grow in knowledge.

As in the past, I enjoyed the walk over to the beautiful, stone hospital. The walks curved gently around the large old trees. I loved the musky smell of the boxwood trees. It was springtime and all the plants and trees were coming to life showing their little leaves. In a way, it seemed like a new beginning for me too. I looked at the large hospital. I always stood in awe of it. So much takes place here every day and so much took place here a few years ago with me. I loved this medical center.

I found myself walking down the hospital hall to the elevator. I pushed the third floor button, as I did so many times in the past. I went to the nurse's station. They were busy, so I sat in the room where the patients congregated to visit, watch TV or play cards. How many times I sat in that room filled with fear and dreading when the nurse would come out and tell me it was my turn to see the doctor. Back then I was terrified of him, not really knowing why, as he did nothing physically to hurt me. But the anguish I felt, the emotions he stirred in me, were frightening. One of the patient's voices broke through my thoughts.

"No. Leave me alone." She was saying.

"But your doctor is only trying to help you", this nice looking woman was saying to this elderly lady. I guessed her to be a patient too.

The older woman in the wheelchair said,

"I don't care. He can't change me. That's how I am. All this worrying depresses me."

The younger woman spoke patiently,

"I think depression and worry are not the same thing. You can worry and not be depressed. You need to tell your doctor what you are worrying about. How can you be happy when you spend all of your time worrying?"

"It doesn't change anything." The old lady grumbled, "I can't help it."

Then with a wave of her hand, she added, "I don't want to talk anymore. Leave me alone."

She had tears in her eyes. How sad, I thought. I sat there and looked at her and wanted to say to her, "Listen to your doctor. He can help you." But I knew she wouldn't hear me. People have to open themselves to help, and she was not willing. She would most probably die lonely and alone, unhappy, as she probably was most of her life. I saw many like her, when I was here as a patient, older people so set in their ways, that they close their minds to any suggestions of help. All the hospital could do, in these cases, was to keep trying and give them medication to ease their pain and suffering.

I walked down to the office of one of the doctors, who had helped me a great deal, but at the time that I was a patient, I did not care for him. He conducted the group therapy sessions. Group therapy was hell to go through, but necessary for me, as I learned to express myself and found a better understanding of others and myself.

The doctor was just closing his office to go home. I walked up to him, feeling happy and confident for the first time since I arrived.

"Dr. Lee, it's me, Veronica," I said, and then realizing how I must have appeared to him, thinking that he did not recognize me, I started over, saying,

"I'm sorry. I was in your group therapy session four years ago."

He smiled and held out his hand, "Of course, I remember you." How have you been?" He asked in his strong Asian accent.

I reminded him of the day I finally broke down when realizing I had to end my marriage, and the fear I had of losing my children.

"They did blame me for the breakup, and my two oldest boys went to live with their father. But the good part is, "I've learned to cope without medication." I said happily.

He smiled and said, "I knew you could do it." You have always been a very strong woman, even though you did not think so."

I told him about the tragic accident my son Tony had and my not being able to see him.

"But I am learning to cope with that too." I added.

"Good for you." he said smiling.

I told him I was writing a book. I felt happy and pleased with myself in talking with him. This was quite different than before, when I was here as a patient. Then I was afraid and lonely, trusted no one and was only able to survive and cope with the aid of pills.

I had indeed come a long way.

Chapter 1

MY BACKGROUND

I WAS BORN IN New York, the eldest of four children. I have two sisters and a brother, and later a half-sister was born from my father's second marriage. I lived in New York for the first eight years of my life, and then my father's job transferred us to a small hosiery and cotton mill town in South Carolina.

From as far back as I can remember it was my grandmother, my mother's mother who supplied me with love and furnished the only happy memories I have of my childhood. Perhaps this is because my grandmother took care of me so much. My mother was only fifteen years old when she became pregnant with me. I remember my mother telling me this only when I accidently found the marriage certificate and then my birth certificate. When I was fifteen. I remember feeling upset and thinking, "maybe this is why I didn't feel loved by them. I wish I could have told someone how I felt all those years. I felt like I was a mistake. I didn't tell my Mom how I felt but wished I could have. I did ask her about it and she explained to me how they felt about each other when they met and that they were very much in love and wanted to marry, but their parents wouldn't let them because of their young age. She said they intentionally had sex to get pregnant, so they would have to marry. Of course both sets of grandparents had to agree to let them marry. Dad was just sixteen years old. They were still kids.

In view of the things that happened in my life regarding my mother and father, I can't help but wonder if her explanation was really the case, or rather was the pregnancy an accident and not planned. (Some years later as we were walking up the back stairs to my grandmother's kitchen, my Mom told me that those stairs were where I was conceived.) I don't believe I needed to know this, but I think she sometimes thought of me more as a sister than a daughter. I immediately retorted,

"Is that why I have always been your step child?

We laughed at my statement as I said it lightly and made a joke of it, but deep down I meant it. I could not help but wonder if it was an accident and that maybe later on they resented being tied down so young and did she resent the responsibilities at such a young age. Then I reminded myself that my parents had three more after me, all of us being born very close together. By the time Mom was twenty-two, she had four little ones.

Maybe this is why I can't think of any good childhood memories regarding my mother I am very sad to say. I think Mom tried to do the right things, like birthdays and kissing us goodnight, but her heart didn't seem to be in it. Mom always did come to our bed and kiss us goodnight with, "Sleep tight, don't let the bedbugs bite."

I wish I had this attention during the day, but as a child, I didn't understand her frustrations and always saying to me go outside and play.

The one lingering feeling I remember regarding my mother was my fear that I would anger her. I did not realize the source of this until years later in psychotherapy, when it came to me that this fear stemmed from an isolated incident that occurred when I was about 3 years old. I have no memory of my mother physically abusing me, and I had always believed that I was extremely close to my mother, especially as an adult. I always sought her approval. I loved her and would do anything for her attention. Much later in life, it came out why I felt so controlled by her.

It took many years to understand and to try to remember what occurred on that day in the kitchen when I was just three. All I could remember was my mother being so out of control and screaming. I remember she was smoking a cigarette and I must have asked her about it and it really set her off. She came at me with it and tried to put it in my mouth. I guess I asked at the wrong time. I didn't know what she was going through, being a child and thought it was something I had done or said.

All I knew for sure was, don't make Mom mad EVER! SO I always did what she wanted me too throughout most of my adulthood. I never spoke back or disagreed with her, except one time, which reminded me why I never would. The result of my doing so, was grave.

Not long before my mother passed, she told me what happened back then, not realizing I remember how upset she was and how I felt about it. Mom told me about a friend she had invited to stay with us at home to help her get on her feet. Her name was Bessie. (She didn't know I remembered that name. It was burned into my mind from back then.) I said nothing and just listened. She said Bessie slept downstairs on the couch and she and Dad slept upstairs. She woke one night to find Dad not in bed. Mom went searching for him and found him on the couch with Bessie. They were making love.

Oh, my gosh, that was it! It wasn't me! Mom had found Dad having sex with her best friend. No wonder she was upset. I probably just asked her a stupid question at the moment her world was falling apart. Like a lot of children would, I took the blame. Now, being an adult I could understand why she was so upset. How many children base their life's reactions on a single incident that is planted in their brain at a tender age? It is very sad.

I do have memories of my father. He always stood out as the most prominent figure in my life, even into my adult years. To me, he was a king. I don't know when I started trying for his love and approval, I have no doubt, it was at an early age. I mostly tried to stay out of his way, because I was scared of him. I know, this is a contradiction, when I say how much he meant to me. He was the one who punished and spanked me. Yet, I wanted his affection and tried for this from a distance. I wanted so much for him to take me in his arms and hold me. I saw pictures of other little girls sitting on their father's lap and this is what I wanted too; but I didn't have the courage to go to him. Much later, as an adult I had a better understanding of things. I started remembering positive things about him I could interpret as love. But as a child, to be hugged and kissed meant love. That is all I understood. Sadly, these feelings stayed with me much too long.

I don't know when or why exactly I started keeping feelings to myself. One thing I knew for sure was not to cry, and not to show anger. I learned at a young age, these were two things that upset my parents and I didn't want to anger them. I was to set a good example to my brother and sisters, since I was the oldest. If I was afraid of anything, I was being silly. I tried to keep my fears to myself.

The first house I remember living in was a pretty white house with shutters and a small back porch off the kitchen. I remember laying in my youth bed peeking through the bars at my father going upstairs into the attic. I didn't know what was up there. I wanted to go with him. I was around three then. I was thrilled and loved what I saw when he allowed me into the attic with him. It was a whole new world. Dad had built a miniature town with a train running through it. It was beautiful! There were houses, cars, streets and little people. I was fascinated by it all. My father would allow me to sit and watch him operate his trains, as long as I was quiet and didn't touch anything. This make believe world made such an impression on me, that later in life, I made up my own.

When I was in the first grade, we moved to a large three-story house. With a tall hedge surrounding the back yard containing swings and a sandbox. I played in it for hours. I remember seeing my mother pick mint leaves from one of the bushes she used for ice tea. The house was very large and frightening to me. We didn't use the third floor. My parents rented it out to a woman friend of theirs. I went up there once but was afraid of the musty smelling halls. There seemed to be something foreboding about the third floor and I always avoided it as long as we lived there.

What stands out, as a memory of this house was the day I was crossing the street holding my four-year-old sisters hand. This was right beside the house. Some boys started throwing stones at us. I let go of Betty's hand to chase them. When I came back to get her, she was in the middle of the street with a car coming around the corner. My father was driving the car! He saw my sister was left there alone, and I had let go of her hand, something I was never to do. He was furious and yelled at me to get in the house. I knew I was going to get a belt whipping and I was scared and upset. It didn't seem fair. I hated being responsible for Betty. I knew I couldn't explain it to him, so I ran in the front door and out the back. I couldn't stand waiting for a whipping. I decided to just run away from home. I ran to nearby park and sat on the swing until dark, trying to decide what to do. I didn't know where to go and I was getting hungry and was afraid of the dark. I finally went home realizing I had no choice. Maybe Dad forgot about it or maybe I worried him so, being gone so long, he'd not spank me, I thought. I was sleepy, tired and cold. I timidly walked up the stairs to the large porch and knocked gently. I could see my father through the large picture window reading the newspaper. He did not get up and my mother came to the door and let me in. She said for me to go to my room. I looked at Dad. He was still reading the paper. I said "Goodnight" quietly to my mother and ran up the stairs to my room and promptly slid under the bed, after grabbing my pillow. I felt safer under the bed. Dad didn't mention the incident any more after that night. He probably knew I had learned my lesson. It took me years before I no longer felt responsible for Betty and my other siblings.

A few days later another incident happened that stayed with me for many years. I thought of it while on the airplane on my way out here to write this book, and the thought of it surprisingly brought tears to my eyes. Dad came home from work one night with the most beautiful doll I had ever seen. It was a Sparkle Plenty doll. Sparkle Plenty was a little girl character in a comic strip, about a detective named Dick Tracy. This was in the 1940s. She had big blue eyes and gorgeous, long blond hair that extended to a point down her back. She had a bottle tied to her arm and when fed, she would wet her diaper. I was happy when I saw her. I was standing in the dining room next to the table and my father and Betty were in the living room in front of me. Dad said,

"This doll is for good girls, and Veronica you have not been a good girl." He gave the doll to my little sister. I was crushed! How can an incident stay in a person's mind so long, that even when I told my doctor about it, I cried as though it was yesterday. I never expressed my feelings back then and they were still with me as though it happened yesterday. I felt embarrassed. Why couldn't he bring two dolls home? I was good most of the time. I tried to be. I felt I had to defend myself even then.

I am sure my father didn't realize that this would have such an effect on me or that I was that impressionable, or he would not have done it. He would have found another way to punish me for letting go of Betty's hand. Was it then that I tried to be the good girl I felt my father wanted? I never did succeed, to my knowledge. Was it then I felt my father loved my sister more than me? No. I believe I felt that even before that incident.

I try to remind myself that Dad did take me shopping for a new dress not long after that incident. I don't think it was any special occasion. We were going to have our kindergarten photos taken and I wore the new dress. Dad picked it out because I didn't know how to choose one. It had small pink, orange and yellow flowers on it and a pleated white trim around the collar and sleeves. Maybe Dad was trying to make up to me for not getting me a doll. I don't know, but I did appreciate the dress he bought for me and it wasn't for any special reason. It was special going shopping with him.

I think it was about this time I started pretending things didn't bother me even if they did. I remember being told by my first grade teacher to leave the classroom and stand out in the hall for punishment. I had failed to turn in my homework. I told myself to just act like it didn't bother me a bit to stand in the hall. I didn't want to give her the satisfaction of knowing she was hurting me and it was embarrassing. I decided to act like I was enjoying it. It worked. She called me in after just a few minutes. Of course my father was told and I was to be punished. A whipping was coming.

My parents had a friend I did not like. He always wanted to hold and kiss me and this made me feel uncomfortable. I walked into the bathroom accidently one day not knowing he was there, and was embarrassed by the sight. He laughed and thought it was funny.

One day he came to the kitchen and said, "Who wants kisses?" My little sister Betty immediately said, "I do."

He looked at me smiling. "Do you want kisses too Veronica."

"No." was my reply. He pulled out of his pocket a bag a candy kisses.

"Too bad." he said as he handed them to Betty. To this day, I don't trust myself with candy kisses. I am afraid I may eat too many.

Chapter 2

MOVING AWAY TO THE FAR SOUTH

ALL OF A sudden it seemed we were in South Carolina. It was such a sudden move and a drastic change in where we lived. Dad bought a small, white frame house with a long front porch and a swing on it. The house stood alone in a field with a narrow dirt road in front leading to a main road. There was a cornfield, wheat field, and a tobacco barn behind our four-room house. I shared one bedroom with my siblings. There were no nice parks or neighbors close by. I didn't understand what happened and never asked. I was eight. The only thing I did understand and was painfully aware of, was that my grandmother was far away and I missed her. I felt alone.

I was put back in the second grade as soon as we got settled because I never completed it. We moved during the school year. I hated starting a new school. I was shy and didn't make friends easily. I remember returning to school after visiting my grandmothers in NJ. My father liked to drive at night because there was little traffic. We arrived back home early in the morning, just as school was starting. Dad drove us to school and said we would be late, but he didn't want us to miss school that day.

I was terrified of the idea of going into the classroom late, but couldn't tell Dad. He dropped my sister and me off in front of the school, telling us to go directly to the classroom. I pretended that I was going in and waited for his car to disappear down the road, then came back out. I just couldn't make myself go into the classroom late and have everyone stare at me. I was so self-conscious. My sister Betty stayed right with me. We stayed out on the porch maybe an hour before I had enough courage to go on in. I suspected the teacher saw us outside and I decided we had better go in. I took Betty to her class then went on to mine. As I expected everything got very quiet. Everyone stared at me. Immediately, the teacher told me to come in front of the class. I was so scared. She started yelling at me and told me I was late, and that she saw me outside on the porch. She said I was going to have a whipping. She went to get the paddle. I couldn't let the whole class see her spank me. I would be so humiliated. It was bad enough coming into the classroom. I ran from the room and down the hall with her shouting after me to come back. I went into my sister's classroom. She was crying. She had already been spanked. I took her hand and said, "Come with me." She didn't question me, but followed. We ran all the way home. A spanking from my father would be better than a spanking from my teacher in front of everyone. At least if Dad spanked me no one would see. I just couldn't let the whole class see me cry and I wasn't sure that I could not cry. I couldn't stand their laughter. My father surprised me this time, when I explained why I came home from school. He didn't spank me, but rather enrolled us in another school. Of course, I just told him we were being spanked for being late for school. I didn't tell him we didn't go directly in, as soon as he dropped us off. I don't know whether or not he found out what really happened. He never said. The new school he took us to was a private Catholic school. I had fallen behind in my schoolwork. This was the third school in which I was placed into the second grade, because of our moving. I was glad to be in this new school. The kids were nicer and didn't yell at us, "Yankees go home." I didn't know what a Yankee was and why were they angry with us. Later I found out about the civil war and we were Yankees. They still didn't like us.

We were baptized into the Catholic faith shortly after starting school. The day we were baptized, Dad and Mom had their marriage blessed. Mom was not a Catholic, but Dad was although he had been inactive. A Justice of the Peace had originally married them. My parents became very good friends with the priest, who was the pastor of the church. This priest was very good to all of us and gave us children special attention. He was to marry me ten years later and became an important part in my life's decisions later on in years. I gave my first son his name, as he was so good to my siblings and me.

I remember well, my first holy communion. It was one of the nicest days I can remember during that period in my life. We didn't have many nice clothes, but on that day, I wore the most beautiful white dress I had ever seen with white shoes and socks. I had a veil and a pretty white prayer book also. It was a very special day to me.

In my childhood years, I found comfort in this new religion, but in later years, it confused me. I wanted to know more. Things looked so much better, but I was to find out that life wasn't going to stay beautiful and all people good, like I thought then. I was protected from life, from reality.

Dad and Mom must have been having a really bad time financially. I didn't have to be very old to realize we didn't have much money, and Dad didn't believe a woman should work back in those days. He had a good job as an engineer, but I am sure it was hard for him to support a family. They were so young themselves when I think of it. They were just in their twenties with four children. Dad wanted Mom to be at home taking care of the home and us children. I can imagine it was really hard for her leaving her home near her parents and friends and moving so far away in a wheat field with no one to talk to, not even a phone. Down the street there was a neighbor. If Mom had to use a phone for any reason the neighbor let Mom use hers. I still remember the ladies name - Mrs. Diggers. Dad got Mom an old car that had a rumble seat and a gallon jug on the floorboard of the car. This jug contained the gas for running the car. Mom used this car to take us to school. I asked my mother to drop my sister and I off a block from school so the children wouldn't laugh when they saw our car. They already made fun of my clothes and shoes, and I didn't want them laughing at the car too. I asked my mother if we could walk home from school with a neighborhood boy who was older than we were and she agreed. It was at a least five-mile walk but I didn't mind it. It was better than having the kids make fun of me. I felt ashamed wearing the second-hand clothes of a girl at school. Her mother gave them to us. They were dresses that her daughter had outgrown. They were faded, but Mom was glad to get them. Thankfully, the girl was older and in a different class, so I didn't see her much. To make matters worse, the dresses were always wrinkled. Another thing that always bothered me was the holes in my socks and shoes. I tried putting cardboard in the bottom of my shoes, but it kept sliding around and it didn't work very well when it rained. I was sliding down the sliding board in the playground one day, and some kids noticed the holes and laughed at me. Children can be very cruel. I felt so ashamed.

Another incident involving the holes in my socks that made me even more self-conscious was the time I was visiting at a neighbor's house. He was a classmate and I liked him very much. His name was Bobby. His mother had invited us in to play, but we had to take off our shoes, as she had just scrubbed the kitchen floor. I hated taking off my shoes because I knew I had holes in my sock and I didn't want them to see them, but I couldn't see any way to avoid it. I tried pulling my socks down over my heal some, hoping she wouldn't notice, but I heard her whisper to her son, "look she has holes in her socks and her feet are dirty." I could have disappeared in a hole. I never went back into her home and she told her son not to play with me. Even into my adulthood, whenever I saw her, I could not forget the incident and I felt I hated her for judging me. I was just eight years old. I had no control over it then.

I don't remember baths being a regular thing when I was a child, or brushing our teeth or keeping our nails clean. Perhaps my mother was taking care of us the best she knew how. I knew she had the four of us with no more than 18 months between us. She was young, and there wasn't much money. It had to have been hard for her. As I have grown and matured over the years, I have the knowledge that being poor doesn't mean you are going to be dirty. All it takes is soap, water and some time. Personal hygiene is very important. I learned in school and from my friends how important it was. We need to start the habit at a young age and for it to be a daily routine. I want to mention that to this day, I do remember my great grandmother telling me when I was around 5 yrs old to brush my nails with a nail brush. That always stayed with me.

I dreaded at school when it was time to pay tuition. The nun would call for it in the classroom and we would all pass our white envelopes up to her. She would always ask in front of the class, if I had one too. My reply was always no. Darn it, I would think. Did she always have to ask in front of the class? Couldn't she ask privately? How I envied those that could pay. I didn't want to be different. I drew more and more into myself, becoming more self-conscious, not wanting to be noticed. I spent a great deal of my recess time in the little brown church, alone rather than on the playground with the rest of the children. This way, they didn't notice me. I thought.

It was about this time that Dad paid attention to my constant bed-wetting. It was embarrassing and I didn't mean to. I would dream that I was going to and wake up wetting my bed. Terror would always fill me, but I couldn't stop it. I slept with Betty and tried saying it was she wetting the bed, not I, but it didn't work. Sometimes I would wet the bed when sleeping alone. Dad would always take me to the bathroom, pull down my pants and spank me. I would just about die from embarrassment. I remember him saying,

"Veronica, you're getting too old for this. You are eight years old now, much too old for wetting the bed and then me having to spank you for it." This hurts me more than it does you," he would say. Betty and I slept together and she sometimes would wet the bed too. Many times we didn't know which one did it. Betty got spanked too.

I would cry saying, "I didn't do it on purpose, Daddy. I don't want to. It just happens."

Oh why couldn't I tell him what I was feeling inside?

How very much I wanted his attention. How much I wanted him to hold me, to love me, to call me "his little girl." I wanted to crawl up in his lap and have him hug me, not spank me. I cannot remember my father holding me as a small child or later on. I craved that. The only physical contact I had was his spankings, and I felt they were better than nothing. At least I was getting some response from him.

Maybe I encouraged the spankings without really being aware of it. I do remember the fear I always felt, when my mother would say,

"Wait until your father comes home. He will take care of you."

The wait was agonizing. Why didn't Mom just spank me and get it over with? She didn't though. That was Dad's job.

About this time, I would get delirious every time I had a little fever, which seemed quite often to me. I used to have very bad earaches and usually ran a high fever with them. It was terrifying to be delirious. I remember the feeling so well. Everything would be out of order. I would see things, objects out of proportion, the room upside down and furniture all over the place. Things kept coming at me, not letting up. Laughing faces, with big heads that looked like monsters I'd try to tell my parents in between screams. I would be physically fighting them. Dad would put the light on to show me things were in order and it was my imagination. Sometimes the doctor would come to the house and give me a shot and put warm medicine in my ear. I never really outgrew this delirium. It just happened a few times as an adult, but then it would be explained to me what caused it. Fever caused the hallucinations.

As a young child, I had tremendous cravings for sweet things, especially cookies. When we did get them, it was always a real treat. On Saturdays, the whole family would go to the grocery store. We children would stay in the car anxiously waiting for the return of our parents, for they always brought a box of Cracker Jacks for each of us. It was a real treat and it was so much fun looking for the little toy inside. I remember when we wanted something we really didn't need, Dad would always say, "I am not going to give you children everything you want. This way, when you grow up, you will appreciate things and not be spoiled." I didn't understand what appreciate meant then, but his statement stayed with me the rest of my life. I heard it often as a teenager. By then I understood what the word "appreciate" meant. However, at the age of eight, all I understood was that I wanted good tasting things to eat. I still appreciate Cracker Jacks.

I went into the store with my parents once and took one white grape that was on display. I loved it. I wanted them so bad, but couldn't have them. I told myself then when I grow up, I will buy all I want.

One day I wanted some cookies, and we didn't have any. I felt like I had to have some, so I decided to go to a neighbor's house and see if she had any cookies in her home. I did not know her, but the way I felt, it didn't matter. I found a kitchen window open and crawled inside. There was no one at home. I found the pantry and some cookies in the pantry. I ate all the cookies I could find, and then slipped back out the window. I never told anyone about the incident and never heard anything about it. I never tried it again though. Writing this I cannot imagine what ever possessed me to do that? How can cookies be so important that I would sneak into someone's house? That was pretty bad.

This was not the first time I stole cookies. Remember when I spoke of my father buying me the dress after the Sparkle doll incident? I was wearing the dress the very day I was caught taking cookies from the cafeteria and not paying for them. Of all times, we had school pictures taken that day, when I was in kindergarten. The very day I had been caught. I could not smile in my school photo, I was so embarrassed and ashamed at being caught. I felt like it was a "mug shot."

I still remember it like it was yesterday. It was the cookie that has a plain wafer type bottom and a ball of pink or white marshmallow on top and sprinkled with coconut. They sold them in the cafeteria for just two cents, but I never had two cents. I don't know why I didn't ask my parents for money, but I never did. It seemed easier to steal them. They had a metal cup that you would drop your two cents into and then pick up your cookie. I would get in the cookie line with everyone else and when it was my turn to drop my pennies in, I would pick up two pennies and then re-drop them in the cup, so they would make a clinking sound. No one questioned me and I would enjoy my cookie. Well, I got away with it for weeks and then one day, I found myself first in line. I did my usual thing. There was already two pennies in the cup. I was "set up." After my "clink clink", the lady looked in the cup expecting to see four pennies and there was just two. They had found their thief. They knew someone was doing this and it was just a matter of time before they found the culprit or the "Cookie Monster." I was caught! Of course I was scolded and then told to go into this room and have my photo taken. It will be posted for all to see. Yes, I look guilty and very ashamed, a reminder that crime does not pay.

I don't remember my parents being told. I don't believe they were, as I don't remember a punishment; but I will never forget the shame I felt when I was caught.

When I became Catholic at the age of eight and went to my first confession, I said, "Bless me Father, for I have sinned. This is my first confession. I steal cookies." At that stage in my young life, that was the worst crime I had ever committed.

I felt very lonely as a child and missed my grandmother very much, when we moved to South Carolina from New York at the age of seven. It was 1948 and I was going to be eight this year. I played mostly by myself because there were not many neighbors, and even if there were, I don't think I would have had many friends. I was so shy. Outside in the back yard one day, standing beside my sand pile, I cried. I didn't go under the house this time, as I normally did, to hide when I cried. There was no one around to see me. It seems as though it was yesterday, when I remember the incident, and how I felt and what I was thinking. It seems I'm crying most of the time, I thought. Why do I cry so much? No one sees me or even cares about me. I hate being the oldest. I hate being responsible for my sisters and brother, when I have to babysit. I am only eight years old. I didn't feel like a carefree child. Sometimes we had a sitter, but when we didn't, I would have to watch my siblings. My parents went out a lot. Mostly just down the street to a lounge, where they had many friends. I just stood there crying quietly looking down at my sand pile. After awhile, I sat down in the sand and started pushing my little green metal car. I liked the way it left tracks in the sand, like a road. I started pushing my hands in the sand making roads, then a tunnel, and a bridge. I was getting excited at seeing what I was creating. I pushed my little car on the roads that I made. It looked so real to me. I loved it. All I need is a person. I thought. I ran into the house and cut out a paper doll from a book. I put her in the car. I was so excited at seeing what I had done. I'll make my own little world. That is what I will do. I didn't like the world I lived in, so I decided not to just go along with it but to escape to my own world when I was unhappy. I could make things like I wanted them to be in the world I made. I could always escape to this new world that I made up, and to me it was wonderful. It was there all the time most of the time, trying to block other things out.

From that day on, I did just that until I received psychotherapy twenty-seven years later when I was forced to face reality. I had long ago stopped playing with paper dolls and cars. I was now acting out pretending in a different way. No one knew me. I tried to be exactly what was expected of me. Whatever it took to get approval and acceptance, I used, for I craved it so desperately. When elements of my fantasy world touched on reality, and things did not go as I planned them, I had difficulty. It was terrifying. I had no control over what happened sometimes and I didn't like that. I didn't know how to handle pain. When this happened, I would have to ignore the reality and make something up, so I could live with it. My make believe world was my escape, my salvation, but it couldn't last forever. It was not healthy.

When I was nine years old, we moved from the small house into a very impressive two-story house that was over a hundred years old. The house had a long porch that ran from one end of the house across the front. The porch also had tall columns on it. Each room was very large with high ceilings and there was a fireplace in all the rooms. Upstairs each bedroom also had a fireplace. Each one of us children had our own room, but Betty and I decided we wanted to share the same room as we always had done in the past. There was a closet in our room that led to an attic. We never went up in the attic. I didn't care for the house. To me, it was too large and open. I didn't feel comfortable in it and there was no place for me to hide. I could no longer go under the house as I did in the past, as there was a musty dark cellar. I was afraid to go down into it.

Something strange happened at this house that was never explained. I was lying in my bed one night trying to go to sleep, when I felt there was someone else in the room other than my sister and me. I looked down at the foot of my bed and it looked like the figure of a man standing there. At first, I told myself, "No, it can't be. It must be a shadow." I closed my eyes and looked again at the same spot. He was still there! I couldn't believe it. He wasn't moving. I kept watching him, trying to make him out. He was wearing a hat and a long coat. I couldn't make out his face, because of the darkness. I kept real still, afraid to move. I wanted to scream, but was afraid to. I kept telling myself, he would disappear. Suddenly, I saw his arm raise up and he had a knife in his hand. I felt I was smothering. I started screaming and screaming. I saw him run into the closet that led into the attic. Daddy and Mom came running into the room and switched on the light. They both just stood there, looking at me and asked, "What's the matter? Why did you scream?"

When I finally could stop crying and catch my breath, I told them, "There was a man standing by my bed. I saw him. He had a knife," I cried. My sister Betty was now sitting up in her bed looking at us.

"I didn't see him." She said.

I cried, "You were asleep."

Mom came over and covered me up and said,

"Lay back down now and go to sleep. You were just dreaming." "No, I cried, Mommy, I was not asleep. I was awake. I saw him. He ran into the closet."

Daddy went over to the closet and looked in.

"See, there is nobody here, Veronica, you were dreaming." "Daddy, he must have climbed up into the attic." I said pleading. I could tell they were getting a little impatient with me, as it was late. "Go back to sleep now dear," Mom said kindly as she and Dad left the room.

I appreciated her being tender with me that night. I heard them going back downstairs and wished their bedroom were on the same floor as mine. I closed my eyes and was afraid to open them the rest of the night. I finally drifted off to sleep.

The next day, I was still convinced that I was not dreaming and dreaded going to bed again that night. I put off going to bed as long as I could, but finally I ran out of excuses and had to go. Later on that night, I felt I was going to sleep when suddenly, I had that feeling again, that someone was in the room with me. I was so afraid I could feel my heart beating. Again, I slowly and reluctantly opened my eyes and looked towards the foot of my bed. I couldn't believe my eyes he was there again! This time was worse than the last time, for it confirmed what I had seen the night before. I didn't wait this time to scream. I yelled as loud as I could. As before, he ran into the closet. I kept screaming until my Dad and Mom appeared at the door.

"He was here again. I'm telling the truth. I was not dreaming. Please believe me." I cried sobbing. Daddy seemed more patient this time and said,

"Okay, let's go in the closet and look." He made me go with him. "See, there is no one here," he said. I looked up to where the opening went into the attic.

"He went up there, Daddy. I know he did. He must live up there and just comes out at night."

"Veronica, now think, how can a man live up there? It is not possible. You had to be seeing things. Now go to bed. Betty can sleep with you tomorrow night if this will make you feel better," he said.

"I'll show him to Betty, then you will believe me," I said looking at my sister.

"I don't want to see him." Betty added quickly. "Now look what you have done. You have your sister scared." Mommy said as she covered me up and kissed me goodnight.

"Go on to sleep and don't have any more bad dreams."

The next night Betty reluctantly went to bed with me. She was getting put out with me for waking her two nights in a row. I felt better with her in the bed with me, but didn't know what protection she could be. Well, if it happens again, she will see him, and then they will believe me, I thought. I waited a long time to feel sleepy. I was so scared. I kept looking down at the foot of my bed and was afraid to look away. I didn't see anything. After awhile I felt it was safe to go on to sleep. I felt I was going to sleep when suddenly I was wide-awake! I had not looked at the foot of the bed for a while and I was afraid to. I was afraid he would be there. Suddenly, I felt he was there again. My chest hurt so, I was so afraid. I slowly turned my head and opened my eyes. There he was! I saw him. I told myself I was seeing things, that it was a shadow, or maybe I was asleep and dreaming, but none of it worked. He started to move towards me slowly. I told myself again that I was imagining it. I felt he was mocking me and laughing at me because no one believed I saw him. I thought I saw his face and he was smiling.

When he started moving towards me again and I clearly saw the knife in his outstretched arm, I nudged Betty and whispered,

"Betty, Betty, wake up. Please wake up."

She didn't respond. I looked up. He was still there. I couldn't wake her up! I panicked and started screaming. When I started yelling, I saw him run again into the closet, my sister started running too and ran to her bed. I heard her fall, and then she was crying. My parents came running up the stairs, as before, and asked what happened. I was trying to tell them as they ran over to my sister. Her lip was bleeding. She had fallen when running to her bed and cut her lip on the bed railing.

She cried, "Veronica scares me." I was crying too, but for another reason.

"Did you see him Betty? Did you see him? Tell Mommy and Daddy what you saw." I said to her between sobs.

"I didn't see anything. You scared me." She cried out angrily. Suddenly, I felt in trouble. I knew they would never believe me now and my sister was hurt because of me. I was so frightened. I wanted them to take me in their arms and comfort me, but that wasn't going to happen. Especially now, since my sister was hurt because of me. I didn't know what I was going to do.

This happened several more times and it was getting on everybody's nerves, but I couldn't help it. It got to the point where my parents were angry with me and I can now understand their frustration. My solution was to just stop looking down at the foot of my bed and simply sleep under the covers. We moved several months after that into a different house out in the country. I don't know why we moved, but I was glad and didn't question it. My sister had a scar left on her lip from the accident and I felt very bad about it. For the rest of our lives she took great delight in letting me know I was the cause of it. It wasn't a bad scar, thank goodness, but the memory was bad enough. I always felt so bad as no one believed me. To this day I don't know what caused it, but it is a memory I'll never forget and because of it, I keep an open mind when people talk about bad spirits, but I'd rather hear about the good ones.

Chapter 3

HOUSE IN THE WOODS

THE NEXT HOUSE we lived in, I was to live in until I married nine years later. I was to dream of this house many years after I left it. I still do at times today. I loved this house and what surrounded it. It was placed in the middle of hundreds of acres of woods. We just owned four acres, but woods on every side surrounded us. It was built just off a long dirt road that led to the main highway. There were not but three houses on the whole street and we were not close to them. The house was fairly new and not quite finished but enough to live in. Dad planned to finish building the living area himself, so he got the house for a good price. It was a ranch type home in a T-shape. There was a small door at the back of the house that led to a large crawl space under the house. This was going to be my place to hide, I thought as I walked around the house. There were so many beautiful trees for as far as you could see. Huge trees that towered towards the sky and smaller ones that were covered in dogwood blossoms. They provided a canopy of white blooms overhead. I felt happy as I walked into the woods, wanting to explore.

I found some little purple blooms growing out of a carpet of green moss. The moss felt like velvet to my touch. I had never seen anything like it. I found a small stream, with crystal clear water. The banks were covered with the green moss also. Oh, my paper dolls will like this, I thought. I can make them a boat to float in and they can swim in the clear water. I felt like I found a haven. I tried to imagine myself small like my paper dolls and being in these surroundings. My paper doll will take my place, I thought to myself. I walked to the edge of the woods and found a golden wheat field. The wind was gently blowing and it looked like a golden sea, with gentle waves. I walked into the field to lie down. The wheat felt good beneath me and it stayed flat for me and created a little room. All I could see now was the beautiful blue sky with the white puffy clouds, and I was surrounded by a golden wall. It seemed too good to be real. I lay there for a long time looking at the clouds and making faces out of them and other images. I loved the way the wheat smelled and how I was closed in that golden little room. It felt good and I felt happy.

After awhile, I went back into the woods and climbed the oldest and biggest tree I could find. I climbed as high as I could. I was not afraid of the height. The tree was strong and could hold me and it was peaceful up there in that old tree. I could see for a long distance, over the wheat field and to another field of corn. Another place to explore, I thought.

I stayed in the tree a long time watching little and big ants running all over the bark. They fascinated me. I wonder if they know where they are going? I thought to myself. I wondered if ants can think and do they have feelings? Does it hurt when we step on them? I had so many questions about life and no answers. I climbed down the tree and walked across the street to some more woods.

The trees in this forest were different. They were mostly very tall pine trees and then a field of smaller pine trees. I liked the smell of the pine. The woods looked so clean and neat with pine needles all over the ground. It was easy for me to lose myself in these woods. At the end of the tall pines I found some more wheat and corn fields.

I wandered through the fields until I saw an old barn in the distance. My heart skipped a beat when I saw this. I wanted a closer look. I kept walking until I reached the barn. I looked up at it in wonder. I was surprised to see this as there was no house in sight, and I thought this was strange. It was made of old natural wood and had a loft upstairs. I felt excited and felt it was placed there just for me as I climbed into the loft. There was hay in the loft and it smelled sweet. Oh, how I love this, I thought as I lay down in the soft hay. This is better than under the house on the dirt floor. This will be my place to come to. (This barn meant so much to me years later. As an adult I found myself going back to a barn, when I was troubled.) I left the barn after a while and went further out into the fields. I found not one, but three ponds that I could swim in. I felt like I had found my own world that no one knew of, My Secret Place.

When I wasn't playing with my paper dolls, trucks and sand piles, I was out exploring. I mostly went alone. After awhile, I shared it with Bobby, my little brother. Bobby was just three years younger than I and I loved him very much. I always felt sorry for Bobby because he was sick a lot, and he didn't have any friends to play with, just his sisters. I felt he was lonely for a boy to have as a friend, but I knew he was shy. We only had two neighbors, and they were not that close by. There were no other children. Somehow, I felt we had something in common. I remember whenever Bobby got a spanking, I would cry too, and wish I could take that spanking for him. Maybe I felt close to him because I wished I had been born a boy. My mother told me Daddy and Papa Tom, my Dad's father, had hoped I'd be a boy and they were quite disappointed that I was born a girl. Mom said they had already picked out a name for me. They were going to name me "Patrick" after my great grandfather who was born in Ireland, but since I was a girl they named me Veronica. I thought I'd name my son Patrick someday. I thought this as a child. I'm sure my mother didn't mean for me to take the news that Daddy preferred a son to a daughter, the way I took it. Immediately, I told myself that is why he doesn't love me. He wanted a son. I thought about it a long time feeling very hurt, when I came upon the decision, well, I'll just have to do everything I can to make him glad I was born. I have to prove to him I'm as good as a son. I have to make him proud of me. I want him to love me. All these things went through my young mind and stayed with me making me determined to win his approval no matter how long it took.

Even though I knew Dad wanted a son when I was born, I also knew he liked for me to look feminine, because when I was around ten years old, he passed by the bathroom. The door was opened and he saw me combing my hair.

He stopped and said to me, "Veronica, always take good care of your hair and keep it clean."

I always did try to keep myself looking nice from then on, hoping he would notice. Much later in life, as a woman, I had the drive and ambition of a man in my career. It was of the utmost importance that I prove to him I could succeed in a man's world. Every time I received a promotion on the job, I couldn't get to the phone fast enough to call my father to tell him, hoping I would hear those magic words, Veronica, I am proud of you." But they never came. Others told me he was proud of my accomplishments. Dad just wanted me to be a housewife and a mother, as he felt all women should be. I found this out much later, but it was too late, I was too involved in my career. I needed it. It was an escape from home life.

Betty, my younger sister was just 18 months younger then I. Our mother used to dress us alike when we were small. I remember well, the new dresses whenever we received them on special occasions, like Easter, Christmas and May Day at church; which was a big celebration in the Catholic Church. I loved the smell of the new dresses and the newness of them. One Easter I received a pretty yellow dress with a large ruffle around the skirt. It had some small lace sewed in it. Betty's was just like mine but in green. The dresses we received at Christmas were black taffeta with different colored polka dots on it. These crinkled when we walked but were pretty. We both received beautiful dresses the following year for May. They were white with white overlay floral brocade. I still remember the fragrance of that particular new dress. I felt beautiful in it, but was envious of my younger sister Betty as she was chosen to crown the May Queen, the statue of the Virgin Mary. It was a large outdoor celebration and Betty was dressed as a bride, which was the greatest honor on that Holy Day. I said I envied her, but really I was proud of her, and happy for her. It was an honor. I thought of my new dress and the flowers in my hair and I felt good. Betty's personality wasn't as reserved as mine, and it seemed she got more attention than I, but then she said what she wanted. I tried hard to be friends with Betty, but she rejected any signs of affection from me, and we mostly fought.

I remember our fights so well and wish I didn't. It makes me sad. It seemed whenever we fought I mostly got punished because I was the oldest and should set a good example. I was responsible for them. Throughout the years, as an adult, whenever we all got together, both Betty and Dawn would remind me of how I hurt them when we were children. I could never understand this, because anything that did happen was an accident. I would never hurt them intentionally. I do remember when we were children and playing cowboys and Indians, we needed a victim to rescue, so Dawn played the victim. We tied her to a tree and sprayed her with the hose, but not in the face. Then we rescued her. I saw this in a drive in movie once. I thought she would like it. It was a hot day. The only other time I can remember was when we would climb a young tree and it would bend over; then we would call Dawn as she was little and light and when she grabbed hold of the tree it would take her up in the air for a ride. She would cry out in surprise, as the tree lifted her up into the air. But we always got her down safely. These were childhood games and fun, but she never forgot them.

I accidently hit her with a baseball bat when I was playing in a ball game and swinging at a ball. This was something else she thought I did on purpose. I loved my baby sister very much and would never hit her in any way. Our parents were at the ball game and saw it was an accident. I was not punished for it. I felt terrible that I had caused it. I did not know she was behind me that close. Why would she think I would do that on purpose? This was one of the reasons I hated family reunions. My two sisters took such delight in reminding me of what I used to do. I always got sick to my stomach when I had to attend them. I hated hearing them laugh at my make believe world I used to live in as a child. They didn't' realize they were also intruding in my present life. They were a constant reminder, and as an adult, I hated it.

Around the age of ten, I started playing more and more to myself, with my paper dolls. The only thing needed was a home, not one like I always made for them out of a shoebox. My happiest Christmas I remember was when my father bought me a dollhouse. Of course I thought it was from Santa Claus. I liked believing in him and did until I was about eleven or twelve. It was easier believing in this make believe world. I liked it. I still remember the excitement when I saw the beautiful Christmas tree, with the toys under it that Christmas morning. I ran to the dollhouse fascinated at the miniature rooms and furniture. Again, I wished I could make myself small and enter this beautiful house. My dolls have a home, I said to myself. I loved it. I no longer had to use the shoeboxes. I used to cut out the doors and windows in the boxes, and use strips of toilet paper for the curtains on the windows. I made my own furniture out of cardboard and scotch tape. My paper doll lived inside the house that I would make. I never understood then, why I always set fire to my cardboard house, nor really cared why I did it. I would have my paper doll inside, but I always "saved" her from the flames, not wanting her to burn. Watching the fire burn and curl from outside the windows always fascinated me. I loved to watch it destroy the house, but there was always something sad about it too. I always made another to burn at a later date.

    I loved taking my paper doll out to the beautiful spot I found in the woods, with the green moss circling the pool of clear water. I built her a small boat, and put her in it. I could really put myself into that doll. I would be lost to reality and any unhappiness I had. One day I felt like I wanted some excitement for my paper doll, which I had named Veronica. I took her to a drainpipe, which carried water under the dirt road from a large pond, into a small pool of water. I placed Veronica in the small boat that I made and let it go into the pipe that went under the road. I ran to the other side of the street, waiting for the little boat to appear, so I could catch it in the nick of time to prevent it from tumbling over the water falls, that fell into the small pool below. I waited with great excitement for my doll to appear. The stream was faster than I anticipated, and I missed her. Veronica went over the waterfalls, with great force. I was really scared as I ran down the bank to the bottom of the falls. I fished in the water for her, feeling very frightened. I found her, but she was torn in two, by the pressure of the water. I felt great sadness. It was as though a part of me died.

I took her home and held a real funeral for her. I put her in a box, and had my sisters and brother attend the funeral for her. I even hummed a sad tune. I remember my five-year old sister Dawn crying, as I pushed dirt over what was left of my paper doll. I really felt like I had lost something very close to me. I cried and cried after the funeral. I felt so alone and lost. A part of me felt like it had died. It was painful for me, when my sister, much later in life made fun of this incident. I was embarrassed by it and understand now as an adult, why I did it.

After the incident with my paper doll, Veronica, I started playing with small wood dolls, about 6 inches tall. I enjoyed playing with them more, as they seemed more realistic to me. I liked combing their hair and making clothes for them. The only thing I didn't like about them was I couldn't make them fit in the dollhouse and I couldn't imagine myself being small, like them. I couldn't put them in the boats and cars I made either; but I could tie them to stakes, and I liked this. It was like they were captured and I was going to free them. I would set a small fire beneath them, as they were tied to the stake, and just in the nick of time, I would save them. I had an incident once, when I couldn't get my doll untied fast enough to rescue her. The fire burned her. Her legs were blistered, and the wood looked awful. I felt as bad as the way she looked. I had to bury her too. After that happened, I stopped trying that; but it escalated. I started setting fires across the street in the woods. I would choose a field, with just a few small trees in it and set the fire. I loved to watch the fire burn away the dry tall grass until it caught a beautiful pine tree on fire. This scared me and I had to work very hard to put the fire out with the broom I always carried with me to beat the fire out. Those pine trees were our Christmas trees, and I didn't want to destroy them. I loved them. They always brought happiness to me at Christmas time, when Dad would take us children over there to pick out a tree for our Christmas. He took such care in decorating it on Christmas Eve.

As a child I did not understand why I was doing these things, and why they held such fascination for me. Much later on, as an adult in psychotherapy, it was explained to me why I did these things. Many of you may have already guessed. I was the doll, and I wanted to be rescued. I explain in more detail later on and it makes so much sense.

Children that set fires are disturbed and it is important to find out why they do it. My parents did not know I was doing it, so I am sure my guardian angel looked out for me and protected me in many cases.

When I was around ten years old, I started visiting my grandmother for the summer months. My sister, Betty always accompanied me on these summer vacations. I was always so happy to leave home, that I didn't mind leaving my dollhouse and my dolls. I didn't have to pretend at my grandmother's, as it was a happy place to be. I didn't seem to upset my grandmother as I did my mother. I never understood why my mother always seemed upset with me, because I tried very hard to be good. I just felt in the way and I felt like a bother. Sometimes I wanted to disappear. Mom was always saying to me, "Wait until your father gets home." It was always a threat and I feared seeing him, as I knew it meant I was going to get a whipping. Many years later, I was asked what did I remember most about my mother, and I was surprised my only response was,

"She used to always kiss me goodnight, that's mostly what I remember, then I added, "but I didn't like it."

My therapist Arielle would ask" why didn't you like her kissing you goodnight?"

"I don't know." I just remember "I didn't like it" was always my response.

"Think." Arielle would say. "How did you feel?" she'd ask. "Guilty." I said. "But I didn't know why I felt that way."

"Keep thinking about it." Arielle would say. "Maybe someday it will come to you why you felt guilty."

Many years later the answer came to me why I felt that way and I later explain it in another chapter.

I always felt great anticipation in the ten hour drive to my grandmother's. There, at her home, I didn't get into trouble and I felt loved.

Chapter 4

SUMMERS AT MY GRANDPARENTS

I CALLED MY GRANDMOTHER Grammie when I was small, and when older, called her Gram. She and my grandfather who was Pop-Pop had a large white house on a hill and corner in New York. Oh, how I loved that house. It was in a nice, neat neighborhood, with tree-lined sidewalks, where I could roller skate. There were old gas lamps alongside the road, which were made into electric lights. In the backyard there was beautiful grass surrounded by sweet smelling rose bushes. My grandmother had planted pansies, Lily of the Valley and buttercups. There was a pussy willow bush beside the stairs leading up to the backyard and a huge snowball bush. Pop-Pop took great pride in his rose bushes and gladiolus plants. To this day, I love these plants. The whole yard smelled of flowers. There was a hammock in the back yard that my sister and I always tried to beat each other to. We knew when Pop came home from work though it was his. Everything was in such order at my grandmother's home and I especially loved getting into fresh smelling bed sheets at night. I liked the way they felt smooth and crisp next to my body. Gram made us take a bath every night, so I was clean when I went to bed, and I felt so good, snuggly and secure.

There was a lot of love between my grandparents. I can't ever remember them arguing. I always saw Gram kiss Pop-pop goodbye when he was on his way to work. I would kiss him goodbye too. I felt free with him and loved walking to his service station sometimes during the day. It was a long, beautiful walk on the sidewalk to his station, passing by many beautiful homes. He was always glad to see my sister and me when we arrived. I felt proud for his customers to know, I was his granddaughter. He always introduced us.

He would say, "This is Veronica and Betty, my granddaughter's from South Carolina. They are spending the summer with us."

I knew to stay out of the way when he was busy and we never stayed long. Pop-Pop had a huge raspberry bush behind the gas station that he had planted himself. We would go out there and pick berries for him and he would pay fifty cents for a basket full. He loved raspberries on his morning cereal and on his ice cream at night. To this day, I dearly love raspberries. I can taste them, close my eyes and the memory comes back. Pop-Pop had rosebushes at his station also, and everyone would marvel about how beautiful they were. He loved flowers and it showed in the manner he cared for them. It was a family trait that he shared with his brothers.

Every evening preparing supper with my grandmother was exciting waiting for Pop-pop to come home. When I heard him coming up the steps outside the kitchen door, I would run to greet him. I would throw my arms around him. Pop-pop was reserved but I knew he liked it. I still remember the twinkle in his blue eyes. How much I wish I could have done this with my Dad. Even when I was older, I never had the courage. Now, thinking about it, I am sure my Dad would have loved it.

Pop-Pop and I would sit and watch the ball games or wrestling on TV together and either eat Vanilla Cherry, Butter pecan, coffee, or banana ice cream every night. I didn't understand or really like the games on television, as I was only ten, I just enjoyed sitting next to him, saying nothing. I did this until he passed away when I was fifteen.

Pop-pop died of a heart attack. I don't remember being told or even remember the trip back to New York for the funeral. I remember well seeing Pop-Pop lying in the casket. I knelt down, beside the casket and prayed. I stood up, bent over and kissed him on the cheek. I wasn't afraid to do this. I loved him so. I can't remember crying. I don't believe

I did. I never told anyone how bad I hurt inside. I am embarrassed to admit this, but I feel it is important, as I never told anyone that I tried to take my life after I got home. I took a scarf and tied it around my neck and pulled it hard and tied a knot. I didn't want to live. I remember my head pounding and hurting really bad as the blood filled my face. It hurt so much; I frantically tried to untie the knot. I got it loose and was able to breath. It hurt too much to try to choke myself. What was I going to do? For years after that, I would cry in my room at night and pretend that Pop-pop was right there with me and I would talk to him and tell him how much I missed him. Even as I type this now, my chest hurts remembering, and tears are in my eyes.

Later on when I got more counseling and understanding, I realized why I would always get depressed every February for many years. That is when Pop-Pop died. I never openly grieved when he died, but did every February (without realizing that was the anniversary of when he passed.)

I wanted to mention how I felt above and my experience so that the readers will understand how some children may feel when a family member or a friend has died. Many times, someone is so lost in their own grief that they don't think about what a child is going through. Children won't usually let you know. It is important for them to express how they feel and grieve also. If it is not dealt with, then it may stay inside and affect them in different ways in years to come.

I want to get back to the happy memories at my grandparents home before I finish about our summers. I continued to visit for the summer until I was married. Betty went to live with Gram when she was fifteen. Not long after Pop-pop died.

During the week, Gram worked as a checker at a nearby grocery store. She was able to walk to work just down the street. The icebox was always filled with good things to eat. We always had to ask for permission to take something out, and most of the time, Gram would say it was okay, but not right before supper. Once when we were waiting for a bus at the bus stop. I was eating an ice cream cone and I said,

"Grammie, you are the best grandmother in the world."

She hugged me affectionately and said, "you say that because I give you most of the things you want."

"No, Grammie, that is not the reason. I love you. I am so happy when I am with you."

Our grandmother was taking us to the city to see a movie and do some shopping. Oh how I loved that. The only time we went shopping at home was at Easter time for a new dress, and whenever our shoes gave out, and we needed new ones for school.

We knew not to ask for anything though. Gram would pick up something and say, "Do you like this?" Would you like to have it?"

I don't know why I would feel a little guilty saying yes, but I did. I don't think Gram spoiled us really, because we always appreciated everything we got and my grandmother was not extravagant. I wanted a pair of black patent leather shoes so bad, with a strap across the front. I could never tell her or anyone. I knew Dad must have been having a hard time, financially, because whenever we got shoes back home, they were usually brown ones that laced up because they lasted longer. I hated them because they were ugly. Not black and shiny. Sometimes we got oxfords, but they didn't stay looking nice for long. I never could keep the white part clean, and it was so hard trying to polish them. They had two colors and you had to stay in the line.

I would really get excited if my grandmother would get me some new paper dolls. At home, I cut them out of magazines. But here I could get a whole book full, and they were real movie stars. They were so pretty with lots of clothes. All I had to do was cut them out. It was really fun changing their outfits. I pretended again they were me, but I didn't lose myself in them as I did back home. There were too many good things at my grandmother's home.

The front porch of the house was large and screened in and I slept on it every night. There was a wind chime on the porch and whenever there was a gentle breeze, which was often, it would tinkle. I would go to sleep at night snuggled under the blankets to keep me warm on the cool summer nights, hearing the wind chime.

To this day, I like coffee, cherry vanilla, pecan and banana ice cream, raspberries, wind chimes, clean, crisp bed sheets, flowers and cigar smoke that reminds me of my grandfather, and my happy childhood summers at my grandparents' home.

Whenever it came near the end of summer, I would get a knot in my stomach. I didn't want to go home.

"Oh Grammie, please let me stay with you I want to live with you and Pop–pop," I'd cry.

"You can't dear, your mother needs you at home, and I want you to promise to be a good girl for her and help her all you can," Gram would always say to me.

I didn't understand why my mother needed me, but it stayed in my head what my grandmother said, and I wanted to please my grandmother. She did once say to me, maybe when you are older, you can come live with me. Every year as we would start to cross the river, in leaving New York, I would turn around with tears in my eyes, and say to myself, Someday, I will live with you, Grammie.

Chapter 5

GOING BACK HOME

THE TRIPS BACK to South Carolina were long and tiring. When my parents came to pick us up, my brother and youngest sister were with them too, so it was crowded in the back seat with the four of us. We would take turns sleeping on the floorboard of the car, and there was that darn bump. We dare not fight or push in the car. We were to sit still and be quiet. People were always telling my parents how well behaved we were. If we ever went to someone's house to visit, we always sat very quietly on the couch unless we were told we could go outside and play. We knew when we left for our trip; we were to go to the bathroom last thing, as Dad did not like to stop unless necessary. We always drove straight through at night. This was in the early 1950's to 1954. I was ten to fourteen yrs. old. My siblings were all younger. Back then it took longer to drive from New York to South Carolina as the roads were not as good as they are now.

Grammie would pack us sandwiches to eat, beverages to drink, and fruit. We would stop sometimes along the road to eat, but most of the time, we ate in the car, while Dad was driving. Sometimes when it was so hot, I would get thirsty and was afraid to tell my father. I knew he wouldn't stop just because I wanted a drink of water and I didn't expect him to. If I had to go to the bathroom, I would just try to control it and hope Dad would stop soon. If it got real bad, I would tell my mother and she would tell Dad to stop.

The worst experience I ever had was when I was fourteen years old and Dad came to New York alone to pick my sister and I up. Dad had won an airplane that summer and had even been on television when it was presented to him. Anyway, as I was saying, he flew the plane up to pick us up and fly us back home. As we were leaving the airport, we were running late and Dad was in a hurry. I had to go to the bathroom, and I was so afraid of telling him. I knew he'd get mad, so I didn't say anything. A friend of Dad's was with him and that made it even worse. How stupid was that? I got on the plane having to go to the bathroom! I worried and worried. At one point it started hurting so bad, how can I go and no one notice? It was just a four-passenger plane. No bathroom.

I whispered to Betty, "I have to go to the bathroom so bad."

She was angry and said, "Well, you should have gone before we left." She was right, of course.

"I've got to tell him." I told her. "You better not. You'll make him angry." She warned.

"I'll just have to go right here then," I said "and let it fall to earth." I said.

"Don't you dare," she hissed.

I didn't understand why she was so angry with me. I was the one going through it. I held it. I don't know how I did it, but I did. As well as I can remember, it was three hours later when we touched down in my hometown. I remember hurting so badly I could hardly get off the plane to go to the bathroom. I know it was my fault and for being so stupid, but for some reason, that I didn't understand, I just could not tell Dad. I'm sure he would have waited for me to go to the bathroom before we left the airport. He might have been put out, but he would have gotten over it. I still think I have to go to the bathroom before leaving the house even if I really don't have to. It made an indelible mark on me and taught me a huge lesson.

When I got home, it was good seeing my brother again. He always spent the summer and any other vacations with my father's dad and stepmother, Tessie. They really took to Bobby. I knew they loved us all, but Bobby was their favorite. It was really extra special when they came to visit. We called our grandfather Papa Tom. He was a gruff, husky man and very strict, but sometimes liked to tease us. He too, smoked a cigar, but I didn't feel free to hug him like I did Pop-pop. I had great respect and admiration for him though, and I loved Tessie, my step-grandmother. Papa Tom would announce when he came into the house, "All right the old man is here. Is there any dirt under the bed? No money if there is any dirt." I'd run to my room that I shared with my other two sisters. It always seemed to be a mess, and I would try to clean it up as fast as I could, throwing everything into the closet. And then he would say, "I'm checking the closets too." I'd cram them in a box and close the dark green velvet drapes the church gave us to make the room darker. He'd come in and inspect. If he didn't like something, he'd tell me, but most of the time, he would give us a quarter.

Then he would go out into the car and bring in so many groceries. Papa Tom was a manager of a grocery store, and brought us lots of dented cans without labels, because they could not sell them in the store. We never knew what we were going to have for supper. I remember once we had about fifty cans of canned cherries and what seems like hundreds of boxes of sugar pop cereal. They were for in-between snacks. Sometimes Papa Tom and Tessie would take my sister and I home with them for a weekend, but not often. He said we were not as good as Bobby. Betty and I always seemed to get into a fight. Bobby mostly got to go. My poor youngest sister Dawn mostly stayed home. Maybe it was because she was so young at that time.

I was told my mother had to go to the hospital when I was ten years old. I remember this so well, as Mom was giving me my first birthday party where I could invite friends. I was excited and nervous at the same time. I appreciated her doing this for me. I remember her good friend was with us and she had two children, so they would be there and I had a friend I could invite that lived across the field. Mom got sick and had to leave during the party. I don't remember her leaving. I was told this when Tessie came to take care of us. I believe she had her appendix taken out then. We loved Tessie being there with us, but I became very concerned because she said she was going to leave, if we children did not stop arguing with each other. She said she didn't want to watch us anymore as we were upsetting her with the fighting. Tessie never had children, but was very patient and loving. We had never seen her upset, ever! I remember feeling so bad and not wanting her to leave. I told my brother and sisters, "let's try to be real good so Tessie would not leave." We loved her so much and didn't want to lose her.

I didn't know my Dad's Mom, my paternal grandmother very well. I hardly ever saw her. She and my Dad were not close. Grandma Molly and Papa Tom divorced when my Dad was a teenager, and Dad didn't visit her much. I don't know the story there or what happened. It was never talked about. I remember she lived about an hour from my grandmother in New York. She would take the bus to come and see us at Easter at my grandmother's house. I remember one year she brought us a hollow chocolate Easter egg with a beautiful religious scene inside. It had a hole at the end of it and you could peek inside and see the baby Jesus. It was decorated so beautifully. She kept telling us she was our grandmother and hardly ever saw us.

I felt guilty; I didn't love her because I didn't know her. I think I was about eight then. One summer, she asked Grammie if I could come and stay with her a few days. She wanted some time with me. Grammie asked me if I wanted to go. I wasn't sure, but felt I couldn't say no in front of her, so I went, not knowing what to expect. I didn't want to hurt her feelings, but felt a bit uncomfortable. She was my grandmother and I was supposed to love her. This was different.

When we arrived at her home, she introduced me to her boyfriend. I don't think he lived there, as he wasn't there all the time. Her boyfriend brought his grandson over to play with me, but he was a mean child. Grandma would say, go outside and play with Johnny. Johnny would kick me, throw stones at me and spit. He was about six years old. I was always running from him. I could hit him back but knew I better not as my grandmother would not like it. I went into the house and told her what he was doing, but she didn't believe me. She got angry with me and told me to behave myself. She wanted her boyfriend to know what a good grandchild she had. I just had to keep running from him. I dare not talk back. I wasn't allowed or wasn't able to express myself to her.

One day Grandma sat me down in front of her in the living room. She started telling me how awful my father was, that he was her son and he never called her or loved her. She said my grandfather Papa Tom and her sons deserted her for someone else. She said she had been trying for years to find out where my grandfather and Tessie were living. I didn't say anything. I was not expecting this and I was confused. I was just eight years old. She got angrier. She said no one appreciated her and everyone treated her like dirt. She never saw her grandchildren or her sons. I was so frightened and felt awful. I didn't understand what she was saying. I didn't know anything about past circumstances, but I remember thinking, I want to get away from her. The way she was acting, I didn't blame them for not wanting to be around her. Was she always like this? I couldn't do anything right when I stayed with her. She said I was too sloppy. Didn't I know how to eat? I should hold my shoulders back when I walk. I should kneel in church, not sit.

"What was wrong with me?" she asked. "Didn't I have anything to say? Didn't I love her? She was my grandmother," she reminded me.

It was hard to love her. I slipped away from her one day and called my grandmother crying, please come and get me. I want to leave here.

Grammie came to get me without telling my grandmother I called her. I never wanted to be around her again, but sometimes, somehow I felt sorry for her and kind of guilty because I didn't love her. I kept remembering her saying, "I am your grandmother."

I tried to visit Grandma Molly when I was an adult, but it was not easy as she lived in New York and I lived in South Carolina. She was a very difficult woman and it was hard to be around her, as she was so depressing. She wanted love, but she was not a loving woman. Eventually she lost her eyesight and died without family being close. Grandma Molly drove people from her and probably never realized it. I wish I'd told her, "Grandma if you would stop complaining and talking about the past so much and show a little love, people wouldn't mind being around you. You demand love and respect." Sadly Grandma Molly died living in the past; not knowing all she had to do was show love to receive love.

It was sometime around this period when I was eleven or twelve that Aunt Mamie came to work at our home as a maid. She was a big, black woman who was very kind. Mom went to work for a doctor and we needed someone at the house with us children and to take care of the housework. After Mom went to work things got better all the way around. I knew this because we started all going out to the drive-in movies about once a week. Dad didn't believe women should work outside the home, but she was happier and we had more money for extras. My mother hated housework, and with Aunt Mamie being there, she didn't have to worry about it. I didn't see much of her, but she didn't seem as angry with me for things. It was during this period, I was feeling tired all the time and was so skinny. Mom took me to the doctor she worked for and he said I was anemic and I had to take B12 shots every day for about a week or so. I hated the shots but I liked my mother taking me to the doctor. It made me feel like she cared about me. I have no doubt she did, but I felt like she didn't.

Looking back, as I said, I don't have many memories of my mother, no experiences of just the two of us together when I was a child. I know I was always proud of the way she looked and I liked my school friends to see her when she got out of the car at school. She was pretty and she dressed pretty too. Her clothes with her jewelry and her scarves, always matched. Mom was popular. She and Dad still had lots of parties at home and they liked to dance. Dad was known at his workplace for his special spaghetti dinners he would have at the house. He built a very large and long table outside and invited many men from where he worked to come and have spaghetti dinners. We knew to stay in our room, when he did, but we got to eat earlier his wonderful spaghetti. He was a good cook.

I wasn't doing well in school. The only A's I got were in art, religion and conduct. This really upset my father. He tried making me do my homework first thing when I got home. It didn't bring my grades up. Nothing did. The truth was, and I never told him or anyone, I didn't try. I didn't care. I was glad it was upsetting my Dad. It didn't seem to bother Mom. It was my way of rebelling although I didn't realize it then.

Whenever we would have a special program at school, or open house and my artwork was on display, or I had a speech, my parents didn't come. I would tell them, but something always came up or they forgot about it. I wanted my Dad and Mom to see my artwork. Didn't my A's in conduct mean anything? I was a good girl. Darn them. Once when I was thirteen, I had the leading role in a play. I wanted so badly for Dad to see me, but he didn't come. He won't give me what I want from him, I thought. I won't give him what he wants from me – good grades. I was too young to know or understand I was only hurting myself and I would spend twenty some years trying to prove to him I was as smart as any son he could have ever had even if I was a girl. Dad just didn't know how much I loved him. How much I wanted him to be proud of me.

I don't know how important this is to even mention, but maybe some of you readers might relate to this. It was at about the age of ten years, that I began getting delirious from time to time. My parents told me that one night, they found me, way past midnight, on the telephone calling my friend's mother. It woke them up as the phone was in their room. Dad said I was put to bed and later I was up dialing again. I don't remember any of it, only him telling me so. The earaches had stopped, so I don't know why I was doing it again. Usually someone becomes delirious with fever. It is a scary feeling when everything is out of order, but this time, it didn't seem as scary.

Chapter 6

BECOMING A WOMAN

WHEN I WAS fourteen, I became a woman. I had my first period. I didn't know much about sex at all. I never really thought how babies were created. Oh I knew something went on in bed. I had heard my parents in bed (the bed springs squeaking) at night and I saw how dogs mated. I thought men looked like babies did, only larger. Never did I think they have pubic hair. I didn't know they got hard. I don't know how I thought they did it. I just didn't think about it much. My brother told me a lot about it when I was fifteen years old. I never saw a picture of a nude woman or man until much later on in life. We were taught to be modest and we were.

Wearing a pad was new to me and like most women I didn't particularly like it, but it was necessary. Not being used to having to wear these things I accidentally left it laying on the tub. My mother said my father saw it and said for me to be more careful in disposing of it. I was so very embarrassed that he knew. I didn't want to face him and felt sick inside. I didn't understand why. It was a natural thing to occur, it was just so personal to me.

It was strange that all through my adulthood until many years later, I just had my period three or four times a year and just for about three days. I never had regular and normal periods until I was in my early forties after I made major changes in my life. I was later told that stress alone, can cause your body to not perform normally. It can cause all kinds of true ailments.

Not long after this incident, Dad started taking time to talk to me. I mean really talk to me, and he wasn't scolding. He would talk to me about life and how to work for things that I wanted.

He said, "Veronica, remember this, if you want something bad enough, you can have it if you strive for it and work for it. Nothing is impossible, but do it in the right way. Always be a lady. Keep yourself for your husband. If you don't, he'll never trust you."

I couldn't help but think of him and Mom then. Didn't he trust her? As I mentioned before, I had found my birth certificate and their marriage license. The fact that I was born just a few months after they were married upset me terribly. Why? I felt he like he had to marry her, but I thought they wanted to get married. That is what Mom told me. Somehow I wasn't too surprised. It confirmed what I thought. Had I heard them arguing about it sometime in my childhood. Why was I not surprised? Is this why Dad was telling me this? I promised him I would not be with a man until I was married. I would make him proud of me. This was the first time I can recall my Dad really talking to me. He acted like he really cared. He did care. I felt it then without a doubt.

I was still taking my long walks in the woods though, in my fantasy world. It was about this time that I got my first kiss at a birthday party. We were playing "spin the bottle." I was scared when I had to go out in the hall and let this boy kiss me. I told him to "do it right." I don't know what I was expecting. He said, "What do you mean, do it right?" I always kiss right." I had always looked forward to my first kiss. I thought it would be wonderful and magical. Well, it wasn't. Uck! I hated it. It wasn't what I imagined at all. No bells went off, no lights flashed. Is this what kissing is all about? How disappointing. When I returned to the room the kids asked me how it was. All I could reply was, wet. (It wasn't a French kiss I found out later, it was just a sloppy one.) The boy never did like me after that. No wonder. I had embarrassed him. Poor fellow. He was probably as inexperienced as I was. He was supposed to be the lover of the neighborhood. I liked my fantasy world better. I had an imaginary boyfriend that I pretended to meet in the woods, across the street. I even had a name for him. I would hold my fingers to my lips and pretend he was kissing me. I loved lying in the wheat field, feeling the warm sun and the gentle breeze and pretending he was lying beside me.

A sixteen-year-old boy moved next door to be with his aunt for the summer and the school semester. He was from Brooklyn, New York and so very handsome. I really liked him, but he told my brother I was too young and inexperienced for him, that he wanted a girlfriend with experience like the ones he had back home. My brother, sisters and I played in the woods a lot and we saw him out there one day smoking a cigarette. He seemed so grown up to me. One day he pulled me behind a tree, so my sisters and brother wouldn't see us and gave me my second kiss. Oh, I liked it. It was warm and sweet, but he never kissed me again. Maybe he didn't like it. It was after this incident that he told my brother he wanted an experienced girl.

I let him think I didn't care; that I had someone else. I let him believe I was meeting a boy across the street. I even showed him a photo of a young man, pretending that it was the boy I was meeting. He started laughing and said, "This photo is so old, it has turned brown." I felt like a fool. It was a photo of my father when he was seventeen years old. I made up something like, Okay, this is not his picture, but I do have a boyfriend. I never did let him know how he hurt me.

We all left for New York that summer. Every July 4th there was a large family reunion. I hear a lot of people don't like family reunions and I was no exception. As always, I'd get sick. I'd have a hurting and nauseated feeling in my stomach, and emotionally felt so uncomfortable. I'd try to stay out of the way and not be noticed. I felt like I was undressed or something and people could see through me. I was always glad when the reunion was over and everyone was gone. My sister and I stayed with my grandparents as usual. I liked being alone with them.

That summer, it seemed that as Betty and I got older she liked me less. We had always spent the days at the park with friends in the past, but this year she didn't want to go when I did, and I couldn't go without her. Betty wasn't as quiet as me and she made friends easily. I felt left out a lot with her, it seemed she just didn't want to do anything much with me.

I had met a boy that summer at the park. Harry was an Italian and so good looking. He liked me and I was on cloud nine. Of course my sister was always there with me. We'd just walk around the park or sit on the bank by the little stream and talk. He never kissed me, but I was his girl he told the other kids at the park and that thrilled me. One day Betty, Harry and I were walking home and Pop-Pop came by in his car. He was angry and told us to get inside. Betty had told him about my boyfriend and he wanted to see for himself. He didn't want me to have anything to do with boys at that age. I was too young, and even if I wasn't, it wasn't going to be an Italian boy. He never did trust Italians for some reason. I told Pop-Pop that we didn't do anything wrong and that I wouldn't, and please let me go back to the park. He did let me go back with Betty, but he didn't have to worry about Harry any more. He dropped me after that. I was so hurt. I really liked him. He just acted like he didn't know who I was after that incident. (As I think of it now, it probably brought back memories of what he and my grandmother went through when Mom got pregnant at the same age as I was then, just fifteen years old. Pop-Pop nipped it in the bud.) I'm glad he cared enough now to do that.

It wasn't long after this, Betty and I were doing the dishes. She was washing and I was drying. I was so mad at her for getting me in trouble. She had told Grammie something that made her angry with me also. Oh no, I thought, she is not going to do this to me. I won't let her mess up my relationship with my grandmother. The sink was in the middle between cabinets. I was on the right and had to open the cabinet door to put the dishes away. If I swing the door open hard, it will hit her right in back of the head, I thought and I did just that! Needless to say, she ran screaming to Gram, but I just said it was an accident and to make it look good, I even said I was sorry. It was the first time and the last time I did something deliberate like that, but I was not sorry then. Later, much later, I truly apologized because I could have really hurt her and would not want to do that. Betty didn't remember the incident. Thank goodness.

When we returned home after that summer, something was wrong, but I couldn't put my finger on it. I just tried to stay out of the way and kept to myself a lot. By now I had long stopped playing with cars in the sand pile. I still liked paper dolls even if I was fifteen. Now I was designing their clothes and drawing them myself. Mostly, I stayed out in the woods or across the street in the barn.

I liked being alone. I remember that winter, it snowed and there was ice frozen on all the trees. I slipped out of my bedroom window after everyone was asleep and went for a walk in the woods. The moon was full and I could see so clearly. Everything was so beautiful. It was all shades of blue, white and glistening icicles. The moonlight made definite shows of the trees. I lay down on the ground in the snow. It wasn't cold. I had never seen anything so beautiful. It was like another world.

I went for walks often at night, but I had to slip out because we had to be in bed by nine o'clock on a school night and Dad didn't like me walking around in the woods after dark.

"It is dangerous, Veronica."

I liked him worrying about me, but I wasn't afraid. I was in my own world where I thought nothing could harm me.

I started having some boys take an interest in me, as I looked older than my age. I wasn't allowed to date until I was sixteen years old, but I could have friends come to the house. Dad would take us to the skating rink and pick us up afterwards. I met a lot of friends there, but I was still shy when it came to boys. I met one nice boy there and he asked to take me out and I told him I couldn't date, but he could come to the house. He did, and I got my first and last French kiss from him. We were in the living room and Dad just walked in and said hello to him and sat down to watch TV. The boy left and I never saw him again.

Another boy liked me from the skating rink, but he was twenty-three years old. He was the best skater at the rink and very popular. I was flattered he wanted to date me. All the girls liked him. When he first came to the house, I was showing him my dad's workshop that he had built himself and a small business he started on the side that later turned out to be very successful, but he wasn't interested in seeing the workshop. He pulled me to him and kissed me. He kissed me so differently, it kind of scared me. It must be because he is so

much older, I thought. It really scared me to be truthful. When Dad met him, he didn't like him at all.

He said, "Veronica, he is much too old for you and too experienced. I know his kind of people and I don't want him coming here, understand?"

A friend of Dad's, a police officer, even came to the house to tell me he knew of the boy and his family and they were no good, that he had gotten several girls pregnant. I asked him about what I had heard the next time I was at the skating rink. He said yes, he had, but he had changed. He asked would I just let him call me once in awhile. I said okay. He made me feel sorry for him somehow. I was so naïve.

Chapter 7

TROUBLE AT HOME

THINGS WERE NOT good at home with Mom and Dad. I don't know when I really started to notice it. Sometimes we know things as children, but just pretend it doesn't exist, as we don't want to believe it. I always bragged about my good-looking father and mother. I told everybody how happy he and she were together. They always had parties and lots of friends and went out together often. I can remember this now. I had blocked it out for a long time. I knew Mom and Dad's friends because we saw them frequently, even on vacations, but I suspected there was something between my mother and a friend of theirs. Mom would stop by his service station quite often after she picked us up from school. I kept pushing the thought away. I knew there were phone calls. The phone would ring once and she'd take the telephone from the hall, go into my brother's room and close the door. I never told anyone about it, or the time I came into the kitchen and saw her in his arms. I didn't want to remember it, so I conveniently put it out of my mind for many years and forgot about it.

Sometime during this age, (I was around fourteen), I asked my mother, who was Bessie? She looked at me with the color draining from her face.

"How do you know anything about Bessie?" she asked.

"I don't remember well," I answered. "I just remember standing on the stair steps at Papa Jim's when you and Daddy were having a terrible fight." The name "Bessie" stood out in my mind."

Mom said, "You were only a few years old. Did your father tell you about her?"

"No, Mom honest, I just wondered who she was," I answered.

"Well, she was one of your Dad's girlfriends," she replied.

Maybe Mom told me this at this time because of what I suspected she was doing. I didn't tell her I knew she liked this friend. The name Bessie was stuck in my brain all those years since I was just a few years old. Now I knew who Bessie was. I would ask Dad about her later.

Dad was gone a lot at work or at the airport. He was an engineer for a large corporation and loved to fly small airplanes, since he got his pilot's license. When he was home, he was in his workshop. He had started a small model train business on the side, and it was becoming quite successful. He would sell his model train kits to people all over the world. Sometimes I would go out and help him in the shop put the kits together, but he didn't talk much. My father became more and more involved in his work, which later led to great success.

At this time, I was attending an "all girls" Catholic boarding school in a nearby town. I was fifteen. I guess Dad thought I'd be safer there with the nuns after this encounter with the twenty-three year old. I was surprised they thought of sending me but thought it was pretty special to go and be there all week and come home on the weekends. I know Dad must have hoped I would get better school grades going there, but I didn't. I was failure, a complete failure there as a student.

I was always getting into trouble without meaning to. I liked to wear lipstick and lipstick was not allowed. I was caught having a make-up party in my room one night by the Mother Superior. I was grounded and my parents were told. I broke about 50 dinner plates one time, pushing a tray loaded with dishes from the kitchen down a ramp. Of course, they slid off. I was doing dishes as punishment for sneaking across the street to the bakery when I was not allowed off campus. Now, it was worse because I broke the plates.

I kept to myself more and more once again, and my parents were told I was not participating in activities and that my grades were poor. To make matters worse, this boy that my father told me not to see, called to me from the hedge of the schoolyard one afternoon as I was at recess. He told me that he and another boy wanted to meet with me and another student later that night.

I was hesitant, but said I would. He said that it was important and he had to talk to me. That night, we slipped out, but I met him outside alongside the school building. I got scared and went back inside after just a few minutes. My friend did too. I don't think he even kissed me. I can't remember what he had to tell me that was so important. It was stupid for me to have done that. Well, a passerby saw us outside. All Sister Superior was told was that two students were seen outside late after hours. The Sister didn't know who it was for sure, but she suspected as she opened a letter that was addressed to me from this boy. All mail was opened, as they were responsible for us. I never read the letter. I never really saw it. I was told that the letter said that he was asking me to marry him and to run away with him! It never entered my mind to marry him. I hardly even knew him. I was just fifteen years old. This was all told to me in Sister Superior's office in front of my parents.

My father was furious. How could I do that after he trusted me? He had spent money for me to get a good education and to better myself. He was upset that I didn't get good grades and said all I had on my mind was boys. I couldn't talk. I couldn't talk. I couldn't say anything but cry. They left. I went to my room there, at the school and wrote Dad a letter. I told him I didn't want to come home the next weekend because he didn't trust me.

Dad, I never planned on running away. I wrote. I know I have to get my education before anything else in this world. Your trust means everything to me. I felt I had lost what short-lived attention I got from him the last year and all our good talks. I didn't blame him for being disappointed and I begged him in the letter to believe me. I'd try harder. I did try. I just couldn't concentrate. I couldn't remember what I studied.

After a few months, understandably, I was taken out of the Catholic school and put into a public school. I was glad to be out. That Nun did not like me and I hated having to get up every morning at 6:00 A.M. We were on a constant schedule. I thought as a young girl, going to the Catholic elementary school, that maybe I would be a Nun one day. Maybe every little girl thinks of that when they are taught by them. My experience was good up until then with them, and I was a spiritual person. I changed my mind after this experience. Truly, I wanted children someday and looked forward to that.

I was not prepared for public high school. It was so different. The kids were different. It seemed everyone cursed a lot and I was not used to that. I never heard cursing in our home. We were not even allowed to say, shut up. If we back-talked we were slapped. These kids were disrespectful to the teachers. I was shocked at the way they talked to each other and to the teachers. I remember thinking it reminded me of a movie I saw named Blackboard Jungle, where there were many delinquents and rough necks in the school. This was in the 1950s. Even the girls cursed a lot in the bathrooms and there was a lot of talk about sex. This was all very new to me and made me feel uncomfortable. At first, I kept to myself.

Later during the school year, I got in with a good group because I knew one girl who was a neighbor down the road from where I lived. They were a wealthy family. I was told later he made his wealth being a bootlegger. A lot was new to me. She introduced me to the other girls. I didn't think them to be friendly. They dressed well and made fun of those who couldn't afford to. I didn't think that was right. I went home and told Dad I really needed some new clothes, that the girls dressed fashionably, and couldn't I have little something new? I was still wearing hand-me-downs.

"You don't need new clothes. You have clothes to wear. People should like you for yourself, not for what you wear. If they don't accept you, they are not your friends."

"But Dad, I'd plead. "You don't understand."

"That's enough," he said and I left it alone. I couldn't argue with him. When Dad said, that's enough.

He meant just that. The one good thing about my size at that time was that I could wear my mother's clothes. She had lots of them. I tried to make do the best I could and wore scarves with sweaters like other girls and roll down my Bobby Socks. Mom had wide full skirts that were also popular.

I don't think the girls really accepted me in that group, but my friend was popular, so they accepted me. One day I became friendly with a girl who was poor. I felt sorry for her. People stayed away from her and she was always alone.

In Glee club, later I felt a tap on my shoulder. "If you want to stay in our group, you'd better stay away from her. Her mother is a tramp and she is no better," she whispered. Well, that did it! "I'll be her friend if I want to," I said.

She couldn't help what her mother did, and I didn't believe it about her. We became friends. Even my sister Betty stayed away from me. She was a friend with the sister of the girl who brought me into the snobby group. My sister didn't like her either.

The girl never hurt anybody. She always kept to herself. How could they be so cruel? Of course I was out of the group after that, but I didn't care. I felt like I didn't belong anyway. My sister Betty stayed in the good group. It hurt when I would see her in the hall and she would not talk to me.

I had other friends at school too. Close friends who were not poor, but not wealthy either. Some of the students thought I was stuck up. I guess it appeared that way to them since I always had difficulty saying hello first.

My grades picked up. I was good in English, Art, Home Economics, Geography and History. I no longer took religion, but still stayed close to the Catholic Church as my faith was very important to me.

Dad and Mom didn't attend church, but always took us. Sometimes they would go if it were a special occasion, like Christmas, Easter and Holy Days. My mother wasn't Catholic, but she went along with us in what we believed as far as I know. I never heard her say anything against it, but then not for it either. I appreciate the fact that she did take us to church even though she didn't go.

I loved going to the church services. I loved everything about it. The candles burning, the different color votive lights, the statues, the fragrance of the incense and the flowers. I sang in the church choir and loved the Latin songs. We learned most of them as children and had them memorized. The same priest that baptized me and saw me through my childhood was still pastor/priest of this church. We were so close. He knew our family well. I gave my first-born son his name.

I remember when I first went to the public school in the tenth grade when asked my religion in class. You're what? Was the class response, after I stated I was a Catholic? They acted like I had something bad wrong with me. There weren't many Catholics in that town then, and I believe we were the only ones in that entire school. They would make fun of me, but I would just ignore them or at least pretend to.

Chapter 8

THE YEAR MY WORLD CHANGED

THE NEXT YEAR, 1956, I remember so well. I was to turn sixteen years old. It was a traumatic year for everyone in the family.

My maternal grandfather, Pop-Pop died in March of that year. As I said, before, I can't remember this time too well – his funeral. I do remember bending over the casket and kissing him goodbye. I loved him so much and couldn't believe he was gone.

I just didn't want to believe it. After returning home, I pretended for a long time that he was still alive and it worked. I wasn't able to see him but once or twice a year, so I could do that. Then, after awhile, I'd feel he could hear me talking to him. I felt his spirit there with me. This helped too. I guess I never really let out the pain of losing him. I never told anyone how I felt and no one asked. I found out much later on in therapy why I would always get depressed In March for many years after that, not knowing why. I never connected the two.

It's called an "anniversary grieving." Your subconscious knows even if you don't. If you do experience pain and don't acknowledge it, you will later in one way or another. It will manifest itself in depression or physical ailments. This experience has made me very aware of little children who have lost a family member. Many times they are forgotten about because the adults themselves are going through the grieving process. It's important to ask children how they feel also and let them express their feelings of loss.

It was that following May I met the boy I was to marry and to father my three sons. It's funny how I felt when I first met him. What did I have in mind? I surely did not want to get serious after what happened with the other boy who was twenty-three years old. I remember saying to myself, it will be nice just to have an innocent teenage romance. I wanted nothing serious, just something to tell my husband about someday. How very wrong I was. I wish I had turned and run in the opposite direction. He was cute, dark and quiet. This attracted me to him. He had a broodiness about him. I met him through some friends of his that knew my girlfriend. At this time, a lot of kids were coming to my home on Friday nights. Dad allowed this, as I was fifteen and my sister, Betty was thirteen. My brother was now eleven and little sister Dawn was ten years old. We'd build a campfire outside and roast marshmallows and sing. Three of the fellows would play their guitars. Ronald was the quiet fellow's name. I asked his cousin why he was always quiet. He told me he had a girlfriend, but he had a car and because of that, they would ride with him. I walked over to him and asked him why didn't he bring his girlfriend too? We broke up, was his reply. I knew my girlfriend liked him a lot and wanted to date him. I found out later, he liked me and I was flattered that he wanted me to be his girl over her. He came over to the house on Friday nights more often and then we started going steady.

When my father heard this, he said, "Veronica, I don't want you going steady. You are too young, and I don't like this boy. He's not for you." I don't care if he comes over to visit with your other friends, but that is all." I said to him, "Dad, I am fifteen years old, almost sixteen. You married Mom when she was about my age." I was getting braver, and I am sure he did not like hearing that. Dad responded, "We were too young too. That boy quit school. He paints whenever he does work, which is not often. None of his people ever amounted to anything, and he's no different. You're making a bad mistake." He closed with, "His people are not our kind of people."

He didn't forbid me this time to see him. I was out to prove my father wrong about him. Ronald couldn't help that some of his family served time in prison and that some of his family were alcoholics. I don't know how my father knew this, but he did.

As Dad walked away, I said, "Dad, I am not going to marry the boy, we are just going to go steady. That's all." His last words on the subject were, "You are making a big mistake." Oh how I wish I had listened to what he had said. He was so right! It turned out to be the biggest mistake of my life.

Ronald and I started to go steady. I felt like I finally had somebody. He said he loved me and to me, at that time in my life, it was enough. Ronald was a different kind of person. I never knew what was going on in his head. He was so quiet. He didn't like friends. He was mostly with his cousins who were his age. I really felt sorry for him without realizing exactly why.

He took me to his mother's house to meet her and the rest of the family. The house was old and small with thin boards on the wall. They didn't have much money to live on, and it showed.

Ronald went into the kitchen where his mother was preparing dinner. "Momma, this is the girl I told you about, - Veronica" Ronald announced as we walked into the room. His mother was a short, kind of stocky Indian looking woman with shoulder length wavy hair. She had a sweet smile, but was embarrassed and started apologizing for the mess in preparing dinner. I didn't want her to feel uncomfortable, and I tried to put her at ease. It didn't matter to me that they didn't have much. I liked her immediately and came to love her very much.

"Won't you have some supper with us? It ain't much though." She said in her Southern accent. "It smells good. Thank you," I replied. This was my introduction to my first Southern meal. Pinto beans, collard greens, fat back sliced and fried crisp, corn bread and bread pudding. I had never had these things before.

I thought it was delicious and told her so. Ronald's little sister Mary kept staring at me throughout the whole meal. She was a pretty little girl with dark skin, and pretty long dark hair. Mary was about nine years old at the time.

"You're pretty," she said to me. It took me by surprise her saying that in front of everybody. I was not used to hearing that. I said thank you and hoped that they didn't think I was stuck up or thought I was better than they were. Seems I heard that a lot from kids and I didn't know why. Ronald's brother came for dinner too. He was younger and he and Ronald looked very much alike. He too, was reserved but friendlier then Ronald. I liked him immediately.

He smiled and said it was nice to meet me. Ronald's stepfather came in, as we were about to finish. He was drunk and cussing. He was a short, sloppy overweight man, and badly in need of a shave. His hair was messy. Up until then, I had never seen a person drunk to the point of being loud and disgusting. Ronald's mother was very patient with him, and took and quickly put him to bed, like it was normal occurrence. No one said anything. I felt Katy, Ronald's mother, was embarrassed. I thanked Katy for the dinner and helped with the dishes, and then we left.

I had a sick feeling in my stomach.

Ronald had told me his father died when he was fourteen years old and his mother had married his father's half-brother, Ike. He told me Ike had served time in prison and was an alcoholic, but Ronald's mother loved him and it was her life.

That was another reason I felt sick. I had seen the man before. Right after I started going with Ronald, before I met his family, my friend asked me if I wanted to go to the beach with her and her mother. Her mother said we could take our boy friends. Oh, that would be great, I told her. I still wasn't allowed to date yet and it would be wonderful to walk on the each with Ronald and my father wouldn't know.

Ronald knew my friend and her mother before I did. This was the same girl I stood up for at school. If her mother was a whore as everyone said, I didn't know it. This friend of mine never told me of anything wrong her mother had done. Well, her mother called my mother and asked if I could go to the beach with them. Mom said it was all right. Ronald had agreed with her mother to get her a date also. The six of us took off for the beach. Her mother had her own private quarters that she and this man shared. Judy my girlfriend and I shared a room and Ronald and his cousin shared a room.

It was the first time I was alone with Ronald. We were sitting in the back seat of the car. I didn't know where Judy and his cousin were. We started kissing and hugging. Ronald started to pet me and he was kissing me so long and so hard it hurt me and I was scared. I started crying and told him to stop. I told him I was a virgin and had never done it. I wanted to wait for marriage. I felt very strong about this. He didn't try to talk me into it. He left me alone and told me he would respect me. After that we would just go for long walks on the beach and go to the amusement arcade. He didn't try again, and we went home.

After walking out of Ronald's mother's house that evening, after seeing this drunken stepfather, I screamed at him, "How could you? He is your mother's husband. How could you do this thing?" The man I saw at the house, his stepfather, was the same man he "fixed up" for my girl friend's mother! This incident alone should have warned me what kind of person he was. How stupid I was!

"Oh, he runs around all the time, and Momma knows it. It's no big thing."

"But did you have to be a part of it?" I cried.

What was he thinking? I thought it was terrible. Was there no loyalty to his mother?

"I'm sorry," he said. It won't happen again and it has nothing to do with you and me." This was a huge red flag. I foolishly, let it go and tried to put it out of my mind. I didn't want to believe that he could be so cavalier about this.

It wasn't much fun going steady with Ronald. He never wanted to go anyplace. I wanted to go to school activities, like ballgames or school dances. He never wanted to go and I didn't want to hurt his feelings by going without him. I wish I had. We mostly sat at the house and watched TV. Dad still took my sister and I to the skating rink. Ronald would meet us there but he never would skate. He'd watch us. Sometimes I felt I was the best thing that ever happened to him and he loved me so much. He said he needed me in his life. By this time, I was able to talk him into going back to school. He was attending night classes. His mother said I was a good influence on hm.

Chapter 9

MEETING BRENT

WE WERE ON our way to New York, as we did every summer, only this time it wasn't Dad driving and the rest of the family in the car, just my sister Betty and me and a man friend of Mom and Dad's. I knew this man and his wife as they had been over to the house on many occasions. We had even gone on vacation trips together. What I didn't realize at the time, as that was the man I saw my mother being hugged by. I had really blocked this out of my mind successfully. I supposed because I didn't want to believe anything could happen to Mom and Dad's marriage. My memories of negative things didn't come back to me until I was at Hospital Medical center undergoing treatment for severe depression.

I didn't know where Dad was or why the trip wasn't as it used to be. I assumed he was aware of who was taking us and it was ok with him. It was a pleasant trip with my sister and I reading the road map and telling him what turns to take. This man just sort of disappeared after taking us to our grandmother's. He said Goodbye to us all and I didn't see him again until many years later. (He was to become our forth stepfather.)

It was a good summer. I was so glad to be with my loving grandmother again in a home I felt comfortable in. It looked the same, only Pop-Pop was missing.

My grandmother and I talked about since I was older, maybe I could live with her and be of some help since Pop-pop was no longer there with her. Maybe Dad would consider that possibility. My heart leaped with joy at just the thought.

That summer was extra special in many ways. That also was the summer Dad sent my sister and I the most beautiful letter ever. It was addressed to The Two Southern Belles in care of my Grandmother's home. He drew funny cartoons on the envelope. It was written in light blue ink. Gosh I thought Dad's changing. This was not like him, but I didn't question it. I was thrilled to receive such a wonderful letter. I remember the letter so well. I did carry it for years until it fell apart, but how I wish I had it now to hold in my hands I have the words etched in my heart. He thanked us for his Father's Day card, and said that there should be a "Daughters Day" celebrated. He said that we were two fine daughters. Dad had never said anything like this before. He went on to say that he and my younger sister had been to church and asked if I still wanted to be a Nun? He needed to know if I had not changed my mind, as he needed to make arrangement at "St. Mary's in the Woods" a convent school in Indiana. I had not told him I had changed my mind. By now I wanted to get married someday and have children. He also said that Ronald and some of his cousin came by the house and he tried to make conversation but Ronald was still very quiet and didn't talk much. I thought Dad's trying. He closed the letter by reminding me to eat bread with butter, and for my sister to eat her green peas. Later, I realized Dad must have known by then, he was going to leave us, and wanted us to know how he felt. I was so happy after reading the letter, I cried, not realizing it was my one and only letter from Dad. Things were about to change drastically.

My sister and I went roller-skating one night and I met a very nice young college student by the name of Brent. He was attending Seaton Hall University and was studying to be a doctor. Brent was an only child and a Catholic like me. He was tall and handsome and came from a very good family. What impressed me the most was that, he was so polite and a real gentleman.

My sister met Brent's friend that night too and wanted to see him again. He was in the armed forces and home on leave. Brent asked me if I could date. I told him I wasn't sixteen yet, but would be that August. I did tell him I was going steady with someone. Going steady to me meant you don't date anyone else. He informed me his friend didn't have a car and would be bringing him over to my house to see my sister. Could I just sit and talk to him? Yes, of course that seemed all right.

After awhile I really got to like Brent a lot. He asked couldn't I just go to a movie with him? I told him I would think about it.

After he left, I went to my grandmother, "Gram, Brent asked me if I'd go to a movie with him," I said to her. "Why don't you go, dear?" she asked me. "I can't Gram. I really want to, but I'm not sixteen yet and I am going steady. I can't go behind Ronald's back. It would be dishonest," I answered.

"Veronica I am sure your father would approve of you going to a movie." You will be sixteen in a few weeks and Brent seems like a fine young man." As far as you going steady, you're much too young," she told me quite firmly.

"Well," I said. "I do want to go." I'll just have to call Ronald and tell him to date too. I will tell him I am going to a movie with another boy."

Aunt Margo, who married my uncle, was there too. She heard me and said, "are you crazy? You don't have to call him. Just go and have fun." I looked at Gram who agreed by nodding her head yes. I thought about it, and then said, "No, I have to tell him." How dumb was I? I was to have it thrown up in my face for years to come.

Brent and I really had a wonderful time. We went to a movie, and then stopped at a soda shop afterwards. We had a lot of things to talk about and I laughed with him. I didn't give Ronald a thought and didn't let his response over the phone ruin the night.

When I called Ronald, I told him that I wanted to go out with a boy. "Ronald I could have gone and you would have never known; but I want to be honest with you, because you trust me, so I had to call. Why don't you date other girls while I am here also? When I come back, we can still be together."

"Veronica, I love you, I don't want to date other girls. You said you loved me. Don't you still love me?" His voice was breaking.

"Yes, I still love you. We'll still be together when I come home," I told him again.

"Do you promise?" "Yes," I replied feeling very sad.

I continued to date Brent. But said nothing more to Ronald about it when he called. The nights I knew he was going to call, I'd stay home. I didn't want to upset him.

I met Brent's parents and really got along well with them. They liked me and invited me to a family get-together that following Saturday at a club. There would be a picnic, boating, swimming and games. We went and I had such a good time. Everyone was so nice. Brent and I went for a swim and then lay on a quilt sunning ourselves. "I love you, Veronica," he said. I heard it and really couldn't take it in. All I could think of was, oh no, what will I do about Ronald? I had promised I'd stay his girl. I told Brent about him, so he knew the situation. "I care about you an awful lot too, Brent." I said. "Do you love me?" He asked. "I don't know. I think so, but how can I love two people at the same time?" was my reply. He didn't answer to that.

He just said. "I have plenty of time. I have my schooling to finish before I can think of anything serious, but I'd like for you to wait for me if that is possible."

"Oh, Brent," I said.

I was overwhelmed. I felt happy and free with Brent and very comfortable. Here was everything a girl could ask for and I didn't feel free to be his girl. What was wrong with me?

Later on that summer, Dad and Mom came up. Brent and his parents were there at Gram's at the time visiting, so they got to meet Brent and his parents. After they left, Dad said, "Now that is a fine young man." I even got Dad's approval. What more could I ask for?

Brent and his family left for vacation and Brent sent me two Indian dolls for my sixteenth birthday. I treasured those dolls and kept them until eleven years later when I gave them to a friend's daughter who admired them.

Before leaving to go back home, I asked Dad if I could live with Gram. He said, "No Veronica, it's best you come home." Something, in the way he said it, I knew something was wrong. When I left, I told Gram I couldn't live with her yet. She said kindly, "I know, dear." And said the usual, "Be good and help your mother all you can." She needs you." There was concern on Gram's face. Her words stayed with me for years.

Later crossing the bridge, as we always did, I turned around and said goodbye to New York. Little did I know I was saying goodbye to the last kind of happiness I was to know for a long, long time.

Chapter 10

DAD'S MISSING

THINGS WERE NOT good at home when we returned after summer break. It seemed very tense at home more than ever. Things seemed to escalate between Dad and Mom. They both were short tempered when they spoke, but they didn't have much to say to each other. Dad was gone now more than ever after winning the airplane. Which is understandable. He wanted to be at the airport, when he was not at work.

I should have paid more attention to what they were going through and not have pushed the envelope where Dad was concerned. Me being a teenager, I didn't want to think about it and was involved with my own problems, I regret to say.

Not long after school started, I was saying goodbye to some of my friends on the front porch. It was Sunday evening and they were not allowed to stay past 5:00 o'clock because of school being the next day. We had to get ready for bed and be in bed by 9:00 o'clock. Dad was strict about us being in our room on school nights. Well, Dad must have had a really bad day.

I guess I was taking too long saying goodbye, because he said the second time, "Veronica Ann, I said get in this house." Without thinking, I said, "Just a minute." He was out there in two seconds and slapped me in the face.

"When I saw now, I mean now!" He said angrily.

He told Ronald and my friends to leave. How could he do this to me in front of my friends? I was so ashamed and embarrassed. He told me to get to my room. Later when I thought he was asleep, I sneaked out of my room to call Ronald. I didn't know what he was

thinking and I had to talk to him. The phone was in the hall. I quietly tiptoed in my bare feet, down the hall to the phone that was just outside my brother's room, and slowly closed the door.

"Shh." I told my brother.

I dialed the number as quietly as I could. I had just got Ronald on the phone, when the door swung open and the light went on! In a flash Dad had the phone out of my hand and out of the wall. He tore the phone loose. I had never seen him so angry. This time I got a whipping with the belt.

"Sixteen years old and I still have to whip you." He yelled. He whipped me hard.

"I won't cry. I won't cry." I thought to myself. He could have killed me and I wouldn't have cried. I kept telling myself. I won't give him the satisfaction of knowing he was hurting me. "I hate you." I shouted at him. "I hate you."

He spanked me harder. I didn't hate him. I hated him not showing me love. To me, back then, love was being held by someone who loved you. He never held me. (I feel bad writing this, as I know now, what Dad was going through, and I just added to the stress.) I was to find this out later when I was going through the stress of a divorce and I over reached with one of my own sons.

After the whipping, I laid in bed about an hour, then I got up and yes, I climbed out the window. I didn't know where I was going, but I wanted to get away from there. I felt so alone. I thought I had just found Dad's love by his letter and now this happened. I felt so lost. It was very late. I imagined about eleven o'clock. I wanted to go further than the woods this time. Where will I go? I wondered. I know, I will go by Judy's house and then I'll worry about it in the morning.

Judy must have lived at least ten miles away and it was dark outside. That walk was a nightmare. I was afraid of being picked up and I was afraid of Dad finding out I was gone; so every time I saw a car's headlight approaching, I would run and hide in the side ditch. These were country roads with no houses in sight. The roads there had deep ditches, so I was easily concealed. The night air was cool. Why didn't I wear a jacket? The ditches were dirty and I was getting all scratched. I couldn't see very well in the dark. I was lucky a snake didn't bite me, but then I didn't think of that. I finally made it to Judy's house. The house was dark. They must be asleep, I thought. I walked up to the door and knocked. No one answered. I knocked again. No answer. I walked around to the back of the house. Their car was gone. No one was at home. I had not thought they might be gone. What was I going to do? It must be around one o'clock in the morning. As I was walking around to the front of the house, I saw car headlights turn into the drive. I jumped back behind a bush to make sure it was them coming home. It was a man and he was alone. It wasn't Judy. My heart sank. It sank further when I heard, "Veronica." Oh my God, it's dad! Pure terror went through me. What will I do? It never occurred to me to keep my mouth shut. He would have left and I would have been safe. But then maybe, I felt going with him was better them staying out all night in the cold. I don't know what I thought.

Fear gripped me. "Veronica," he called again, and I meekly walked out. His hand was like a flash of lightening when it hit my face. I was on the ground. I had pushed him too far.

"You just don't give up, do you?"

That is all I can remember him saying. I just blocked out anything else he had to say. I know I tried to jump out of the car and he caught me and hit me again. When I got home, I went to my room exhausted and he went to his. I am sure he was exhausted also. The incident wasn't brought up again.

All of a sudden Mom was gone. We were told she went to visit Gram for a while. I don't remember having any feelings about it. It never occurred to me that she left because of the tension between she and Dad. Once Ronald told me he heard they were going to break up. My response was of great anger when I asked him,

"Who told you such a lie? They get along fine. I would know if it were true." I accused him of making it up because he kept talking about us getting married. He just kept at me about it.

"You think if they break up, I'd marry you now?" I said to him with anger, feeling afraid. He wouldn't tell me where he heard it.

One day my siblings and I came home from school, and it was like we came to the wrong house. Everything was so shiny and clean.

Everything! I had never seen it like this. I didn't know it could look like this. Everything was in such order. All the dresser drawers had clean clothes, freshly ironed and neatly folded in place, scarves, sweaters and underclothes. All the dirty clothes in the hamper had been washed and towels folded and put away. I know things were messy before, and we kids tried to keep things the best we knew how, but I didn't know it could look like this. It was like a fairy godmother came. I asked Dad who came and did this. He said some friends of his, where he worked. I remember thinking I wish the house could always look like this. I wish I knew how to keep it looking like this.

I remember one day about this time, I started to go out into Dad's workshop, but stopped when I saw my father sitting on the edge of the doorway with his head in his hands. I just stood there looking, and then I realized my father was crying. Dad was crying. I never saw a man cry. I guess I must have thought men didn't cry. Oh Ronald cried a lot it seemed; but this was my father crying. I had so many mixed emotions. I know I couldn't let him see me. He wouldn't want me to see him cry. Why was he crying? I felt so sorry for him and I didn't know why. A great sadness was in my heart. It felt heavy. I went back in the house and never told him. I understand now, so many years later, why he was crying. I wish I could have put my arms around him.

Dad came home one day and said, "How would you all like to go square dancing?"

"All of us? Ronald too?" I asked.

"Yes, Ronald too," he said with a smile. I knew Dad liked to dance.

He and Mom were good dancers, but he never asked just us before.

The next thing I knew, Mom was home before we were to go to the dance. I heard she and Dad arguing loudly before we were to leave.

Mom was screaming hysterically. I ran into the bedroom where they were. Mom was next to the wardrobe. I can still see her face, wet from crying and she was screaming so. It was frightening. Dad was trying to calm her and Mom kept crying, stay away. Go to the dance.

Dad said,

"Come and go with us."

I couldn't stand seeing my mother like that. She was wild. "Mom come go with us," I pleaded.

Dad said for us kids all to go out of the room and he'd be right with us. We still were going to the dance? What was wrong with Mom? Why was she acting like this? Did she come home unexpected? Was she angry because we were going? Dad asked her to come too. We all went to the dance without Mom. I tried to put the scene in the bedroom out of my mind.

It was fun at the dance. Everybody was having a good time. Dad asked me to dance with him. I never danced with my father and felt kind of self-conscious. I didn't know how to act, but tried the best I could. I wanted him to be proud of me. Ronald wasn't a dancer, so he just watched. I don't remember what happened with Mom after that night? I can't remember if she was still angry or if everything was okay. I guess it was just a time in my life that I still won't allow myself to remember.

The next thing I knew Dad was gone, just gone. "Mom, where is Dad?", I asked puzzled. "That's a good question." I'd like to know the answer to that question myself." She replied angrily. What was happening? I turned to Ronald, and asked him.

"Where is Dad? Why isn't he here?" He made a face by rolling his eyes and said, "you know good and well he left. You saw him and your mother."

"What are you talking about?" I said panicky.

"Don't you remember? Are you telling me you don't remember seeing him put his clothes and things in the car? He answered. Then he added a bit impatiently, "You watched him pack the car full of things the day he left. Your mother was screaming and begging him to stay. She ripped the back of his jacket as he walked down the steps in trying to stop him. You stood right there on the porch and saw the whole thing." Then he added, "What's wrong with you?"

"I can't remember. Did I say anything?" I asked him. "Yes, you said he would be back." When he didn't come back a couple of days later, you tried to jump out of the car, on the highway. Now, don't tell me you don't remember that too?" he said a bit sarcastically. "Are you telling me the truth?" I asked him, my voice rising. "I have no reason to lie," he said calmly. "Ask your mother if you don't believe me." he replied.

"Mom?" I said looking at her pleadingly. She was in the kitchen and didn't even look up as she said simply, "it happened."

Through out the years I would ask, Ronald "are you sure I was there?" Did I really try to jump out of the car? His answer was always the same as above. For some reason, I let the whole thing go, not wanting to think about it. I didn't even question why Ronald's response was of impatience with me when I questioned him about the incident.

After that I don't remember having any strong feelings one way or another after Dad left. I didn't understand that. I must have really blocked out my feelings then along with unpleasant incidents. I felt shut down. I do remember vaguely a feeling of relief, which I did not understand until after getting help. Subconsciously, I was afraid of my father finding out about Mom's man friend. I had blocked out the day I saw Mom in this man's arms. I didn't even remember the phone calls until I went into therapy. Little by little I started remembering things. At the time these things took place, it was all too painful and frightening. It was reality.

My mother told me, Dad left her for a much younger woman he knew at work. She left her husband, too and a two year old son behind. Your father's been seeing her all this time. "He didn't have time for his own family, but he did for her." She said bitterly. I don't remember feeling anything when she said this to me, just numb. I do remember how very much I hated hearing my mother talk about it on the phone to all of her friends. I said nothing, but I felt angry with her and didn't understand why.

Mom seemed to change quite a bit after my father left. I believe my mother loved my father even though she may have cared for someone else, but she was mostly angry then as opposed to grieving. Perhaps it was a way to cover up her real feelings. I don't know. I only know I felt as though I had lost her too. She never seemed to hear what I was saying. I drew more and more to myself and closer to Ronald. I felt he was the only person I had in the world. I could never let my grandmother know what all was happening. I didn't want to worry her. She was worried enough about my mother after my Dad left. My sisters and brothers and I never talked about what was happening, and it wasn't long before my brother was leaving home too. Mom said we were having a hard time financially and it would help for my brother to go live with Dad's father and stepmother in another state. This was so sad because we children were close and I missed my brother terribly. He was my friend, my playmate from childhood. He was just thirteen years old. In some ways, I felt he was lucky though to be able to go live with my paternal grandparents. They loved Bobby a lot and would take good care of him. It was always a joy to go and visit them. Our step grandmother, Tessie, was kind, loving and a great cook. Papa Tom was gruff and strict but funny too. He loved to fish and Bobby could go fishing with him.

We knew Dad was someplace in Florida, but did not know what part of the state. The money orders that my father sent were always from a different town. Every month the money came regularly for the home payment and for support for each of us. Dad wasn't forced to do that by a court. They never went to court. He did it because it was the right thing. He can't be all that bad, I thought. He cared enough to see we were taken care of. This made quite an impression on me at a young age. Dad was doing this on his own and not because there was a court order making him. He did care, is the way I felt then, not understanding Mom could have the law after him for not supporting us.

My mother got a job at a local restaurant as a waitress. Money was still tight, but we weren't hurting. Dad sending money along with Mom's wages worked, but Mom was still angry saying he didn't send enough. If I needed something for school or any clothes, Ronald bought them for me, making me feel more and more obligated to him. He was still working as a painter for one of his relatives. I did babysitting whenever I could, and just continued with my schooling.

Chapter 11

GOODBYE BRENT

THAT THANKSGIVING WE went to my grandmother's as we did every year. Mom asked Ronald to go with us to help her drive. She didn't ask me how I felt about it. She liked him and they always got along well together. She approved of me going steady with him. She often said it was good to have him around because he took care of things around the house that needed fixing, now that Dad was gone. She said she felt secure with a man around. Holy cow! He was just Seventeen years old. She said if we had car trouble on the trip that he could take care of that too, since he knew car motors so well. For some reason, I wasn't very happy with him coming to my grandmothers with me. It was a strained trip to New York and my sister, Betty did not care for Ronald at all, and it seemed she and I were not getting along. I still didn't know what the problem was with her.

I was glad to get to Gram's for several reasons, one of them being that I couldn't wait to call Brent. I still cared for him very much and could not forget the wonderful carefree time I had with him. It was always so serious and heavy with Ronald. There was no comparison. Ronald did not know how I felt about Brent, as I did not want to hurt his feelings. Whenever he and I had a bad argument and I would threaten to break up with him, if it didn't stop, he would cry and beg me not to. It always made me feel so guilty, and my mother would say I should feel sorry for upsetting him. She would tell me, be glad you have someone who loves you so much. You should be grateful. Those words seared in my brain.

I went into my grandmother's bedroom as soon as I had a chance to get away from Ronald and call Brent. As I dialed his number, my heart was beating so hard. I was nervous. He answered the phone, "Hello." Oh it was so good to hear his voice. I felt warm all over.

"Brent, it's Veronica" I said quietly.

"Where are you?" he asked.

"At Gram's." I answered.

"You are here, in Jersey?" He sounded surprised, but pleased. "I'll be right over." He added.

"No, Brent, you can't." Ronald is here", I whispered.

"Well, tell Ronald you want to see me. He doesn't own you. You want to see me don't you?"

I responded, "yes, of course I do, very much. It's just not that simple. I can't."

I felt so controlled by them. I truly felt like I couldn't and it was killing me!

"All right, I won't come over now, but I don't understand you," he said somewhat resigned for the time being.

"Brent, Mom and Dad broke up." I said suddenly, changing the subject.

"What?" he said surprised, adding, "I don't believe it. You must be kidding."

"No, it's true. I felt al choked up saying the words and tears were filling my eyes for the first time. Hearing the words made it seem even truer.

"I'm really sorry Verionica. I am so sorry,' he said to me very kindly. There was a brief silence, and then I remembered I had to hang up before someone came into the room and wondered why I was sneaking to use the phone.

"I have to go Brent, before they find out I am on the phone," I whispered.

"I don't understand why you have to be so secretive about it," He said. "Promise you'll call me when I can see you. Okay?"

"Yes", I answered. "I'll call you."

I kept waiting for the right time to come so I could call Brent, but it never came. Ronald was always there. I kept hoping he would leave and go somewhere. I couldn't get away from Ronald without him being right there with me all the time. Finally it was time to go home. I felt panicky. I had wanted to see Brent so bad, and I had not even called him back. I had to take another chance. I waited for Ronald to leave the room, and then I closed the bathroom door, so he would think I was in there and I slipped into my grandmother's bedroom to once again call Brent. Mom and Ronald were packing the car. I didn't have much time.

As soon as he answered the phone, I said, "Brent, I called to say Goodbye." What do you mean goodbye?" He asked with his voice rising. "Are you going already?" You said you would call me when I could see you. I have been waiting for you to call." Veronica, I want to see you. Now!" he added.

I was crying.

"I know you love me, Veronica." He said more softly. "I'm coming over." He said.

"No, please don't. We are leaving in just a few minutes." I pleaded with him. "You are right, Brent I do love you so much, but I can't go with you. I promised Ronald I'd marry him. I have to." I heard my mother and Ronald coming back into the house. "I have to go now. Please take care of yourself. Goodbye," I said as I hung up the phone, afraid they would walk into the room. I was able to come out of the room and open the bathroom door, without Ronald thinking anything. I was so relieved.

We got into the car and made our usual stop at Pop-Pop's service station to fill up with gas. My uncle was now running it since my grandfather's death. While sitting in the car waiting for the tank to be filled, Brent drove up! I was so surprised to see him, but happy too. He got out of his car and came over to where we were parked, and politely said he wanted to talk to me privately. I was so impressed that he did this. Ronald didn't say anything. He had to get out of the car to let me out as I was sitting in the middle back seat.

"Ronald, this is a friend of mine. This is Brent." I said feeling very nervous. Ronald reluctantly shook hands with Brent, when Brent held out his hand. We walked over to his car, and he sat down in the driver's side, as I stood next to the door, my back to Ronald and my mother.

"I couldn't let you leave without seeing you. Brent said. I had to see you. I called your grandmother not long after you hung up from talking to me. She told me I could find you here. Your grandmother likes me. Your parents liked me when I met them last year. Why don't you feel free to see me?" He asked.

I couldn't answer, as I didn't know the answer to that question myself.

"Do you love this guy?" He asked, nodding towards Ronald.

"I think so. I don't know. But, I love you too." I said looking down at him in the car, wishing I could get in with him and drive away from all this.

"Well, he has some kind of a hold on you." Brent said. I noticed he still had one of my earrings clipped on his sun visor. It made me feel good to see that. He noticed me looking at it and said he was going to keep it there.

Mom yelled at me to come, we had to leave. How very hard it was saying goodbye to Brent. He had tears in his eyes and I felt like my heart was breaking. How much I wanted to be with him. Why couldn't I be? I had to say goodbye to this fine young man.

The ride back home was terrible. Ronald was mad at me of course for talking to Brent and acted all hurt. Mom was mad and said I was inconsiderate and selfish. How could I ask Brent to come over in front of Ronald? It didn't matter I didn't know, but inwardly I was so pleased he had the courage to do that. It showed me how much he cared. My sister Betty was mad too. No one was speaking to me. I didn't care, but I felt stuck. I held on to the knowledge that someone good and decent loved me for all the right reasons. It felt good to be loved and not feel so responsible for someone's life. Ronald always told me, he couldn't live without me and I believed him. He said he would kill himself if I ever left him and I believed that too. It was a sick, controlling love. Not a healthy one.

Not long after this, Mom had a friend of hers move in with us. She said it was to help with expenses. I didn't care for this woman at all. She was too loud and she was always cussing. She drank a lot and before long, my mother was doing the same thing. I had never heard my mother cuss before and hearing it was very unpleasant. She and Bunny, her new friend, started often having long and loud parties. I hated seeing the men put their hands all over my mother and her laughing at their dirty jokes.

One Sunday morning, after one of their parties, I went into my mother's bedroom to wake her up as she always drove my sister and I to church. I froze at the sight that I saw from her bedroom door. Oh no, I thought to myself, not this too. Not my mother! I couldn't believe my eyes. My mother, Bunny and Bunny's boyfriend Roy were all in the bed together, nude. They didn't see me, as they were all three asleep. I can't explain how terrible I felt and how very much the pain in my chest hurt. All I could think was, mothers don't do things like this, especially my mother. This was the woman, who along with my father taught me to be good. I tried so hard to please her and do what she said. Didn't I count? Didn't the same rules apply to her? How could she do this? It was wrong. I kept the scream inside me, as I didn't want them to see me. I felt like the room was closing in on me. I had to get out of there. Was no one who I thought they were? Was everything a lie?

I ran as fast as I could from that horrible sight and out the front door. I ran crying from the house into the woods and then the fields across the street sobbing, Mom, how could you? Oh Mommy, don't you care about us? What's happened? I ran to the barn and climbed up into the loft and threw myself into the hay. I felt somewhat comforted by the softness of it and the way it seemed to cuddle me. I felt so alone as I sobbed my mother's name over and over. I wanted my father. I wanted my grandmother. I wanted someone, but how can I ever tell anyone what I saw? I felt so ashamed and didn't know why, but after awhile, I quit crying and felt calmness, a resolve. I felt God knew and how very much I needed Him to be with me.

I wondered, didn't Mom care about herself anymore? Didn't she care what I thought? What about my little sister? I hoped Mom would get up before Dawn saw too. She was only ten years old. I couldn't even approach Mom about it. I didn't know how. I was afraid of making her angry. What was I going to do? I felt so helpless. I

reminded myself, my mother was drinking. I felt for sure she would not have done that if she had not been drinking too much, but still it was bad. I stayed in the barn all day until late afternoon. I finally went home.

My mother was in the kitchen when I walked into the house. "Where have you been?" She asked. "I was just across the street." I went for a walk and then I stayed in the barn for awhile." I answered. She went on cooking at the stove. Bunny and Roy were gone.

"What's your problem?" she asked angrily, when I didn't have much to say. This was my opening. "You know." I answered.

"No, I don't. I am not a mind reader." She said still sounding angry.

"What you did last night," was all I could get out.

"Look here young lady. It's my business what I do. I work hard trying to make a home here. I do the best I can since your father took off and left me holding the bag. I don't need you to tell me what to do." she said, with her voice rising. "Do you understand?" She shouted.

"Yes." Was all I could say with tears in my eyes. I felt hurt. I couldn't reach her. This was not the mother I knew. Mom was gone too.

This incident stayed with me until my adulthood. When I was twenty-nine years old, and was talking to my doctor about it, I was crying as I had in the barn. The pain had stayed with me all those years. Now I realize that Mom was not herself and was having a very hard time adjusting to being on her own. Dad had left her for a much younger woman. She herself was only in her thirties and had four children to care for. She felt very rejected, helpless and alone. I realized much later that parents are human and can make mistakes just as well as anyone else; but at the age of sixteen, I was so sensitive and impressionable that it hurt me terribly to see my mother in this position. I couldn't understand, as I had been protected from things from the time I was born and this behavior was all new to me. There were more changes in my life at that time, than I could keep up with.

I didn't tell anyone of this, with the exception of Ronald, for a very long time. I told him everything, as he was all I had.

It wasn't long after this incident that Bunny moved out. I was glad to see her go, but Mom had other plans that I was not aware of. She asked Ronald to move in with us, before she said anything to me about it. They just assumed I wanted it too. I was not happy about it, but didn't know how to tell them so. It was the last thing I wanted. I wanted to break up with him, now he was going to be living with us? Why did she do this? They thought it was a great idea. Mom said she felt safer with a man around, and Ronald could fix things around the house when they needed repairing. I thought, a man around? He was just seventeen years old! How many mothers would ask their daughter's boyfriend to move in with them? This was weird to me, but it made perfect sense to her. As they both were sitting at the table talking about their plans, I was thinking what are my school friends on the bus going to think when they see Ronald's car at my home early in the morning? I know that they would think he spent the night with me. They would think we were sleeping together. What would his family think? I was worried. I cared about my reputation and I knew how mean the kids at school could be. Mom said Ronald could take my brother's room, which was just down the hall from my sisters and mine. My brother was now living with my Dads parents. I missed Bobby.

I resented it very much that they had made this decision without talking to me about it. I already felt obligated to Ronald; now I would be getting in deeper with him living in our home. I had just wanted an innocent teenage romance. A happy one and it wasn't working out like I planned. I would think these thoughts and then feel guilty, reminding myself that he loved me and he was all I had. Without him, I would really be alone. I couldn't hurt him but telling him how I felt abut him living with us, and besides it would make my mother very angry. She wanted him there. It was her decision. I kept silent, and he moved in.

Every night when it was time to retire, Ronald would walk me to my bedroom door, and kiss me goodnight. We talked sometimes of the day we would marry and then we would be able to sleep together. We talked about how important it was that we wait for marriage. He knew how much that meant to me, and he never tried to push me into having sexual relations before we were married. There were many times I felt my mother wouldn't care if I had slept with Ronald or if we did make love, as she never spoke to me about it. We were left alone in the house often and it would have been so easy. I felt bad she didn't care. I kept remembering what my father had told me and I was determined to stay a virgin. There were times I was tempted when Ronald would hold me and kiss me, but I just couldn't go all the way.

My sister Betty really resented Ronald moving in with us. She never did like him and now she liked him even less. She had a steady boyfriend who was in the Navy. Her boyfriend was a friend of Ronald's and mine, who attended the same school we did. He was now stationed in Greenland.

One day Betty and I got into a terrible argument that lead to a physical fight, that I would dream of for many years to come, as it changed our whole relationship for most of our adult life. I don't remember how the argument started, but what I do remember is that she called me, dirt. I know this would seem minor to many people nowadays, but remember, we did not curse in our family or call names. This hurt me deeply. When we were arguing, I had said her boyfriend would be surprised at how she was acting. That is when she said, "He wouldn't talk to dirt like you and Ronald."

When she said that, I ran up to her and slapped her in the face yelling, "How dare you call me dirt? I am as good as you are."

She was hitting me back and we were exchanging blows when Mom heard us and said, "What's going on in here?"

"Veronica hit me." Betty wailed. "I'll hit you again if you ever call me dirt again." I said.

Betty said to Mom, "She is dirt." "I heard her ask Ronald to sleep with her the other night."

I was shocked at what she said.

"You're lying. Mom it is not true." I never asked him to sleep with me." I cried.

"Yes, you did." She said with a smile. I hated her for lying.

Mom just said, "I don't want to hear any more about it." I have enough problems without you two causing me more. I don't need this on top of everything else." She dismissed it lightly. I lived with it for many years.

After this incident, Betty left for a few days to stay with her boyfriend's sister at her home. There was much tension at home with the two of us. Mom had to separate us she felt, to prevent any further incidents. I would see Betty at school. On a couple of occasions, I would try to approach her to talk about what happened. I loved her and felt bad about what happened. I felt she had misunderstood Ronald and I one night when we were talking about some day being married and sleeping together. I though maybe she really did think I asked Ronald to sleep with me, and for some reason it was important that she not believe that. But she would not talk to me. She would walk past me in the halls with her friends and ignore me in the classrooms.

It really hurt. After a short while, her friends stopped talking to me too. Oh no, I thought. She told them too. I was miserable.

When Betty was gone from home, Mom started dating this young college student. His name was Mark. She still worked at the drive-in restaurant where the high school and college students hung out. I was embarrassed that she would date a college student who was so much younger, but now that I think about it, she was just 32 years old. She was a pretty woman and many men found her attractive as Mark did. Mark was 28 years old. He started college late. I could never get used to seeing her in Mark's arms. Once I saw them lying on my brothers bed. It just didn't seem right. It wasn't right. Mom did everything for him. She washed and ironed his clothes. She cooked for him. I didn't like him. I felt he was taking advantage of my mother. I didn't feel that he really cared for her, because word was getting out at my high school that my mother was dating a college student. One of the boys on the school bus told me about it one morning. I guessed that Mark had bragged about my mother and I hated him for it.

One day I was going up the stairs at school, when this boy asked me for a date. He said it in a nasty, laughing way, in front of some other students. They were all laughing. I said no, that I had a boyfriend. He said, "I don't know why you act so "stuck up." You are no better then your mother. You're a whore just like her."

When he said this, I slapped him as hard as I could. "That is not true!" as I turned to run up the steps. I was afraid that he would hit me back, but he didn't. Later, I was told by my girl friend that he heard that kind of talk at the drive-in restaurant where my mother worked. I hated him from that day on.

I never told my mother what happened that day at school, but I did try to tell her how I felt about Mark. She was my mother and I loved her. I didn't like to see Mark using my mother and then bragging about it. I tried to talk to her about Mark, but she resented it and told me it was her business who she saw.

I guess at this time in her life, she felt Mark made her feel desired and happy and she didn't want to hear anything against him. I didn't tell her what he was saying, it would have hurt her too much and I didn't want to hurt her. Now in retrospect, I should have told her, but just didn't have the nerve. Perhaps, back then, I sensed that she needed someone, but I needed her as a mother and it was as if she was not there. I knew she was unhappy and kept reminding myself of this.

Betty came home after about two weeks. It was very uncomfortable sleeping in the same room with her and neither one of us speaking. One night Mark came over to see Mom and met Betty for the first time. He was attracted to her and made some kind of pass, which Betty resented, and she let him know how she felt by jabbing the scissors into his hand, as he approached her at the sewing machine. Needless to say, Mom was very upset and tried to calm Mark, as he was claiming he meant nothing by his motions towards Betty. She had misunderstood. A few days later Betty was sent to live at our grandmother's home in New York. Mom said it was because of financial reasons. Shortly after this incident, Mark's visits became less frequent and eventually stopped. There was just my youngest sister Dawn and I left at home now.

Betty and I never made up. Now she was gone.

I was truly heartbroken when Betty was sent to my grandmother's home to live instead of me. Mom knew how much I loved my grandmother and how close we were. I had always wanted to live with her. Gram and I always talked about it. I wanted to go so badly, but couldn't. How could I explain to my grandmother why Betty was coming instead of me? I was the easy one to handle for Mom. I didn't make any waves. Betty was causing problems for Mom. I couldn't run out and tell Gram what all was happening. I knew it would upset her very much. I don't know what my mother told her, or even if she asked my mother why I was not sent? It was never mentioned again and my grandmother never questioned me. My mother did tell me she needed me at home and that I had Ronald to think of. I felt trapped more then ever.

To make myself feel better, I couldn't help but remember what my grandmother always said to me ever since I was a child, "Help your mother, dear, she needs you." I guess somehow I felt my mother did need me, and it was my duty to stand by her no matter what. I felt resigned, but inside a voice wanted to scream, "but I need my grandmother." I felt Betty was the most fortunate person in the world. How I envied her, to get out of this mess and to live with our loving grandmother.

Chapter 12

BETTY IS GONE

AS I PREVIOUSLY stated, now that my sister Betty was gone, that left just my mother, youngest sister Dawn, Ronald and me. Dawn was about 11 years old at that time. I remember going into the bedroom one night to get ready for bed, and just standing there looking at my little sister asleep. I always thought of her as a baby, and now all of a sudden, she looked so grown up. It was as though I was looking at her for the first time. She was always the tag along. Poor thing, I thought, how is all this affecting her? She really had no one. She spent a lot of her time at her girl friend's house and her mother kind of adopted my sister on weekends. I really felt sorry for Dawn. I loved her so much, and felt like I needed to pay her more attention. I promised myself that I would.

Not long after Mark left, my mother met Dean. Ronald was having trouble with his car one day and asked his Uncle Dean to come over to the house to help him. This was Mom's first meeting with Dean. Mom was having a hard time. She was still working at the restaurant, but she was drinking more and whenever she had too many drinks, she'd get on the phone and call her friends and talk about Dad leaving her. She was always angry and bitter, but more so when she was drinking, so I was kind of happy when I saw she liked Ronald's Uncle Dean. I thought to myself, maybe he can make her laugh. If I had only known what lay ahead….. I would not have been happy. I didn't realize at the time, how much deeper this got me into the situation with Ronald, and how much more this arrangement was going to complicate my life in years to come.

It wasn't long after meeting Dean that mom had him move in with us and into my mother's bed. Only this time, it was a permanent thing. No, they didn't get married. They just decided to live together, and it didn't matter how I felt about it. I tried to talk to mother one day about it, handling it as gently as I could, so as not to upset her.

"Mom, I worry about you." I said.

"What do you mean, you worry about me?" She snapped.

"You and Dean." I answered.

"Look young lady, what I do with my life is my own business. I have enough to worry about without you causing me trouble." If you don't like it, it's tough." She flared. She knew what I meant.

"I'm going to school." I said as I spun around to go to school. She followed me into the hall.

"You don't turn away from me like that Miss High and Mighty. Who do you think you are?"

I was terribly upset. There seemed to be no way to reach her. "Mom," I pleaded. "Do you know what you are acting like?"

I didn't have to say a word. She knew exactly what I meant. She slapped me across the face. I ran from the house crying, but there was no way I was going to catch the school bus for school. I ran across the street into the woods and spent the day in the barn, once again. The subject was not brought up between my mother and I again until 21 years later.

If I thought it was bad before, I had a surprise coming. Living in the same house with Dean was a nightmare. I thought Mom drank, what she drank was nothing compared to him.

He had been married several times and had served time in prison for bigamy, another time for non-support, and disturbing the peace. He wasn't ashamed in the least. He often talked about his experiences in prison, and he knew more about anything than anyone else did, especially when it came to women. I found it disgusting the way he fondled Mom in front of my sister and me and then look at us and grin. I also found it hard to adjust to the way he had no table manners. Another thing that changed in our home, was Mom started spending hours cooking anything he wanted, and what he wanted was food we were not used to, but we were having to learn to like it if we were going to eat. I could hardly stand to sit at the table with him when he had been drinking. He was extremely sensitive and was easily offended, so I had to watch what I said.

He had a violent temper that changed his whole personality, which wasn't good to start with. I remember on many occasions seeing him hit my mother and on two or three occasion he threatened her with a knife. He was always so repentant afterwards saying he didn't realize what came over him and begged my mother to forgive him. There were times he would create a scene at the place where she worked, when he had been drinking, but she always forgave him and it was like nothing happened the next day. Dean would always say he couldn't remember what he did or said. These times didn't happen often, but when they did, it was always the smallest little thing to set him off and you never really knew when he was going to lose his temper.

I tried to stay away from him, as he always wanted to hug me or kiss me on the cheek. He always did this in front of Mom or Ronald, but I didn't like it. I would get a hard knot in my stomach, but I couldn't say anything. Dean and Mom drank all the time. Mostly he wanted to talk and he wouldn't stop talking. I would be trying to think of a polite way to get out of it, when he was talking to me, without offending him.

I just couldn't see what my mother liked about him. He was constantly putting her down, in a kidding way, but it would be in front of other people. Mom said it was because he felt inferior. I asked her what she meant by this. She said he couldn't write because he only had a third grade education, and she had to write things for him. I was shocked. I had never heard of a man having just a third grade education. How did he get along all these years?

When I told Ronald abut his uncle only having a limited education, he wasn't surprised. He said most of his relatives didn't even make it to high school except two aunts. Ronald was the first boy to graduate. That's what his mother meant when she said I was a good influence on him. I found out later that she just went to the third grade also.

Back then, she said. You didn't need an education. I never heard tell of such a thing. It seemed it was really different in the South. I had great Aunts in the North that had college educations. That's all I heard about was finishing school, by going to college. This was a whole new world. Is this what dad meant when he said to me that Ronald people were not our kind of people? I did not understand when he said it, what he meant. I was beginning to now. There was more to come.

Something else really disturbed me. Ronald's people all knew Dean was living with my mother, and some assumed I was sleeping with Ronald. It was just awful. I couldn't run around and tell every one of his family members, I was not sleeping with Ronald, and I am sure most would not even care. I do know that Ronald's mother did not think it was right for her brother, Dean to be living with us. They were not close and I could understand why. She disapproved of his actions. She also did not care for her son, Ronald to be living with us. I wanted to tell her I shared her feelings, but somehow I couldn't bring myself to do it.

With Dean living with us, we had a little more money in the house, but if I needed something, I still had to get it from Ronald. I remember so well when I asked my mother for a dress for the Junior-Senior prom. It was a big deal. It always is, when you are planning on going to the prom. I was excited and asked Mom if I could get a dress. I didn't have any formals. She just laughed.

"Where do you think I am going to get the money?"

"Mom, Dad sends you checks," I said back to her. She was still getting child support checks from Dad. I knew she was because I would be with her when she picked them up from the post office. She was still also getting Betty's, my sister's even though she no longer lived with us.

I had asked Mom for money at the wrong time. Dad somehow found out Dean was living with us and discontinued the house payments. She was furious. Later, she said she would get my dress. We went to an inexpensive department store and I got a used prom dress for $5.00. I don't think I ever told anyone my dress only cost $5.00. I was pretty and no one would know it was second hand. It looked brand new. It was strapless and a pretty shade of coral with ruffles and little silver threads.

I remember I had some white linen shoes I wore on a May Day at school from three years ago in a box. I was getting excited. I had them dyed to match my dress. The two together looked really nice, and I was told how pretty I looked in the dress and shoes at the prom and no one knew it wasn't new. Ronald took me to the prom. He didn't know how to dance then, so we didn't dance and he was very quiet. He just wasn't one to socialize. It was an uncomfortable evening, but at least I got to go, and I did take a couple of pictures to remember how pretty I looked anyway.

It was time to go to Gram's again. Only this summer was so different from the others. This time it was Mom, Dean, Ronald, my little sister and me. I really dreaded this trip, mostly of seeing my sister Betty. As we rolled up to gram's house, this beautiful girl came down the steps. It was Betty, "Gosh, I thought, she looks so pretty."

She looked like another person. She had lost a lot of weight and had a very neat looking suit on. Her hair was long, caught in a ponytail with one long curl. She looked gorgeous. She wasn't coming to greet us though; she was in a hurry to go to work. She quickly said hello to Mom and Dean and a cool hello to me. As she rushed to her car, she said. "I have to hurry. I'm running late for work."

She has a job and a car too, went through my mind. What more could she ask for on top of living with Gram? I just hurt so bad inside and felt no one cared. After hugging Gram hello, I went down into the dark cellar into Pop-Pop's old workshop, and just cried. I don't think I even told Ronald how I felt. It would hurt his feelings if he knew I'd rather live with my grandmother then be with him.

I wanted to talk to Brent so bad, I could hardly stand it. I kept waiting for the chance to slip away un-noticed to call him, but Ronald was always there. It just seemed I couldn't get away from him. When we all went to the park for the usual July 4th celebration, I excused myself during the fireworks, saying I had to go to the bathroom, and went to the phone booth and dialed Brent's number with my heart pounding.

"Hello," I said when the phone was answered. It was his mother. "May I speak to Brent, please?"

"I'm sorry Brent is gone for a few days, may I take a message?" All I could say with my heart sinking, was, "No thank you." In a few days, I'd be back in South Carolina. I hung up the receiver with such disappointment.

I had to talk to someone who would listen. I walked to the church just a few blocks from Gram's home. Ronald walked with me. I just told him I wanted to talk to the priest there. The priest was a stranger, but I heard him speak during the Sunday service and decided I would talk to him. He is someone who would listen and I wouldn't have to worry about hurting his feelings or him getting angry with me. I mostly talked about my sister Betty and our bad fight, and how awful I felt about it. I wanted us to be close and didn't know why Betty did not want to be friends. She was just so cold. I tried to make conversation, but she was always so short with me. I felt like she couldn't wait for Mom and the rest of us to leave. She was gone from the house most of the time. The times she was there I could see she and Gram were not all that close, so I didn't think she had taken my place in my grandmother's heart. Oh I knew she loved Gram, but it was different with the two of us. It always was.

I felt somewhat better after talking to the priest. I didn't tell him everything. I couldn't, and there were things I still couldn't talk to anyone about. I mostly just told him about my sister and I, that I was unhappy at home and didn't know what to do. He said if I ever needed a friend, I could write to him and he gave me his address.

A few months later, I wrote him and told him I couldn't stand it any longer and I was running away, or I might get married. I didn't know what to do. Ronald kept asking me to marry him, but felt I wasn't ready to get married. I kept remembering what Dad said about getting an education first. Somehow, it still seemed so important for me to do this, but if I ran away, where would I go? The priest wrote me back telling me not to marry, that God wanted me to finish my schooling before I took such an important step. Most children my age think of running away at some time or another, but that was not the thing to do. He didn't want me to disappoint God by getting married so young. I must be strong and do what was right. I was seventeen then. The letter said much more, and I kept it to read for many years whenever I needed encouragement. I still have it twenty-two years later. I no longer need it, but for some reason, I can't throw it away.

A few times I tried breaking up with Ronald, whenever we would have an argument, but then everyone was mad at me. He'd always cry and say he was sorry. His mother would tell me how much I meant to him. She'd say how she never saw him care for anyone like he did me and how he was always trying to better himself for me. Mom told me I was lucky to have someone love me that much. I should appreciate it and him. I just wasn't happy with him. He wasn't any fun. Wasn't I ever going to be able to enjoy anything with him? I thought teenage years were supposed to be ball games, dances, movies and such.

Whenever I would bring it up to Ronald, he'd say, "Is that all you can ever think of, is having fun?" I enjoy just being with you. Aren't you satisfied just being with me?" he'd ask.

"It is just that everything is just so serious Ronald. I want to laugh sometimes," was my reply.

"Why can't you laugh with me?" he'd ask.

I'd get so discouraged. I'd feel, what is the use? He just didn't understand. The only good thing I can say about our dating days was that he didn't try to get me to go to bed with him. It was difficult sometimes not to give into temptations, but I felt this was one thing that I could keep for myself. I couldn't give myself completely. I felt it was all I had left. Nothing else belonged to me.

What really got me at my grandmother's was Mom wasn't sleeping in the same room as Dean. Dean slept on the couch. I was so mad inside. She doesn't want her mother and other daughter to know she sleeps with Dean. It didn't matter that I knew. Didn't I matter? I wondered how my mother was going to handle that because she knew Gram wouldn't approve. Gram didn't know Dean was living with us. I could never tell her, as it would upset her greatly, if ever she came to visit. Dean would not stay there. I could see that Gram already had some doubt regarding Dean, as he was so different. Whenever Mom would spend time with her mother and leave him alone, he didn't like it. He was like a child. He was very jealous of any attention Mom gave to anyone other than him. This carried on for years.

Oh I wish I could have run to Gram, to feel her hold me in her arms, as she used to when I was a child and let me tell her my problems. She'd say, "It's ok, dear." Everything will be alright."

I always felt comforted. I could no longer do that.

Chapter 13

HIDING BEHIND MY TOE

IN 1957, WE received some wonderful news. My grandmother was getting married. I was so happy for her, as she had been very lonely since Pop-Pop passed away. Now, I wouldn't have to worry about her so much. I was excited to meet him.

I was told that Gram used to go with this man she married when she was in high school. They both grew up in the same town. Gram was there visiting an old friend, and while attending a dinner together, she saw "Gramps" we came to call him. They had not seen each other in thirty plus years. They had broken up sometime during the last year in high school and later Gram moved away. They both had married someone else. Gramps wife had died of cancer some years before, so like my grandmother he too was alone. He started asking Gram out and they both fell in love all over again. He bought her an engagement diamond ring, and after a very short few weeks of engagement, they married. They were to stop at our house in South Carolina on their way down to the Bahamas for a honeymoon. I thought that was about the grandest thing I've ever heard of. What a fairy tale romance! I waited with great expectation to meet my new grandfather.

I was at my Aunt Ginger's, my mother's sister's home when they arrived. We had planned a big meal for them. When they arrived, Gram looked so happy and radiant. Gramps was very tall with the whitest hair I had ever seen. He gave me a strong hug when Gram said, "and this here is Veronica." He was warm and friendly. I liked him right away. At that time, they seemed old to me, but then I guess most grandparents do to their grandchildren. Really they weren't old at all. They both were around fifty-five years old. I didn't think that anything better could have happened to my grandmother. They had almost 20 years together, and I never ceased to marvel at how they loved each other. Even after nineteen years, they held hands while watching television. Whenever I rode in the car with them, and a car would pass by with only one headlight, they would kiss. It was a game they played, and they were always calling each other "honey" or "dear."

I took to Gramps right away and I was to learn to love him more and more. I couldn't help but love a man that would give my grandmother such happiness.

Even after I was married, we visited them in the summer and I never once heard them argue. Gramps used to always say, "Everyone is entitled to their own opinion." Even though he didn't always agree with my grandmother, he respected her opinions, and she had plenty of them.

Gram and Gramps stayed at our home on the way back from their honeymoon. Again, Dean did not stay at our house when they were there. Ronald did, but he slept on the couch and Mom slept in my brother's room, which Ronald usually slept in. Gram and Gramps had Mom's room. Mom is such a hypocrite, I thought. She knew I would never say anything, so she never even mentioned the arrangement to me. I don't see how she had the nerve. It made me feel like I wasn't even there. Like I didn't have a mind. Didn't she care what I was thinking or feeling? Didn't she care what my classmates were thinking and saying at school? It seemed everyone knew. I just kept to myself and was glad when the school bell rang each afternoon telling us classes were over.

It was about this time I started having severe headaches. I had always had them for about as long as I could remember, but now they were getting really bad. Sometimes, I would call Mom from work to take me home, if I couldn't get Ronald. I just couldn't see with the migraines to do my schoolwork, and I would be sick to my stomach. I bet they all think I am pregnant. I'd go into my room at home and close the dark green bedroom drapes. A priest at the church, who we considered a close friend, had given us these drapes from church. They were heavy and made the room darker then I usually wanted, but I welcomed the darkness when my head hurt so much. It seemed like I went into another world, whenever I had my headaches. Everything seemed far away.

I wasn't menstruating but every three or four months. I knew it wasn't normal, but I didn't have to worry, as I wasn't crazy about having my periods anyway. I knew I was never pregnant and didn't have to worry about being late, as I was not having sex. Girls at school seemed to have a really bad time with their periods. It never bothered me as I didn't have cramps and it didn't last over three days, so I figured myself lucky.

My little sister Dawn was upset by our living conditions at home too. Dean scared her and she didn't understand him. She spent more and more time at her girlfriend's home. I would check on her from time to time at school. I was really concerned about her, but didn't know what I could do. She was better off at her friend's home, where I am sure she was more comfortable. I could tell she didn't like Dean hugging her either. Whenever Dean would get mad, when he felt we were rejecting him, he'd say, "You all think you're better than me." Mom would take him aside and try to calm him down. It seemed harder for my sister and me to keep away from him.

It was also about this time when I had a serious toe infection from an ingrown toe nail. I've always felt funny saying I had a toe problem. A toe seems so small and I always felt so silly whenever I was in a wheel chair at the hospital, and people would come up to me with concern and say "What is the matter?" Why are you here?" they would ask. "I have an infected toe," was always my reply. Really it was much more than that, but that is what I was there for. The infection just wouldn't clear up, after three operations and having the bone scraped. The doctor asked me was there something bothering me that I wanted to talk about. I couldn't talk. Here was my chance and I couldn't talk.

"There is something else that is going on with you than I know about. There is no medical reason why that toe should not heal after 6 weeks. If this last operation doesn't work, I have no choice but to amputate it," he added.

I had the ingrown toenail for years; really before Dad left and I just kept trying to take care of it myself. Sometimes it seemed to get better then it would swell up again with infection. It had been doing this for a very long time. The doctor had taken the nail beds out and scraped the bone, and of course removed the nail. It did look awful. It was gray and dead looking.

When my mother finally took me to the doctor to find out about it, I was seventeen years old. It was a terrible experience. I had always been very modest. When I entered the examination room, the nurse told me to get undressed.

"Get undressed?" I asked with a shock. "Why?"

"You have to. The doctor has to examine you." She said.

"I don't want to get undressed," I pleaded. "Veronica, you have to." Mom said. "Do what the nurse tells you." I left my panties on. "Off with your panties too," the nurse said.

"On no. I can't please don't make me." I cried. Both she and my Mom were getting impatient with me. The nurse gave me a sheet, and I tried to cover myself the best I could while I took off my panties.

It's necessary." The nurse said.

I couldn't see what was necessary about it at all. The doctor came in. He was tall, in his sixties, with gray hair and a very stern look on his face. He looked at my toe and squeezed it. I let out a cry of pain. He was so rough. He scared me terribly. He came up to the front of the table and lifted the sheet down and squeezed around my breasts. My face was burning and tears rolled down my cheeks. Then he went down and examined my bottom. I looked at my mother.

"Why, Mom?" He can't". I pleaded with her. She knew what I meant. "He won't bother you there," she said.

I just could have died. It wasn't right. It wasn't necessary. I just couldn't understand. Wasn't there any protection for me?

After that experience, every time I heard my doctor's voice coming down the hall, I physically had to have a bowel movement. I was that frightened of him. He was kind then, and would joke with me, when I was in the bathroom. "I'm just going to stand out here until you come out" he'd say.

When I was in the hospital for three weeks because of the infection, a letter came addressed to me from my new stepmother, Liz in Florida.

I had not heard from my father since he left. He sent checks to my mother, but that was the only connection I had with him. It was a very nice letter. They had been married about a year and a half now. Dad, somehow found out I was in the hospital. Liz wrote to say how sorry they were to hear I was in the hospital. She wrote that Dad loved me very much and that she loved me. I was so happy when I read the letter, I cried. She went on to say they both would like very much if I would come and visit with them that summer. Would I like to? My heart took wings! It was too good to be true. Dad loved me. They wanted me to visit, I said over and over in my mind.

I guess I wasn't thinking very clearly, because I left the letter out and Mom saw it when she came to visit.

"What's this?" she said as she picked it up. "A letter from her?" Who the hell does she think she is?" She screamed as she read it. She looked at me with such anger. "Well, are you going?"

I was so frightened by her anger I couldn't answer. The nurse called the doctor. Several nurses and the doctor came in and made Mom leave. I was hysterical. After I calmed down I begged the doctor to let me stay there. "I don't want to go home. I hate it there." He said not to worry that I would be in the hospital awhile yet. He was going to talk to my mother and tell her it would do my toe good to have some sunshine and salt water. And Florida is just the place for you now, he added. "You need to see your father." By this time he knew it had been two years. I don't remember what all I told him when I was crying.

My mother and Ronald told me for years that I shouted, "I hated my father" one time when the doctor took my stitches out. It hurt terribly, as the toe wasn't healing properly, and I was screaming. I don't ever remember those words. Years later, long after the doctor passed away, I was holding my records (waiting to see another doctor) and I opened the folder. I saw where it was written; my mother said I had said, "I hated my father." This is not the same as the doctor hearing it and recording it. So all I had to go on is what Mom and Ronald said, and I resented that being in my hospital records. It was made to sound like I blamed my father for my toe condition. I heard my mother say on any occasions, she could not get the money from him to take us to the doctor.

As far as I know, I wasn't blaming anyone for it. I was the one that let it go, and as it stood now, I was glad it was badly infected. It got me at the hospital and away from home.

During my stay at the hospital, I wanted to draw something special for this doctor. I drew a tree on the edge of a very steep cliff overlooking mountains. There was a stream at the bottom of the cliff and mountains. The sun was setting with a small thin cloud passing by it. There were no other trees in sight. The doctor liked it very much and said that he would frame it. I found myself drawing this sketch for the rest of my life over and over. If I were in deep thought, or on the telephone, I would sketch this. I realized after many years that the sketch must have meaning and perhaps words to go with it. In 1970, I wrote the words to go with it. That sketch and the words have had great meaning and importance and still do in my life today. This poem is in the book at a later time.

After six weeks in the hospital, the doctor said I could leave and he had spoken to my mother about my going to visit my father. It would do me good. He told me I was not to worry about it. I don't know what else he said to her. I could tell she was angry, but she was silent about it. I didn't want to hurt her and I didn't want her mad at me. Why couldn't she understand? These things kept going trough my head. Before I left for Florida, she did say, "If you go, don't bother to come back." This hurt me, but I didn't think she really meant it or why was she so upset about my going? My Aunt Ginger and Ronald took me to the bus station to leave. "Don't be upset with your mother, dear," Aunt Ginger said. "She says things she doesn't mean when she is upset and worried. She wants you to come back. She loves you." Aunt Ginger did not really know what all was going on. I know she really would not want to know. She liked peace and everything nice. I looked at her and asked, "Why can't Mom understand that just because I want to see Dad, doesn't mean that I don't love her too?" "She'll get over it," was my aunt's reply.

After promising Ronald I'd write often, I kissed him and my aunt goodbye. I got on the bus feeling torn, guilty and frightened. As the bus pulled away, I thought before long I'd see my Dad. I was to be eighteen that summer, and I would be spending my birthday with Dad and my new stepmother. I was nervous, but excited in a good way.

Chapter 14

VISITING WITH DAD

THE BUS TRIP to Florida was long, but pleasant. I enjoyed the scenery, and I enjoyed the feeling of freedom. I was "almost" on my own, I thought. Even though I felt chained to Ronald and Mom. I am not going to feel guilty. I kept telling myself over and over. Oh it was so nice being away from all the ugliness. I looked down at my toe, in my open-toed shoes and felt like saying, thanks. It really helped having the doctor tell Mom she ought to let me go. I don't think I would have had the nerve to do it myself. I was grateful for that letter from my stepmother. I can't help but wonder if (without realizing it) I left that letter from out on purpose for my mother to see.

I kept to myself while riding on the bus. Toward the end of the journey, the bus driver started talking to me. I was sitting right behind him and I had been quiet all the way.

He asked me, "Don't you ever talk?"

I smiled shyly, and said, "Yes." I didn't know what else to say to him. He just asked me some of the usual questions, and I'd answer. I felt so awkward. As we turned into our final stop, he said we were running early and if my Dad wasn't there yet, would I like to have a cup of coffee with him? I said simple, "Okay." It didn't really matter to me and it was the first words that came out. He said he'd be back in a minute, as he had to check in.

I turned around and there was Dad! I was so surprised. It's like I couldn't believe it. I could tell he was glad to see me. I just kept looking at him, not moving. Dad was acting cheerful, like everything was fine. He reached over and gave me a quick hug. It was as though no time had passed and there was so much I wanted to say.

Would I have the chance? I had missed him so very much. Why couldn't I just let go? Dad couldn't do it and neither could I, but we knew the love was there.

Dad grabbed my suitcase before leaving the bus terminal and I suddenly remembered. "Oh Dad, I forgot, the bus driver. I told him I'd have a cup of coffee with him." What a dumb thing to say. Why was I worried about telling the bus driver I couldn't? He was no one I knew. Did I think I had to keep my word to everyone? Dad said lightly, "Oh, forget about the bus driver, he'll find someone else." For some reason, I was glad Dad was there early.

I don't remember what we talked about on the way to the house. I am sure it was polite conversation. One thing I do know for sure, there was no talk about the past. As we pulled in front of the house, I remember how pretty I thought it looked with flowers planted, green grass and palm trees. I liked the white sand in this part of Florida. Everything seemed so clean and fresh.

When we went into the house, Dad yelled out, "Anybody home?" He had a habit of saying this when he knew there was someone home. Beth, my stepmother came out. I don't recall having any negative feelings toward her. I thought she was pretty and seemed friendly. She was about my height 5'7" tall with a nice figure. Beth had short brown hair and was suntanned. I could tell she wanted to please me. As I think back, she must have been terribly nervous about meeting me too, and wondering what I would think of her.

It's strange, but I really don't remember having any bad feelings when I was told Dad left with a younger woman. That is a time in my life that I didn't want to remember. Maybe deep down inside, I didn't blame Dad for the breakup entirely because I knew Mom cared about someone else. At this time in my life, I had blocked that out, but subconsciously, I knew she was seeing someone. I know now, that was why

I had a feeling of relief when Dad left. I was afraid he was going to find out about Mom and this other man. I didn't know he already knew. It was many years later, when I asked him about it. I could see, even then it was hard to talk about the breakup.

Dad and Beth showed me my room, which was fixed up very nicely. Really the whole house looked nice. Everything seemed cheerful and bright; the house, the conversation and Dad and Beth's relationship.

Beth started to prepare dinner. It seemed she was trying hard. When a little something happened like supper starting to burn, she would get upset. I didn't want to make her nervous, and I guessed my being quiet, and she not knowing what I was thinking or feeling. I found myself liking her and in a way feeling sorry for her, not knowing why. I wish I could have expressed my feelings more to her and that way she wouldn't feel uncomfortable. I just didn't know what to say. I wasn't very good at conversation.

While I was there visiting, my brother, Bobby came to visit also. I was so glad to see him. He was now living with my paternal Grandfather and step grandmother in Florida. We were just three years apart and very close. I missed him so much. He was now fifteen years old.

Everyday, we went to the beach. Dad was at work, but Beth, Bobby and I went. It was a lot of fun. Oh, how I loved the ocean. To me, it was beautiful and exciting. I liked to lie on the blanket and hear the sounds of the waves on the sand with the sea gulls above me. The sun felt so warm and good, and there was a gentle breeze. It was so peaceful here. I'd think to myself. It's like a whole new world. There was no complaining and no talk of the past. I almost forgot about my home in South Carolina. The only reminder I had was Ronald's letters, which arrived every day.

Dad was concerned about my relationship with Ronald, but he didn't try to get me to break up with him. He mostly told me of things that Ronald could do to better himself. He wondered if we had ever thought of moving to Florida. He told me of jobs that were available if Ronald was interested, not necessarily in that town, but other towns too. Dad asked if I had thought about college and told me about the University of Florida. He really wanted me to go. Oh that sounded like that was just too good to ever be true. I couldn't even think of it for a minute. Not even the slightest possibility of it. Mom would never accept that. What would I do about Ronald? Why, oh why couldn't I ever be free of them? I'd ask myself, what is this hold on me? More then anything else, I would have loved to live in Florida and go to this university. I visualized a pair of scissors, in my mind, and cut the strings attaching me to them. I felt so compelled to go back.

On my eighteenth birthday, Dad asked me if I'd wanted to go to the store with him and pick up a few things. I responded with my usual, ok, and got in the car. We were not gone long and after we got back home and I was in the kitchen, Dad and Beth called me into their bedroom. I can still feel the surprise as I write this. There were so many clothes laid out on the bed. There was a beautiful two-piece light blue dress, a light gray dress, slips, hose, panties and a bra. Oh, I was so happy. I just couldn't believe my eyes. They both smiled and said, "Happy Birthday." After trying on my new clothes, which were a little big on me, because I had lost so much weight at the hospital, we went out to eat. Before leaving though, Beth took in the sides of the light gray dress so I could wear it out to dinner. After dinner, the waitress brought out a birthday cake with candles burning, and everyone sang "Happy Birthday." I was now eighteen years old. I didn't feel like an eighteen year old. I still felt like a scared, unsure little girl in a woman's body. It was so hard to believe I was eighteen.

At times, I felt a little guilty, because I was enjoying being with Dad and Beth and because I found myself really liking her. I remember thinking; they are not so bad, like Mom acts out. At home, everything seemed so horrible, the whole situation. Why couldn't the entire ugliness stop? It's not ugly here. They're nice people, I'd say to myself.

The salt water and sunshine did do my toe well. It was starting to heal. It had some color in it now and didn't look so gray. It also had stopped hurting.

When it was time to leave, I got that hard knot back in my stomach. Maybe it won't be so bad when I get home. Maybe things will be better, I'd tell myself. On the way home, I started to feel guilty again because I really liked Beth, and I wasn't supposed to like her. I really didn't like it when she introduced me as her stepdaughter, because I didn't think of her as a stepmother. Stepmothers are supposed to be horrid and I didn't see her in that way. She was just seven years older then I. I thought of her more as a friend. There was something sad about her.

When I got home nothing had changed, if anything it was worse. I didn't like the familiar smell of the house. Not that it was bad; just every home has its own odor. I felt smothered when I walked into the house, and especially when I walked into the bedroom and saw the dark green, heavy velvet drapes.

Mom was quiet when I got home. She really didn't have much to say. She asked me what "she" was like and I said she was nice to me. Mom didn't like me saying that, so I knew it was best I didn't say anything at all.

When I was visiting Dad, he told me he was going to continue to send my support check as I was still in school. He didn't have to, I knew, after I was eighteen. Really he didn't have to support any of us and make the house payment, as there were never any papers served on him or a court ordering him to as he just left the state and no one knew where he was for a long time.

Dad did it because it was the right thing to do.

He wanted to. I didn't tell mom what Dad was going to do of ending the check directly to me. I knew it would upset her. Of course when it did come, I had to sign it and give it to her. I felt I had no choice. What I resented was, I still didn't have things I needed for school from her. She said she needed it all to help pay bills. What is Don going to contribute, I'd think. He lived and ate at our home all the time. What really upset me about Don was that Ronald told me his Uncle Don was still seeing his ex-wife who still loved him. Everyone in the family knew she wanted him back and he would go see her often. I would see his car parked at her home often. I told Mom once about this feeling she had the right to know. As it turned out, he had some good excuse to be there and I was accused of trying to make trouble. I learned to keep quiet.

I went back to school and tried my best to do well, but I was having problems with my toes again. It kept bursting open with infection, and I had to wear socks and shoes to school. I'd soak it in salt water as soon as I got home from school. It really took a long time before it healed. I think sub-consciously I wanted to go back to the hospital now that I look back on it.

During this period of time Mom and Don were having some really bad fights, and he was making scenes at the place where she worked in town. Some of the boys from school worked there as curb boys/waiters and they would witness this between my mother and Don. It was terrible. He'd be drunk, cursing and calling Mom names.

Once in awhile at school, the hateful boys would make a snide remark to me about my mother. Some of them knew the situation and I wasn't proud of it.

For some time now, I was going to talk to the priest at our church when I was upset. Now, that is putting it mildly. Ronald would drive me to the priest's home whenever I was hysterical and he didn't know what to do with me. Father Edward knew me since I was eight years old. Now I am eighteen. He knew our whole family well. He looked after us, while we all were growing up. He had always told me throughout the years that I did a good job looking out for my brother and sisters and he marveled at the way we all turned out, in spite of the problems. Really several older members of the church would make the same comment to my sister and I. I always felt proud when I heard this.

Father Edward meant the world to me. He was always there for me to talk to and I truly loved him. On this particular night when I was upset and crying to him about the situation at home, Father Edward said, "Ronald, you have no real home life and Veronica you don't either. Why don't you two kids go ahead ad get married instead of waiting." He continued, "Normally I would suggest you wait until after you have graduated, Veronica, but circumstances being what they are, I don't see you both waiting." I know you two kids love each other and you deserve some happiness." Hearing him say that, it just seemed the thing to do. I no longer questioned it. I would marry Ronald and have my own home. I remember so well saying to myself, "I think I love him, but even if I didn't, I'd marry him because he loves me so much." I felt that was something I could always be sure of.

If Father Edward thought it was ok, it must be. The only other personal approval I wanted was my grandmothers. I knew Dad wouldn't approve, but I didn't know anyway out of it. It just seemed the thing to do. I'd just have to show Dad he was wrong about Ronald and that he was different, but he was going to have to make something of himself.

We told Mom that we wanted to go ahead and get married. I no longer wanted to go to this school. I didn't need but a couple of units to graduate and I was going to finish up in night school. It was ok with her that we were marrying. She didn't even try to talk me out of it. I have to say, she did give me a reception after the service at home. She told me it cost a $100. I felt grateful she did try to make it a nice wedding when money was so tight. I had written Dad and asked him to give me away but Beth wrote back and said they were sorry, but they just couldn't come. I felt a little bad about it, I really I didn't expect them to come under the circumstances. I asked my Uncle Jim, Dad's only brother, if he could give me away. He said he would be glad to. I found out later, Dad couldn't come to the wedding even if he wanted to, as Mom had papers out on him for support and abandonment. Mom had said to me several times, "If your Father cares so much for you, why is he not coming to your wedding?" I don't think she knew how much that hurt.

I wore my Aunt Ginger's wedding dress for my wedding. It was candlelight satin and beautiful. It fit me perfectly. I borrowed a veil from a church member whose daughter wore it in the May Day Celebration. Ronald paid for the flowers needed for everyone.

My Gram and Gramps came down from New York for the wedding. I asked my sister Betty to please come too, and be my "Maid of Honor." I wanted things to be right with us. My little sister Dawn was a bridesmaid.

Just before the wedding I asked my grandmother, "Gram, do you like Ronald?"

"He seems like a nice enough boy, Veronica, she replied. What matters is how you feel about him. If he makes you happy dear, then I am happy for you." It's not exactly what I hoped to hear, but that is how Gram felt. She just wanted me to be happy. "Just think, she said, we'll be celebrating our wedding anniversaries just a year apart."

Walking down the isle on my wedding day, I was saying to myself, I'm not sure I'm doing the right thing. The priest during the ceremony, made it extra special, saying personal things about Ronald and I, and how special our love was for each other. I felt it must be right.

After the ceremony Father Edward, offered to let us use his personal car for our weekend honeymoon, since Ronald's broke down just a few days before the wedding. I just couldn't accept his offer fearing something might happen to it. He took out a $20.00 bill and said for us to stay at a nice place. We welcomed the $20.00 because Ronald had just lost his job and I didn't have one yet. I was so worried. What a way to start a marriage!

I remember in the car, leaving town, I said to Ronald, "now we can do anything we want to." Gee, it seemed strange to me now, that sex was okay and I really didn't know exactly what to expect. I was excited and apprehensive at the same time. We borrowed Mom's car for the weekend, and did not go far, just to the next town, a whole 30 miles away!

We checked into the motel. We were alone. Opening the suitcases rice fell out everywhere. My sister, Betty had loaded the suitcases with rice. A jar of Vaseline fell out of Ronald's suitcase and rolled across the floor. A reminder of what was to come.

We decided to just try it before eating and not put it off. Try it, what a way of putting lovemaking. All this time of getting worked up and not doing anything and after our wedding seemed so mechanical. We both were very awkward and fumble. I don't know what I was expecting. I guess maybe bells ringing and my head in a beautiful whirl. It wasn't that way at all. Having sex hurt and I wasn't sure we were doing it right. How dumb. What other way can you do it? It's supposed to hurt. I can't say it was pleasant, but then we both told ourselves, it takes time getting adjusted and getting to know each other in that way. We felt the more we did it, the better it would get, and it wouldn't hurt me so much. We did it every chance we could, which was often. I do remember thinking, "Is this what all the fuss has been about?" Is this all there is to it? After we showered together, we went out to eat. I looked at the people looking at us. I wondered if they could tell that we had been doing it. We just spent one night at the motel and a whole day and then went to our apartment and spent the night. The next day we went to my Aunt Ginger's home where Gram and Gramps were staying. They weren't expecting us back so soon, and were surprised to see us. I didn't want to tell them we couldn't afford but one night and truly I wanted to see them again before they left. It would be almost eight months before I would see her again. As I walked into the dining room and everyone looked up, I felt self-conscience and wished we had stayed away another day.

I was so proud of our apartment. It was my new home. My very own home, I kept saying to myself. We got a new living room suite, on credit. It was Aqua blue upholstery with blond wood. Aunt Ginger and Uncle Jim gave our kitchen table and chairs to us. It was one they had for several years, but in good condition. Some church members gave the bedroom suite to us. Father Edward had told them we could use it as they were getting a new set. All my towels and linens were new. I had had a hope chest for two years that I was so proud of. Ronald had bought it for me on my 16th birthday. So over the years, people would give me little gifts to put inside it. I had some really pretty nightgowns that I couldn't wait to wear. Dad and Betty sent me a beautiful white lacey nightgown and negligee set. I had my own home and I felt happy.

I found a job in the dime store as sales clerk. I remember taking mashed beans and pork sandwiches with salad dressing, and eating fresh popped popcorn from the store for lunch mostly every day and loving it. Ronald rode to work and I walked to work that wasn't far. Before long, he bought a used car and I got a better job at a finance company. Then I went back to school.

I remember walking to the grocery store down the street, the same store where mom and dad used to shop, and I loaded up on grapes, cookies and donuts until I had my fill of them. I really liked having a job, making money and doing what I wanted. My happiness was short-lived. It wasn't long after Ronald and I were married when we had a terrible fight. I can't remember what started it. As I had stated before, I don't like arguing so I tried to get away from him. This was the first time I had tried to physically get away, and he held on to me and wouldn't let me leave him. I know the argument had something to do with my mother because he called her a whore. He knew by saying this, it would really hurt me. I didn't consider my mother a whore. She was my mother and I loved her. I had convinced myself she had been lonely and terribly upset after Dad left and that is why she acted like she did with the college kids and some other friends. She wasn't herself.

When Ronald called my mother a whore, I slapped him feeling he deserved it. I wasn't expecting him to slap me back. We physically struggled. I finally broke away and locked myself in the bathroom. I was crying hard because I was so shocked and upset that he could do and say such a thing. Who had I married?

I heard Ronald go out the front door. I unlocked the bathroom door and ran out the back door. I felt I hated him and wanted to get away. I walked in the dark to his mother's house that was about 8 miles away. I didn't know where else to go. I certainly wasn't going to tell my mother what happened.

When I arrived at my mother-in-law's home very late at night, I was a mess. I had been crying all the way. She looked concerned and said,

"I was afraid of this happening. He has his father's temper. He knows better than that."

"What are you talking about?" I asked with great concern.

She said that Ronald's father was the same in that he was quiet, but when he got mad he exploded and "didn't have good sense," is the way she put it.

Ronald pulled into the driveway as we were talking. He was calm now and kindly told me to get in the car. I told him I informed his mother what happened.

"Ronald, you know better." He ignored her statement and put his hand on my shoulder and said,

"Oh, come on. Lets forget about it. I didn't mean it. It was just words."

"Ronald, of all the things in the world, did you have to call my mother that name."

"Let's forget it," he repeated.

I went back home with him. What else could I do? He said he was sorry and didn't mean it. Don't make a big deal of it, Veronica, I told myself. He did promise it wouldn't happen again. Before long, we moved into a small 4-room rental house. It was fun fixing up the house as we had more money now. Ronald received a raise and I received a new job in a shipping department office.

The fights continued. Ronald would get so violent when all I was trying to do was get away from him. He physically wouldn't let me go. He would hold me and I would try to break loose and then he would really hit me hard. It would infuriate him that I wanted to physically leave. I was used to running away from unpleasant things. Oh how I missed the woods and the barn in the field. I had no place to hide. I'd fight him, trying to break away but the more I did the madder he got. Afterwards he was always so repentant and loving. He couldn't do enough for me, and to my friends I'd say how loving he was.

Mom and Dean were the only ones that knew he hit me. I didn't want anyone else to know we had problems. I would call Mom for help when it got bad. I wanted to know she cared. She mostly wanted me to say I was sorry. She liked him.

I was made to feel by Ronald and my mother that I provoked the arguments. If I did, I wasn't aware of it, but back then he convinced me that I was terribly frustrating and drove him to it. I am sure I was frustrating at times, but not to the point that I deserved to be slapped around. He would always say, "Well don't try to run away. I'm afraid something will happen to you. Someone will pick you up or something. I don't mean to hit you, but I just can't stand it when you fight me."

I would convince myself it was my fault and I did drive him to it, so I stayed. Everyone told me how much he loved me. They didn't know he owned me. I was a possession to him.

It was about this time Mom and Dean were having problems with Dad. Somehow Mom and Dad got into a conversation over the phone. Dean called my Dad one night when he was drunk and told him he was shacking up with his 'ole lady.' (Such talk) My stepmother told me this later. This was a big mistake on Dean's part. All of sudden Mom was concerned about Dad knowing Dean was staying in our home.

Dad said something about taking my sister Dawn from her. She was around 13 years old then. I too was concerned because Dean's son was always there. He was about 15. I thought that's all we needed for Dawn to marry Dean's son, then we'd all be related. I didn't want him messing up her life, too. They were being left along much too often.

Mom called me to her house and told me if I was called to go to court, I was not to tell Dean's was living with her. I was very upset by this. I felt I had to do what she told me, as she was my mother, but I knew it was wrong to lie in court. I went to talk to the priest of my church. He said I should not lie and that it probably would never come to be, and it didn't. Before I left he then said,

"You two kids are much too young to have gotten married," and he never changed his mind right up to my divorce.

The summer after I was married, I was invited to go to Florida to see Dad and Beth with my paternal grandparents, Papa Tom and Tessie. Ronald was going to get off work and come pick me up later to come home. My brother was living with Dad and Beth at the time. My sister Dawn went too. I was 18, my brother was 15 and Dawn was 13 years of age.

I don't know what happened for sure, but the visit didn't go well. My brother, sister and I were at the boardwalk and we misunderstood Beth about where we were to meet them at a certain time. She was very angry when she found us and shouted,

"We didn't know if you decided to go dancing or what."

This hit me wrong as Ronald always got angry with me if I wanted to go dancing. Here I felt she was implying I would go dancing even if I were married. When I answered her rudely and said,

"Well, I certainly would not go alone," she got angrier and said, "Well, excuse me."

She was very angry in the car and started crying and hollering. I was ignoring her, but she kept on and then finally I said something ugly.

"I don't have to listen to you. You are not my mother."

I don't know what made me say that because I really liked her. At that she said to my father,

"You had better do something about her." Dad didn't say anything right then. It was an awful position to be in. Later on that night, I was at my grandfather's. Dad came to the door and said for me to come outside. I did and saw Beth in the car. Dad told me to never talk to Beth like that again, that she was his wife, and I was going to respect her. I apologized and was trying to explain my side. I must have said something wrong and Beth heard from the car. She was out in a flash and came up to me crying. She was screaming at me that Dad loved her and he married her and that is the way it was. I tried to tell her I knew Dad loved her. Somewhere in all this, Dad slapped me. I knew that was for Beth's benefit. It's what she wanted. He had to do it for her. I felt like I lost him all over again. Ronald came to get me the next day. Of course, Mom was delighted that it happened. I didn't tell her a few months later Beth wrote me a letter saying, "Let's try to be friends." I really wanted to and welcomed the letter.

Chapter 15

BECOMING A MOTHER

THREE YEARS LATER, I was expecting our first child. I was so happy and excited about becoming a mother it was not easy for me to get pregnant as I didn't have my period but just once or twice a year I didn't have a monthly. Like most women do.

At this time we were making fairly good money. I was working in the industrial engineering department, do it labor analysis. It was a complicated job but I was proud of myself for learning it on my own, in one day the girl before me just walked out. I was determined that I was going to succeed in everything I did. I had to show those girls at school, who snubbed me, was just as good as they were to finish. I was going to make something of myself and on top of that, the woman who owned my mothers workplace told her I was making a terrible mistake by Marrying Ronald and then I messed up my life. I wanted to show her, but most of all, I want to show dad I was intelligent in spite of my poor school grades, and then I could do whatever a son could. I had my work cut out for me, because I wasn't going to stop until I made it as far as I could go. I was determined to make my dad proud of me. It was that important.

Before my baby boy was born I handmade him many outfits all matching. I made little diaper shirts with embroidery and lace. I had an easy pregnancy and was overwhelmed with joy when Josh was born. He was a little chubby though and could not wear all the outfits I made for him. I enjoyed caring for him as much as any mother could. I don't think I ever had a happier day in my life in the day they handed him to me in the hospital. He was just too good to be true. He was a good baby and I had no problems with him.

The only negative side of my pregnancy was when Ronald and I had a terrible fight and he chased me outside of that house. There was a large tree and a root that was exposed above the ground. I tripped on the root and fell. I remember Ronald coming out of the house and being on top of me and hitting me. It upset me that he would do that with me carrying his baby. Later he would cry and tell me how sorry he was and didn't mean to do it. Again, I had pushed him to it. As always, I let it go, as he was so sorry. I didn't know what else to do, but believe him.

When my son was about three years old, my sister Dawn, came to live with us. My mother was moving to New York and Dawn didn't want to go. She had been extremely unhappy with mom and Dean and many times I was called to the home when Dean had been drinking. Mom and Dawn had not been getting along either. I was really kind of relieved they were moving. I was worried so about mom because of Dean's drinking and his temper. I thought being a New York near my grandmother and Gramps might help them.

Ronald and I were still having problems. I remember going to a close by town one day, the place where the priest that was very close to us was now living. We had been married about six years.

When the priest and I were alone, I said, "Father Edward I just don't feel like I love Ronald anymore."

"Nonsense, he said. It was meant for you two to be together. "All young kids have their bad times."

My sister Dawn knew we were having a rough time because she lived with us. Ronald was working a night shift by then and his disposition was awful when he woke up each evening. It even got to the point where little Josh wouldn't go into the bedroom to call his father. We both just hated waking him up.

We moved from there and bought our first house. Dawn was planning on being married so we were busy making plans for the wedding. She had a very large wedding, and my mother, Dean, grandparents and my sister Betty came for the ceremony. Dad and Beth also came. They felt comfortable enough to be there. By then Mom gave up on taking him to court. Little Josh was the ring bearer and looked precious in his white suit.

It wasn't long after my sister's wedding that I found out I was expecting again. I continued to work into my eighth month. Again and I had a good delivery. My curly headed little baby, Tony was born. Looking at this little miracle in my arms brought tears to my eyes. Now I had two sons. I was so happy. Tony was beautiful, Josh was so proud of his baby brother. I could not wait for dad to come see my new house and how well we were doing.

Ronald and I still had our fights, and I still went for walks. I could feel the emptiness in my life, except with the children. Ronald was taking some schooling courses by then and was going to be away for a few weeks. I was glad to see him go. I did not miss him at all.

Ronald wouldn't do anything with us anyway. He never wanted to go anywhere. I would just put the children in the car and go to the park or the pool and sometimes to visit my friends. We never had friends over to the house. He didn't care for that. We never went to a party or a dance. I was wishing there was someone who would care about me and take me away from him. I pretended in front of his family everything was fine. He took great delight to put me down constantly, but after a while I just didn't pay any attention to him.

I went back to work when Tony was just a year old. We were having financial problems again. I was afraid we would lose the house. Ronald was always getting a new car. It seemed he traded cars at least twice a year. It concerned me but he always convinced me we could swing it.

I lost nearly all of any good feelings I had left for Ronald by this time. Ignoring some of my friend's warnings, I got my brother-in-law's wife a job in the office where I worked (Ronald's brother). Big mistake. I knew she wasn't very friendly and rather cool, but I just figured that she was shy. I should have listened to my friends when they said it was not good to get a relative a job at the same office. This girl didn't have any friends. She quit school, but I knew she was smart and I told her I would talk to my boss about hiring her for the job I used to have. I had been promoted about three times. As it turned out, she was hired and it wasn't long before I started having problems with her. I really hated this as I had been working at this company for nearly eight years, and always got along well with everyone.

She and I always had lunch together and sometimes we went to my house to eat as I lived within walking distance from the plant. After a few touchy situations at the office, things started to get strained. She resented me giving her work, which was part of my job. I had the best job in the office and always got the new equipment when it came in. She thought my boss was showing favoritism. My boss and I were very good friends. He wasn't as old as my father but acted as a father to me. His wife was still a very good friend. One day my sister-in-law told me everyone was talking about my boss and I seeing each other, and that the rumor had been going on for sometime, but she didn't want to tell me. I was really crushed.

At that time in my life I couldn't handle it. I felt like I had worked so hard for these years to live down a reputation and make something of myself. I found myself in this job pretty much in the same situation I was in high school. I was reliving it all over again. It made me sick. I became obsessed with the whole situation. It was worse than terrible. I couldn't eat or sleep.

She stopped talking to me. It just seemed like everyone with the exception of one friend stayed away from me. And practically the whole plant was talking about it. I felt extremely uncomfortable whenever I had to go into other offices because people barely spoke. On the other hand, Elizabeth was a friend to everyone, laughing and talking until I walked in the room and everyone would get quiet

It bothered me so bad that at times I left the office and pretended I needed some files from upstairs. I would go up there in the room and just cry. I didn't know what to do or how to handle it. To make matters worse Ronald wasn't saying anything about it even though he knew. Not anything. I couldn't understand him not defending me. He knew it was ridiculous, not true, yet he did nothing. If it were my brother-in-law saying something like that about my husband, I would defend him. I'd call my sister-in-law at home, but she just cursed at me and said it served me right for thinking I was so smart. She said she was tired of always hearing from our mother-in-law, how smart Ronald and Veronica were and then she added, you shouldn't have been so

friendly with the boss Miss Goody-Goody. My boss was right, she was jealous and I just wanted to be friends. What about everybody else at work ignoring me and talking about me? I wanted to shout, I'm innocent but never had the courage to say that. I went to the plant manager and told him about it. He laughed it off saying "Veronica don't think anything of it. Anybody that knows you, the two of you, knows it's not true. The girl is just jealous." I couldn't brush it off, I couldn't cry, I just couldn't continue to work like that. Seeing how serious I was taking it, he said why didn't I just take the day off.

I don't know what a breakdown is, but I think I must have come close to one during this time. It seemed to me that my world was falling apart. I had worked so hard to rebuild my life since leaving home. I wasn't used to handling something like this. I started being delirious. Usually I would just get delirious when I had a fever. I didn't have a fever this time. I was just terribly upset. I felt so frightened. I was seeing scary, laughing faces and everything was out of order. It didn't last long just an evening, thank goodness. I couldn't handle it all. I quit my job saying I was going to have another baby, which was partly true at the time. I just quit early and never went back. It took me years to get over that experience. I started reading books like "the power of positive thinking" which the kind plant manager had sent to me.

I know now that my sister-in-law was jealous of me even before I got the job there. That how most of the people were talking was my imagination. If anyone did hear it, those that knew me, and most did, didn't believe it. They probably wondered why I was not speaking and acting normally, and in turn they felt uncomfortable not knowing what was wrong with me. If anyone did believe my boss and I were having an affair, I should not have even let it bother me. I had just filled it up in my mind.

I was hurt and stayed hurt for a long time over this, because my mother and sister remained friendly with Elizabeth at family gatherings even though they knew what she tried to do to me and succeeded. I gave up a job of eight years because of her and something I couldn't handle at the time. If someone hurt someone I cared about, I could not be a friend to him or her. How could my mother and sister not care what she did by lying to me? She ruined my work place and I allowed it by not knowing how to handle it. I didn't understand how they could be nice to her.

After getting myself back together with the help of some good books and my own self-instilled determination, I said silently, well Veronica, you just start all over again and don't give up. I was more determined then, than ever.

I remember on one occasion when we lived at this house, a really bad fight. Josh was five years old at the time, and still remembers the incident. We were having an argument and Ronald hit me and I fell to the kitchen floor. Josh just came into the room when his father hit me. I made up something, like I slipped and fell to the floor, but many years later he told me he knew his father hit me because he saw it. I really hated that he saw this happen. I didn't want the boys to ever have any bad memories of their childhood. Little did I know it was just the beginning.

Another time we were leaving my mother in law's house with the children and I had another on the way. Ronald had been putting me down again and this time it really bothered me. We got into a bad argument while riding in the car and when he stopped at a red light I jumped out of the car to get away. I couldn't stand to be around him. He drove on and I walked for hours crying. I tried not to cry too much longer because I didn't want people to notice me. After walking several miles on the way home, I stopped to rest at the cemetery. I was several months pregnant at the time. It was private there, and I really let my feelings all out. I just didn't know what to do. I had two children and another on the way. It was near dark when I got home. Ronald was all concerned by this time. My mother-in-law came to see if I had returned. Everybody was all worried. Again he said he was sorry and I was too tired and drained to think anymore about it. I just hated that I jumped out of the car with the children inside. It must have scared them, seeing their mother just leave like that.

It was now March 1967. I was expecting little Roy in May. We gave up our beautiful home, as we were having problems making the second mortgage. We moved into a townhouse that had a pool beside it. It was smaller than our home but I thought at least the children would have a pool to enjoy and I would too.

It was at this time, the worst incident occurred between Ronald and I. I considered it the worst because I was pregnant with Roy, and just thought Ronald would never hit me again when I was expecting. I was seven months pregnant. We were arguing about him not ever doing anything with us as a family. He said, "Is that all you ever think about, is having fun?" I remember him sitting on top of me, and the baby, hitting me over and over and choking me. It was so painful. I was crying and screaming, "I hate you!" which only made it worse. He was out of his mind, saying, "See what you make me do. Why do you do this?" Again, later he cried and said how sorry he was.

Another thing we argued about was he would not being loving to me except after we had a bad fight. Maybe I did provoke them, as he accused me. I really don't remember starting them. As always afterwards he would be loving for a few days. It seems strange that I could even allow or want him to hold me after things calmed down. I would sometimes pretend he was someone else; I would close my eyes, and make someone up in my head. It worked. I liked the way it felt to be held. Many times, if we weren't fighting, I'd try to approach him if he was reading the paper or watching television, and ask him to hold me.

"Oh, Veronica, why don't you grow up?" He liked to sarcastically call me "Veronica."

Sometimes in the mornings, I would like to make love, I always did, but he would get angry. I would feel like, "What's wrong with me?" Why didn't he want to make love with me? I was expecting Josh several years ago when he pushed me away. I just went to sleep on the couch.

Another thing we fought about as many couples did, was money. We just always seemed to have money problems. I guess Ronald didn't know how to handle it any better than I did. I wanted to always feel like he could handle it, so I wouldn't have to worry about it. Like me, he wasn't experienced when it came to spending money. One thing I always did want to do was pay the bills first. Ronald tended to put it off and I always went along with him, wanting to think, he can handle it.

Money was one of the reasons I'm sure that started our big argument or rather I would say fight. We were at that time just verbally arguing. This particular time when I went to the door to leave, as always, he said, "GO, if you're stupid enough to go out in this weather." We had a very bad ice storm. Everything was covered with ice. I didn't let it stop me though. I had to get out of the house away from him. After grabbing my coat, I went to the door crying and slamming it behind me. He always got so mad when I cried, "Oh don't start that shit again," he would say. This hurt me the worst. It didn't bother him that I was hurting.

I walked to the park that was about 2 miles. I did not have to worry about anyone picking me up at that time. Who would want an eight-month pregnant woman? I headed to the park. It was cold but I tried to block it out. I looked up in the trees covered with ice. It reminded me of when I was a child and would go to the woods. Only this time it was different. The ice was melting and dripping down on me, depressing me further because the trees didn't look pretty. I sat there and cried a while and asked God why was this happening to me. Do I not deserve some happiness in life? I felt so lost. After sitting there a while I went back home. When I arrived he was furious he shouted at me, "What is wrong with you, are you crazy or something?" It was his favorite thing to ask. I ignored him, which made him even angrier. I screamed at him, "I hate you I wish I never married you." Then I slammed a gallon glass bottle of milk on the floor. I ran upstairs because I knew I had said too much. I made it to the bedroom and locked the door. He broke through, threw me on the bed and slapped me. I fought back. Every time he hit me I would hit him back. I hated him. I remember him being over me sitting on my legs and holding my hands down with one hand and hitting me with the other. After a while I didn't even feel the blows. All of a sudden I realized that he was still. He would start crying and saying he was sorry. He let go of me asked me to forgive him. "I'll never forgive you I hate you." That I did not accept his apology infuriated him even more. He was angry all over again. "You bitch," he shouted getting off the bed to come at me again. I ran to the bathroom. I didn't make it in time to lock the door. We were striking each other again. This time he got me by the hair.

I was so concerned about the children downstairs. I went down and acted like nothing happened. Josh was old enough to remember and Tony was nearly two but he was noticing things like at the supper table when we were having an argument and Ronald said something ugly to me. Tony got off his chair and came around to hit his daddy. We were both so surprised I told Ronald, "See even the children know the difference in you." He was working the night shift and he was always so angry. His disposition was always so bad, but I just kept convincing myself, it really was my fault because I started most of our arguments. I'd rather believe it was I than to think I really did have a very bad marriage. I guess I knew I made a terrible mistake marrying Ronald, but I just couldn't let anyone know. I had covered for too long.

I went to the hospital to have my third and last child. Again I had an easy delivery. Little Roy was born just 30 minutes after I got to the hospital. The doctor wasn't even there. I remember the nurses kept asking where the doctor was when I arrived in the delivery room. They hadn't called him as soon as I arrived at the hospital even though I had the baby and was in pain. I barely remember them saying that he was on his way up the elevator. I thought I was going to die and thought of Josh and Tony. I didn't want to die. I felt scared that my doctor wasn't there. When I came to he was stitching me. He told me he was sorry he wasn't there in time. I knew it wasn't his fault, but I felt cheated and never did like him as well as before. His brother, the other doctor who delivered Tony, was so kind to me and stayed with me through my labor that was just an hour and a half. I appreciated that very much and I felt safe when he was there holding my hand telling me everything was going to be all right. This time no one gave me any comfort.

Again I was so happy when I held Little Roy. I wanted to name him Patrick Gray, as I was supposed to have been a Patrick. Ronald said no and that was that, so we named him Ronald Roy. I regretted not naming him Patrick, as I was the mother and had that right. It didn't always have to be what Ronald said, but it seemed at the time I had no more fight me. I just gave in.

When the doctor came into my room and said well are you ready to go home? I pleaded with him to please let me stay a couple four days. He smiled and said all right. I just wanted to stay in the hospital with my baby enjoying him. My mother-in-law was watching out for Josh and Tony with my sister's help.

One time when Ronald was at the hospital visiting, my sister Dawn came in and we were having an argument. I had asked Ronald to pick up a few things to have for the baby when we got home because I forgot to get them. He resented having to do it and said,

"You should've thought of that before."

My feelings were hurt as I felt it was not too much to ask of him. After all it was his baby too, and I carried him and gave birth to him. Couldn't he just do a little something? I was crying when my sister came in and told her what was wrong. She said she would get the things but it didn't make me feel better towards Ronald.

I just couldn't handle things. Everything seemed a mess in the apartment. I was physically weak and having a problem caring for all three children. One day after an argument I called my doctor and asked to please send me something. I was crying so hard and realized I really needed help. This was my first experience with tranquilizers. Everything was much better after I started taking them. I didn't get so upset.

When the warm weather came I really enjoyed taking the children out the pool. I put a little Roy in his carriage under a shade tree while Josh and Tony played in the pool. By that time Josh had learned to swim and he was really a good diver. He was six years old now. I loved to just sit and watch them play for hours. I found great happiness in my children and I was so proud of them. People were always stopping and telling me what beautiful children they were. Tony took to the water and I was teaching him to swim also. Ronald never came out to the pool. He said he didn't enjoy it and didn't see what people got out of it.

Not long after Josh started first grade, He fell from the merry-go-round and cut the top of the head. It didn't seem too serious. The Dr. just put a few stitches and said to bring him back in a week. Before the week was up he started to run a very high fever and his face was swollen.

When he started getting delirious I took him to the regular doctor to look at him. After looking at him she said that a little internal bleeding sometime had happened but not to worry. The swelling would go down and he would be all right. I took him home. Later that day, Josh's fever went higher and he was much worse the very same day. Something told me, a mother's instinct, one might say, that something was really wrong. My intuition told me to take him back again. This time, the doctor said, "take him to the emergency room." I called Ronald and told him I was taking Josh to the hospital. We both went into the room with him. The doctor took one look and said he had to operate right away. Josh looked at me and said; "Mommy please don't leave me." the doctor looked at me and said, "I feel it would be better if you left." "I'm staying, it's alright." I said. I held Josh's hand and told him it was going to be all right. He was so hot to the touch. I knew then for sure there, there was something seriously wrong. The doctor made an incision to the top of this head and infection just poured out. Ronald had to leave the room. The doctor said he was afraid of this. The swelling was all infection. How could the doctor have missed this? My god, I thought he could have gotten blood poisoning. Josh was watching me with worried eyes. I couldn't let him see how concerned I was. I just quietly held his hand and tried to keep calm. I watched the doctor put in a plastic tube in Josh's head to keep it open to drain. I don't know how I did it watching him work on Josh without getting sick but I did. Ronald told me later the doctor said there was something wrong with me that you never see a mother do that. I don't know whether or not the doctor said that but any mother who loves her child, will go through anything for them. I just had to block out the reality of the danger of it then for Josh. He was so frightened. He had to stay in the hospital for some time. I stayed with him constantly. He was being given shots and medication frequently to fight the infection. When they told me he was going to be all right I went home, threw myself on the bed and cried and cried. I thanked God for letting me know that something was seriously wrong.

    Years later when I was fighting for custody of my children, Ronald brought this up and said there was something wrong with me because it didn't bother me. He said the normal mother would not have been able to stay there. I don't think I was abnormal as much as I was just able to block out the reality of the event at the time because I felt I had to. I wanted to stay calm for Josh. It was cases such as this blocking out helps.

I went back to work in the fall of 1967 as a receptionist and the secretary for the office manager for a small textile company. I didn't even consider going back to where I worked before. I was fortunate enough to find a lady to come to the housing care for Tony and Roy. She also did housework for me. Ronald was there, during the day, but he was always sleeping up stairs as he worked the night shift.

Financially things started going better, though our home life was getting worse. I was glad that I had my job to go to every day to get away from him, and I was glad he wasn't at home at night. When he was home all we did was argue. My headaches were getting worse. I would call the doctor and he would call in the prescription for me. I was then taking medicine for my headaches and the tranquilizers helped.

Everyone at the plant was very nice to me and I liked my job. I was glad I made the change. The plant manager was especially attentive to me. I looked forward to seeing him at work even though it was a tension, that scared me. I had never had anyone but Ronald and usually whenever a man would pay attention to me or make small comments, I played dumb because I really didn't know how to handle it or how to respond.

I had always, for as long as I can remember been uncomfortable around men, but this one was different. He was mostly polite, and would just make small comments to me, about looking nice or something like that. Everyone respected Tim and I knew he was active in church. Little by little I started caring for him. I really don't think now it was him as much as I just wanted someone. He seemed to fit what I thought I wanted only I knew I could not have him and never intended to have him. It was mostly something I made up in my mind. Now I realize I really never knew him, but that didn't help me understand back then. One day he told me I was on his mind constantly. That was all I needed. I was in love! He told me the song by Andy Williams, The Shadow of your Smile, reminded him of me. Oh my, I felt that was so romantic.

Every time I heard that song in the store on the radio I would stop in my tracks and listen to every word. I was in dreamland.

How little I knew back then. I was confused, I was excited, and I felt beautiful. I felt a lot of things I didn't understand. Tim told me he loved me too. I felt wonderful knowing a man of his position and stature, such a decent, educated man like him cared for me. Much later in my life, another man told me, that I didn't know my own worth. That was so true when this was taking place. I was surprised someone like him cared for me. We both felt we loved each other, but we couldn't do anything about it. As bad as it was at home I could never break up my family. I didn't want to hurt my children. It was good that there was a change in Tim's employment at the company. He terminated his employment and moved to New York City. Of course I was shattered he was gone just like that. Gone without warning. I had to type his resignation and post it on the bulletin board. I think I made one million mistakes typing up his resignation. We never even had a chance to kiss, but that was for the best because I couldn't have handled anything else. It was two weeks before I heard anything. He called to say he was upset by this sudden change of employment and his move to New York City. We both knew we had to leave it alone as we both were married. I agreed. There, was never any question in my head about that. I couldn't imagine myself having an affair. He said that he would call from time to time to see how I was doing, and he would be thinking of me. I was elated. That was enough to satisfy me just as long as I heard from him once in a while. I felt I had somebody really nice he who cared about me. I was so happy. I felt very noble thinking how much like a fairytale it was. Two people who love each other, but don't do anything about it because they didn't want to hurt their families. They just love each other long distance and relied on phone calls. I'm sure that was not the case as far as he was concerned but that's how I felt and I lived for his phone calls every Friday. I would wait and wait for the phone to ring. This went on for a while and then they got to be less and less. I took this very hard. I called my mother in New York and told her when he said he loved me. Thinking back I got a great response from her. She said something like "well if that makes you happy then I'm happy." When I didn't hear from him, my mother would always said "don't worry he'll call again". I was so desperate, I even told my sister Dawn. My sister always told me the same thing too, "He'll call again." As I think back now, I really was desperate to have told them. I just felt you could always trust your family. One day Dad came to visit and I was a mess. I had not heard from Tim in sometime and things were gradually getting worse with Ronald and I. I told Dad about Tim and how much I loved him and that he loved me, but I had not heard from him in awhile. I was so sad. I wanted comfort or some positive words. I can still remember Dad's words, "Veronica you can't hold on to something intangible. If he really loves you, he'd be camping out on your doorstep. Just try to think of the children put him out of your mind." I tried so hard to do just that but it wasn't working. This was new to me. I didn't know how to handle it. I didn't tell Dad how bad things were with Ronald and I'm sure he suspected something, he must have.

I started taking the boys on many outings with me every weekend trying to stay busy. Sometimes I got together with a friend and we took our children to the beach. Ronald wouldn't go with us. I just took the children anyway. I told myself I am not going to wait for him to change any longer.

At work things were going well. I received a promotion to work in the industrial engineering office again because they found out I had the experience. I had been helping out in the personnel department and manager was what I really wanted to be in the future. I tried to learn as much as I could in helping the personnel manager. When he was out sick and when he had summer camp military duty for two weeks I would fill in. I knew I could do that job if he ever left.

I told them, when they put me in the industrial engineering office that I would do it for a while. I found it boring just working with figures all day and hitting a calculator. I had done that for so many years but the plant manager asked me just to do it for the time being. They really needed me there, so I agreed to do it.

Not long afterwards, the personal manager said he accepted another job and they hired a man to replace him. I was upset. I went and applied elsewhere to work. A few days later the plant manager called me into the office and asked why I was leaving. The place I applied to called him for a reference. I told him "I am qualified for the job as personal manager. I know the job and I can do it. Why wasn't I considered?" For some reason I was not timid in the business world but then I had an awful lot to prove.

"We did consider you to be a better candidate, but you would be intimidating."

"You said intimidating? How? I don't understand." "Because the women commented on the way you look." "What's wrong with the way I look?" I asked.

"You dress nicely and you look good. These are mean people here you will be dealing with."

I did try to dress well but my clothes were not expensive at all. I tried to wear matching clothes and have them clean. I was taught to always try to look good.

He went on further, "we felt the mill hands wouldn't be comfortable with you."

"That's not true." I said. "I don't consider myself any better than them." "Once they get to know me, I know they will like me. I already know many of them by name."

"Alright." he said "the job is yours if you'll stay."

"What about Al?" I asked. "You already hired him for the job."

"No. Al applied for a supervisor's job when he came. One just opened for him."

"Try it for a while. It's yours if you still want it."

Did I want it? I was elated. It was mine to do what I wanted with it. I could use my ideas and express my opinions. I was really happy. I couldn't wait to tell Dad that I was a personnel manager.

Even today as I look back, I'm proud of what I contributed to that plant. While in industrial engineering, I suggested that we should start posting the shifts' production, besides posting each employee's production, to create healthy competition, between shifts. As a result, each employee made more money, each shift had more production, and the plant as a whole made a higher percent efficiency. The feeling was contagious. Everyone was excited.

The first thing I did in the personnel department was change the whole filing system, to make it more efficient. I made new forms, new reports on each employee, got their pictures and posted their name under their photo and what department they worked in. Once a week I would do a write up of an employee on their background. They liked this and it gave them recognition.

The waiting room had only a school desk in it, that's all. I told a plant manager that was the first place for new applicants. It should look good. He told me to go out and buy what I needed only be reasonable about it. I bought office furniture, a sofa and a chair. I also purchased a picture to go behind the sofa, some standing ashtrays and an artificial plant. It looked really nice and he agreed. I then told him it just didn't seem right not to have a flagpole outside at our entrance. He said order one and I did. I wrote to the attorney general in Washington DC to get a special flag for the plant. He sent us one that had flown over the capital for a day.

There was a funny incident I want to share. We all stood outside one morning, waiting to raise the flag for the first time. We were excited when the flag arrived and could not wait to raise it on the pole, which we had just installed. I was not thinking how tall the Washington DC Capital flagpole was. When the flag was raised it came over halfway down the pole. It was so funny everyone was laughing hysterically. Someone said maybe we can starch the flag and it would stand out straight, then someone said, we can attach a huge fan on the roof to keep blowing out straight. I was embarrassed, but just laughed it off. Later on the company built a much larger plant and they were able to use the flag there, on their tall flagpole. We went and purchased a much smaller flag. Years later, people would remind me of the incident and we would laugh.

The people did accept me and I became very close to them. I knew them all by their first names. I loved to go out into the plant see how things were going. I had asked the training department to teach me how to do each job, so I could have a better understanding of everyone's job. I tried to pick the applicants for the jobs I thought they were best suited for. The employees in the plant liked this because they felt like if they had a complaint about something pertaining to the job, I would understand. I suggested an employee appreciation day to the corporate personnel director. He liked it and we did that also. I started a new softball team and I played shortstop. I was one of them. It's strange how different a person I was when I was working. I was always confident and happy. In my personal life I was unsure, confused and extremely unhappy.

I should have learned from past experience not to do what I did. I got my husband and my brother-in-law jobs there. Also a friend, whom my husband had borrowed a lot of money from and did not pay it back. Things started falling apart. I was having problems with my brother-in-law who was in the industrial office where I used to work. He had to work closely with the personnel office, which was me and personal conflicts started occurring. I hated this, as I cared for my sister and her husband. My husband's friend started liking me more than just a friend. He was a supervisor, who I also needed to work with closely. I liked Joe, but just as a friend. He was saying he loved me. I didn't know how to handle that. I didn't handle it very well. Ronald was calling me at work upsetting me and I would break down and cry in my office. At that time, he had moved up to a supervisor's position and was really doing well in his job at another plant but same company. I was always glad to tell dad when Ronald got a promotion. Dad did say, "Ronald did well for himself considering his background." But what a price I had to pay to hear that. How stupid I was.

I want to mention here that Tim, my great love (or I thought so at that time) started calling me from NYC at least once a week to see how I was. He would say how he missed me and loved me. Just the sound of his voice put me in another world. I would feel like I was on cloud nine. All he had to say was, "Hi." I lived for those weekly phone calls, late on a Friday afternoon. My heart would stop every time the phone would ring, hoping it was him, and hoping no one else was in my office when he called. Those calls kept me going. Just knowing someone like him loved me. It made me feel special. A year later, he moved just an hour from where I lived. He was so close but I felt we were so far apart. Yet,

I knew he loved me. Those calls came on and off for eight long years, until I got help. Then the waiting for calls, stopped.

After awhile, it all got to me. My headaches were so severe at times I had to go home. At that time, I was resorting to sometimes walking out of the plant down to the little country pond and sitting on a rock for a few minutes to get away from the pressure, not of the job, but all the personal conflicts with family and close friends while on the job. Another supervisor was putting pressure on me. And he and the other one felt like they had to compete for my attention. I just wanted a good working relationship, that's all. I wanted to scream. I just didn't know how to handle them. I was always trying to be so careful not hurting other peoples' feelings.

I got to doing just what I did when I was a young girl and trying to run away from unpleasant circumstances. I was 30 years old, but I felt like a frightened child. The plant was out in the country so I didn't have to drive far. I knew what I was looking for. A barn. Yes, I found a secluded one back off the road just like I wanted it. I parked my car beside the road and got out. I had to go over a barbwire fence. I tried to be careful so I wouldn't run my stockings. I walked to the barn hurriedly. It seemed I couldn't control my body. Inside I was thinking, I couldn't believe I was doing this. I had to wade through some weeds and then I was there. I could smell the hay. Oh, it was perfect. The barn had hay and even a loft. I climbed up into the loft and lay down on the hay. It was so peaceful. I wished I could stay there all day, but I had to go back. I started to cry. What in the world would they think? Me, a grown woman, dressed up, a personal manager, spending her lunch hour in a barn? They would think I was nuts. The thought of it didn't stop me from going back to the barn. I would go there, from time to time. It was my escape, my refuge. My hiding place that no one knew anything about. I'd stand up brush myself off and then step back "into my other world" where everything seemed okay, but it was not.

I was still sketching my tree, on the edge of the cliff, overlooking the mountains. Then the words came to me, the words for the drawing I had been drawing since I was 18 years old. It seemed I was sketching it more and more on notepads in the office, while on the phone talking to someone about something personal, or just lost in my own thoughts. The words are:

> *"I am like a tree. I have roots I cannot move, but I have branches. Each branch represents an experience in my life. The more branches I have, the softer I will fall.*
>
> *When I was a young tree, my branches were fragile. I fell very hard, for they could not hold me. Now that I am older and wiser, I am stronger.*
>
> *Although I have my disappointments in life, as I go down, each branch breaks my fall. I am able to pick myself up again walk away.*
>
> *I will keep climbing, experiencing life, growing new branches, until I can climb no more."*

How little I knew how many more times I was going to have to fall, and pick myself back up and keep trying. It was only the beginning. I thought I had learned so much and really I knew so little.

I knew at that time I really had to talk to someone. I guess I always knew it. I knew I wanted to. I had so much inside and so many feelings I did not understand. It seemed I was always afraid and I didn't know of what. I had so many uncomfortable feelings about so many things; I just didn't know how to handle them or even why I had them. I had a hurting inside most of the time. I couldn't even enjoy the children like I wanted to. I loved them so very much and felt like it just wasn't enough. I took care of them and never mistreated them. I gave them plenty of love and affection because that was one thing I was going to be sure about. I wanted them to know I loved them. I knew I would make mistakes while raising them but they would remember me loving them.

Chapter 16

MY SECRET DOCTOR

NOT LONG AFTER my third child Roy was born, I met with the doctor that delivered Tony. I called him after Ronald and I had another terrible fight. Things kept escalating and I was getting desperate. The doctor was visiting not far from where I lived, and he agreed to see me there. We sat in his car and visited. I was crying and just spilling out everything that had happened including after dad left, and my marriage. It seemed everything was wrong.

"Veronica" he said, "Has anyone ever suggested that you see a psychiatrist?"

"I once heard a doctor tell my mother I should see a psychiatrist when I was almost 18 years old. It was the time I had my toe operated on and stayed in the hospital for six weeks," I answered.

"Did you go to someone?" he asked.

"No, I answered. Nothing more was said about it and I put it out of my mind."

"I think it would be a good idea, maybe one could help you understand your feelings." He said.

I thanked him for taking the time to meet with me. He must have realized how desperate I was to meet him at such short notice. I went home and thought about what he said. I did want to talk with someone, but whom?

I decided the day had come. I just couldn't put it off any longer. I had no idea who would listen or who to call. I didn't want anyone to know. It was going to be my secret. Someone recommended a psychiatrist that was about an hour away from where I live and not far from my work. I went to see this new doctor and he said it was going to be $30 an hour. Gee, I thought it was so much money. Maybe I won't have to see him but a few times. I called my grandmother. I couldn't let Ronald know. He'd never go for it. I had never asked my grandparents for any money, but I knew they would help me, as they always said if you need us for anything, don't hesitate to call.

"How much do you need, dear?" My grandmother asked in her kind voice.

I responded, "One hundred dollars. I'll pay you back in three installments."

"That will be fine, she said. I hope this helps dear."

How uninformed about things I was to think three times was all it was going to take. Well three times was enough to bring some feelings to the surface and make me more aware of a big problem. Now my headaches were constant I was going to have to figure some way that I can see this doctor and pay him without Ronald knowing. I was tired of living all tightened up. What was it about Ronald that I couldn't break free? Did I have to prove something to the extent of living in misery? Why was it so important? Why was I always so afraid of making people mad? Why did I never say how I really felt about things (outside of work)? There, were so many unanswered questions.

I had so much to talk about. My most recent being, not understanding why I was not feeling guilty about how I felt about the man at work. Tim was still calling me and on several occasions came to town and we'd meet for lunch only. I was so happy to see him. It was eight months since he left town and I had missed him so. I felt he was all I had besides the children to love. To me, he was the strong one to lean on for advice. I admired him so. I needed someone strong like him. I was 27 years old and this was my first experience. He was 35 years old. I was not good at handling it. After a period of time, I was with him intimately. I was puzzled that it felt so right to me. It wasn't about sex. It just followed.

My conscience did not bother me as I had expected it to and I didn't understand that. I needed desperately to talk to someone about it. I felt seeing him once or twice a year was better than nothing. It was a bit of happiness that I was experiencing and I didn't want to let go. Looking forward to being with him each time kept me going. I can honestly say it wasn't about sex. I was so infatuated with him, and I don't remember the sex at all. It didn't seem important.

Funny thing is, I didn't worry about Ronald finding out and he never did. I would imagine a scenario and then follow it through. It was like my fantasy coming true. It was real, but it didn't seem real. How pitiful now when I think about it, that I would settle for something like that. Was I that desperate? Yes, I was.

The psychiatrist I started seeing gave me some medication for my headaches and I could get tranquilizers. My regular doctor had to really cut them down when he saw I was calling too often after he had given them to me in 1967. At this time it was 1971. I had been seeing the psychiatrist Dr. Albert just a few months. It seemed I had to take quite a few of the tablets to just take the edge off my headaches and to give me some temporary relief. The headaches returned very shortly.

I had a constant headache for over a week then. I was really getting rundown. One particular day it just wouldn't stop. It was becoming unbearable. I finally had to leave from work. I can hardly remember driving to my sister's house. I asked Dawn to please take me to the doctor. I remember going into his office. I could hardly see the doctor my eyes hurt so and I was very nauseated. My legs felt so weak. He massaged my shoulders and gave me ultrasound treatment because I was having muscle spasms. He told my sister he didn't know if he could help me or not. It was probably better to take me to the hospital if the headaches continued. I went on home with ice and my sister stayed with me. After a while she called the doctor back because my pain was much worse. He said he felt like I needed to see a neurologist and for her to take me to the emergency room. The pain I felt was so great I just knew something bad was happening. I felt I was going to die and would not even make it to the hospital. I felt something was hemorrhaging in my head. I told her to tell the children what she needed to. There, was no way I felt that I could live until we got the hospital.

When we went into the emergency room they asked me questions like who was the president and what was seven from 100 plus three. I couldn't even think of the President's name but I did describe him. I couldn't figure numbers. My head kept ringing. The doctor asked for my eyes to follow his finger. I just couldn't, it hurt too bad. I kept throwing up. My legs wouldn't hold me up. After having to wait for a bed, I was finally given a room. A neurologist came in to check me out and said they were going to keep me to run some tests to see what was wrong. They gave me a shot and some medication.

For four days I couldn't do anything. I couldn't get up. I could not really talk my mouth was so dry. I could have no phone calls, and no visitors with the exception of my mother and husband. I wanted my sister Dawn, so it was approved. I could hardly lift my arms. What was wrong with me? I had a brain scan, EKG, x-rays, and the works. The medicine they gave me made their voices seem far away, but I could hear them even though I appeared asleep.

I hated it when Ronald came, but said nothing. He always said things that made me feel bad and I would start to get upset. I had this sensation of being thrown out in space and pulled back. It was a scary feeling. Sometimes I would start crying, and the nurse would ask him to leave. I remember my sister Dawn sat beside me on the bed.

"Dawn, the pieces keep breaking off." I said to her.

"What do you mean?" She asked.

I replied, "I feel like I keep trying to hold on to the edge, like the edge of a cliff and the dirt keeps falling away."

I knew I was fighting to hold on. I had seen two people that had had breakdowns and I never wanted that to happen to me, but I felt like I was so near one. I couldn't let it happen.

After about a week, the tests were over. Everything checked out okay. There was no evidence of a growth on my brain or anything physical that would explain my headaches. The doctor came in to talk to me and asked me what my personal life was like. I briefly told him.

He said, "Have you ever considered seeing a psychiatrist?" "Yes". I replied. "I am seeing one now."

"Why didn't you mention it before?" He asked.

"It never occurred to me that was the reason my head was hurting like that. I just knew it had to be physical." I answered.

"Well we find no evidence of that. Who was your doctor so I can call him?"

He told me it would take a while for my system to get back and not to get too discouraged. I would not be able to do too much because I was physically weak. I remained in the hospital a few more days. I could have visitors then.

When I got home I had no idea I would feel so weak. I felt like a limp dishrag. I had absolutely no energy at all. My arms and legs felt like water.

I will never forget the day I was coming down the stairs into the kitchen, and Ronald looked at me disgustedly and said,

"There's nothing really wrong with you, you just want everybody's sympathy. It's all in your head."

I just looked at him and said nothing. What I felt I couldn't even put into words. He resented my friends or anyone coming to the house to see me. One of my friends had not seen me in awhile and she actually cried when she saw me and said,

"What has he done to you?"

I didn't realize I looked that bad. She and her husband had both been very close friends. In fact, they were the only couple my husband would ever consider going out with. Years ago we had lived beside each other and even had our babies just a day apart. We shared the same hospital room. We had not seen them in a while. We had gone to the beach for a weekend together, some months ago. She said she could not get over the change in Ronald. How do I stand to live with him? It wasn't just my imagination after all. She saw it too.

I went back to work, but was having a problem remembering. My medication was really affecting me and I found it very embarrassing not to be able to remember from one minute to the next. The doctor kept assuring me it was just temporary, but things weren't the same at work anymore. I was seriously considering quitting. I had been offered a job at a nearby city.

It was about this time when I was at work that Ronald called me and really upset me. I was so angry I came home. When I arrived home he was on the phone. I strongly suspected he was seeing someone else and really didn't care. I had heard from someone who worked where he did he was seen in the parking lot with a woman but I never followed up on it. I told him I had had it and not to come home; his things would be at his mothers when he got off work. He said that was fine. I left and went back to work. When I came home I took his clothes to his mothers. He didn't take the separation seriously. He thought it would just be a matter of time before I came to my senses. Shortly after this I quit my job and accepted a new job a nearby city.

I liked Ronald gone and out of the house. The pressure was gone. My headaches were not so strong and I didn't have them as often. Things were going well. The children were young and it didn't seem to bother them. At this time, I didn't care what anyone thought. I moved to another apartment nearby. When Ronald saw how well I was doing he started being really nice, coming around more. He said he missed the boys. I let him see them, but then it just got to be he was coming too often and staying too long. I didn't like it. It was just like he was living there all over again. He started getting really worried, realizing that maybe I didn't love him and I didn't want to go back to him. I didn't.

Ronald changed. He started letting himself go. I mean really go. He didn't eat or sleep. His mother said he really looked terrible and skinny.

His mother called me and said, "Veronica, I'm afraid he's going to kill himself. He won't eat with us and he sleeps in the car."

Now that was unnecessary, there was a couch in his mother's house. He started coming to the house crying and begging me to forgive him. Pleading, saying the boys and I were his whole life and he was sorry would I please give him a second chance?

"Veronica, please I don't want the kids to grow up from a broken home," he would say.

This got me and he knew it. I didn't love him. I didn't want to go back to him. I was doing well but if it were I, would I not want another chance? I had to get away to think about it. I called a friend in Virginia and asked if I could come and visit the weekend. She said, "of course." I told Ronald I'd give him my answer when I got back home.

I asked my mother in law to help take care of the boys. She was always willing. I loved her a lot and felt sorry for the hard life she had. She was always cheerful, no matter what. I felt like Ronald didn't appreciate his mother like he should and he was not loving towards her. Kate looked very Indian and she was. She was short and dark and on the heavy side with dark black hair. Her mother was full-blooded Cherokee. She lived next door and they were close. Kate always had a smile for you no matter how hard her life was.

I drove to the mountains and stopped at a little country church along the road. I got out of the car and walked up to the door and knocked. An elderly priest answered.

"Do you have a moment father?" I need to talk to you," I asked. He said, "Yes, come in." I told him my situation. My psychiatrist seemed to think I did the right thing leaving my husband. I was doing well wasn't I? The priest thought I should give him another chance. I left feeling a little confused. I didn't want to go back to Ronald, yet I felt I had to because he was the children's father and I didn't want to rob them of a father.

While I was at my friends, my dad called. Bonnie handed me the phone, and I said hello, puzzled as to who was calling.

"What the hell are you doing there, what kind of a mother are you?" My Dad bellowed.

I could not believe this was my dad. What was wrong with him? I never heard him talk like that.

I said, "Just a minute," and took the phone in the other room. I picked up in the bedroom.

He continued, "What goddamn business do you have leaving?" Something inside of me was triggered. I spoke to him, as I had never had in my whole life. He was attacking me as a mother, not knowing any of the circumstances.

I yelled at him, "you of all people have no right asking me what kind of a mother I am when you never knew how to be a father." The only time I got any attention from you was when I was being whipped. What I do is my business, and I'm not doing a damn thing wrong. You have no right to call me here and ask me such a question when you know nothing of what has been going on. I never want to hear from you again as far as I'm concerned your dead."

It was the last thing I said to him and hung up the phone. I couldn't believe that I said all that, but I did. It was a while before I got over it, and I meant everything I said except the part of him being dead. I felt bad about that.

Later I found out Ronald had called him and was crying on Dad's shoulder. There was no telling what he told him, being desperate like he was. He stopped at nothing to get what he wanted, even using my Dad to reach me.

I went back home and went back to Ronald. My stepmother, after a few weeks, called me and said Dad and I should make up. We both said some pretty terrible things. I was feeling bad about it at the time too, so I called Dad and told him I was sorry. Dad said he was sorry too, and we both made up. It was awkward. I knew he was hurting too, and I wish we both didn't have to feel so reserved with each other.

Things did change after we went back together. He realized during our separation I was serious about not wanting to go back and that he was really losing me. It scared him when he realized I might have really meant it when I said I did not love him. He became overly affectionate, smothering, jealous and possessive, mostly jealous of any friends I had, any outside interest, whether it was sports, hobby or a social meeting. I found myself in a different position. Where I wanted his attention before, it no longer mattered. It was the extreme opposite now. He would tell me how much he loved me and how much I meant to him. I was his whole life. He would physically want to touch me and make love to me often, only then I felt so guilty because I could not respond. I have nothing to give him emotionally or physically. Oh I made love with him. I went through the motions and blocked out that it was him. I could never tell him I didn't want to make love. He would be so terribly hurt whenever I even as much said I didn't want to be intimate, so I pretended he was the person I saw in a movie or read about in a book or just maybe somebody who I admired physically so I could get some satisfaction. This way I was satisfied he was happy thinking everything was all right and it got the pressure off of me by pretending to him, to the children, to family, friends and myself. I could not bear to see him crying and begging. It tore me up to see human beings like that. I tried to talk to my mother about my feelings. She told me to give him a chance, that he really loved me and was sorry for all he'd done in the past. She said I was really lucky to have someone love me that much.

I was still seeing my psychiatrist about every other week. Ronald didn't like that but I insisted that he was the one thing I was going to continue to do. I let him believe that it was all about my father and my mother believed it too.

I looked forward to talking to Dr. Albert and I always felt better after leaving him. But I still had to take medicine for headaches. At times, they were severe. I was also taking more tranquilizers. The doctor tried many different kinds. It seemed they were helping some, but not all that much. It took too many for me to be able to just live in this situation without always crying and being depressed. It seemed if I took enough, I could manage to do my responsibilities at home and on my job without getting emotionally upset. That's what I wanted.

I could not have asked for things to go better for me as far as my career went. I was hired into this large company as a personnel manager and worked under the corporate personnel director. I screened and tested applicants, made out reports, kept all personnel files, and did any typing the corporate personnel director needed. I really liked my job and looked forward going to work each day. I was feeling guilty about that too, but it was an escape from my home life. My children weren't a part of that negative home life. I loved the children so much and felt guilty that I enjoyed working so much. Dad had always said, "A woman's place is in the home."

I tried to make it up to my children when I was home, but sometimes my head hurt so much that I spent a lot of time lying on the bed. I felt guilty about that too.

I could no longer complain that my husband did not pay me any attention or give me love. I could not say he did not take me anywhere, as he did, but I could not even enjoy it if we did go out socially. He did not talk to many of my friends, and if we did go dancing, he was all hurt and upset if I enjoyed dancing with someone else. The only enjoyment I can remember with him over 18 years of marriage was going to the movies. It was another form of escape for me.

I tried so hard not to ever upset Ronald because when I did it was usually a very bad argument with both of us shouting things at each other. All I had bottled up usually came out and then he would start crying and I would go on my guilt trip again.

I'll never forget one day what happened. Now I look back, it's hard to believe I felt so controlled by him then that I would have done what I did.

I usually went across the street from where we lived and hit the tennis ball as hard as I could against the backboard. It was my way of letting out frustrations. It seemed to help, if I did it until I was exhausted. A neighbor upstairs asked if I wanted to play a game of doubles with him and another couple. His wife was and still is, a very close and dear friend, but Ronald did not like him at all. The other couple joined us on the court and we started playing. It was an extremely close game and very exciting. The four of us were playing well together and I was really having fun. The game was tied 5 to 5. Six games complete a set, which was the final game. It was in their add and our add. We were tied.

Ronald came home. I didn't realize we had been playing that long.

I told them I had to quit and go home.

"You have to do what? Quit? Now? What's wrong with you? You can't quit now. We are tied! The game will be over within a few minutes."

I just calmly said, "I'm sorry, but I really have to go, or my husband will be very angry."

I was afraid he had seen me playing with my friend's husband. Hopefully he hadn't seen me yet, and would never know the difference.

As I walked off the court they were angry and said, "you are crazy. No one ever quits near the end of a set like this, especially when there is a tie."

I wasn't crazy but I was definitely sick, and at times I wondered how much of a line there is between being emotionally disturbed and crazy.

The children were outside playing and did not see or hear anything. We had a terrible fight. Ronald hit me and I hit him back.

I was screaming and crying. When he left me alone, I went into the bathroom and took several tranquilizers. After a while I felt "out of it." I walked up to the office and talked and talked to a friend. My friend's husband came there; when he saw me leave the apartment he came in with concerns on his face.

"Veronica are you alright? He asked. I heard you and your husband from upstairs. I couldn't help but hear. He's got a problem and so do you," he went on to say.

"I know" was all I could say.

"I can see why you left the tennis court," he said. It was the only thing he had to say about it and I was glad. I felt very ashamed. For years after that he liked to joke to me about walking off the court. Later I could joke about it too, and asked him had he ever forgiven me, and think I wasn't a very serious tennis player. He told me he understood after hearing us fight, and not to feel bad about it.

At that stage in my life, I had convinced myself that this was my life and do the best I could with it. I would have to pretend everything was okay. I just couldn't see any way out of this marriage. I told myself I had so much to be thankful for and felt guilty for not being happy. What was wrong with me? Yes, I convinced myself the problem was with me. I would have to be careful with Ronald so we would not argue or have the scenes that always followed. All the begging, the crying from him, I couldn't handle. I was beginning to feel I was even doing that to him. Everyone knew how hard Ronald was trying, especially my family, mother, sisters, aunt, and of course his family.

He was always saying, "I'd sell everything I own except Veronica and the boys."

He said, "I would do anything for her or get her anything she wants." He made it appear like that is the way it was. He got to the point if I bought anything at all for myself everyone knew it. He made a big deal about it. I doubt I felt guilty about even getting anything like dress even though I always went to lower price stores. People didn't know how smothering Ronald was.

If I was too quiet, he'd say, "what are you thinking?" If I was gone too long in another room he came in to check on me. If I was trying to read a book he'd say, "is that more interesting than me?" If I was on the phone talking to my friend, it was, "you rather talk to her than be with me?" The phone calls really upset him.

I finally told my friends not to call at night, and they certainly were not going to come to my house. They refused to come if Ronald was there. I had just one friend that would come, but it was to pick up one of my sons or drop hers off. She understood the situation at home. As far as anyone else knew, Ronald was a very devoted husband who dearly loved his wife. I was afraid if I told the truth of what he was like, and had been capable of, no one would believe me. That went for my family more than anyone else.

My mother thought I was so lucky. Dad thought everything was fine. He knew we had some problems but nothing that serious. Oh yes, I did such a good job of holding my husband up to him to prove he was different, that now even Dad thought he was really trying.

On one occasion he even told me, "Veronica you have a husband who loves you and three fine children to care for. Appreciate what you have."

Just a few people knew the truth and I allowed it to happen. I was in so deep. I did such a good job at pretending everything was alright and bragging about my husbands' good qualities, it looked like I would be a terrible person and very ungrateful to even consider leaving him.

Even when the worst time happened, I tried to conceal it. I can even remember what started it. He was gone for the weekend. A couple, man and his wife, asked me if I would like to go to dinner and dance with them. It was an Elk Lodge function. I said yes and went. I didn't see anything wrong with it. I knew Ronald would not like it but I went anyway. When he found out he was furious. He got even madder when I told him I didn't care what he thought and I was going to go where and with whom I wanted to. He slapped me in front of the children. That made me madder than anything. I didn't want the children to hear our rage. We immensely argued about that too, because he was always so loud. They could hear us all over the house. Even when he was pleading and begging, it was as if to him the children weren't there, like they couldn't see or hear. This really upset me when he hit me in front of them. As far as I was concerned that was the worst thing he could have done. I told them to go outside and they did. All hell broke loose. I told Ronald I hated him and hit him is hard as I could. Then we were really into it. It was the worst fight ever. Every now and then he would stop and start crying and say he was sorry. When I didn't accept it he would hit me again, saying I was causing all our fights. It seemed after he really hit me hard and knocked me down, he realized he went too far and then he would do more because I was "making" him hit me. He actually blamed me for it. I pushed him, he would say. And one day he choked me. I couldn't tell him it was okay, that I did forgive him. I couldn't talk. I thought, "He is really going to kill me." It doesn't just happen to other people kept going through my mind. This was really happening. He came to his senses and stopped. We both were exhausted. I couldn't even cry. I felt nothing mentally or physically. I was numb. I looked into the mirror when washing my face. I didn't even recognize myself. Oh I knew I would look terrible, but that look in my eyes was frightening to me. My eyes look dead. I felt dead inside. My face was swollen, especially my eye, and my mouth was bleeding. When he went out of the room, I called my girlfriend to come get me. When she came to the door Ronald was surprised. I told him I was spending the night with her and we would talk the next day.

My friend was horrified when she saw me and could not control her feelings. She told him what she thought of him. To this day he detests her. When I got to her house she got her camera and took a picture of me. I felt too tired to even offer any resistance.

"You may need this in court someday," she said.

"Keep it. Don't let him know you have it." It was a Polaroid picture. Little did she know five years later I did need that picture when I was fighting for my children, but because of certain individuals with influence, in the court system, it never got shown. Only my attorney saw it. I gave it to her thinking it might help prove something to someone. The judge never saw it, and again if he had it may not have made any difference; finding out what I did later during the trial.

Now as I look back, I don't see how I did what I did. After that incident, I decided to leave for a two-week vacation in two days. The plans were to go to Florida to visit Dad and Beth and my grandparents. I was to see my brother, also. They were expecting the children and we were all excited about going. I didn't see any way out of not going. I told Ronald I would still go as planned, but he was not to touch me at all, and I didn't even want to discuss what happened.

We both went to a doctor the day after it happened to see if there was something he could do about my eye and bruises. I didn't want anybody to know what happened. The doctor also was a good friend who knew our circumstances and tried to talk to Ronald about being so possessive of me. He was really trying to help us. Ronald was very repentant in his office and said he was really ashamed about what happened. I convinced myself for the time being, again, I was responsible for what happened.

Anyway I had a lot of tranquilizers to take if I needed them. For now they were my companions. I'd take one, and if I got no results, I'd take another and another, until things didn't bother me, but I was still able to appear not drugged. The doctor gave me some kind of medication to help make the bruises go away quicker. Most of all I didn't want my father to notice.

Ronald kept his word on the way to Florida and didn't bother me physically. The children were happy and excited and I'm trying to think of our trip and not what happened. I, too, looked forward to that vacation. We were going to stop at Disney World on the way south.

I put lots of makeup on my face hoping no one would notice. I made it past my brother, my grandparents and I thought past dad. We had been there two days and nothing was said and the bruises were fading. With makeup you could hardly notice them at all. My stepmother notice though. We were sitting out at the pool.

"Veronica, where did you get those bruises?" She was looking at my neck. I must have forgotten to put makeup on my neck and she could tell or maybe they just seemed faint to me. There, were finger marks from where he was choking me. I couldn't think of an explanation.

She asked, "Did he do this?" "Yes, but please Beth you have got to promise you won't tell Dad." I pleaded. "I've got to take care of it."

"How long has this been going on?" she asked further. I couldn't tell her. I was so ashamed that I could live like that. I just replied, "not long." I told her I was partly to blame.

Beth promised she wouldn't tell Dad. She said it would really upset him and neither one of us wanted to do that. He would feel it was something I had to handle. I just didn't want him to know for any reason. I remember thinking he wouldn't be proud of me. I had led him to believe everything was all right for so long. I knew I should have done something about it long ago no matter what anybody thought. I was living my life at that time though I wasn't thinking or feeling that way. Much later the term "it's my life" and the full meaning of it really penetrated my mind. The realization of that brought me so much joy.

I went home from our vacation and did my responsibilities without much feeling. I just thought it was my life and I'm so tired of fighting. I was glad that at least I had my job. There, everything was going well.

I was given a big promotion to be the corporate personnel director when the acting director resigned to accept other employment. I learned much from him, as I assisted him in training sessions of supervisors and other management personnel. I knew what his responsibilities were. I had attended several seminars on public speaking, management courses, employee relations, understanding motivation of minorities, and working with the underprivileged. The upper management at the company believed I could handle it, since I had already been working there, and knew the personnel and procedures. I also knew they understood they could have me for less money then they would have to pay hiring an outsider. I didn't want that part, but it was an opportunity for me to get the experience I knew was valuable; there was more I wanted to learn. I figured I'd get things running smoothly and then hopefully get a raise.

I couldn't wait to tell dad now. I thought he would really be proud of me even though I wasn't the son he wanted. I called him. I was so nervous.

"Dad, I said excitedly, I got a great promotion. They made me Corporate Personnel Director." I have this plant of 850 employees and another plant with 425 employees in the New York office at 35 employees. I keep all the records. Of course I won't need to go to New York. I'll just keep the records here at the home office." There, was a long silence.

"Dad?" "I heard you" was his reply. That's a big responsibility." Then he tried to be lighter about it. He said something about me being a mother and housewife with sisters. He wasn't angry or anything. It was more like it's too bad you couldn't just be satisfied being a housewife. It hurt so deeply I tried to block out exactly what his words were. I stammered something like, "I'll do that too."

When I hung up I felt like the wind had been kicked out of me. Of course dad didn't realize what I wanted was his approval, for him to be proud. If he known that I'm sure he would not have said what he did, but at that time it really hurt. I felt like I would never get his approval. Well, I wasn't going to give up. At this time it was much more than Dad I wanted to please. It was important to me for a lot of reasons. Now it seemed I was going to give that job everything I had and do it as well as any man.

I was the Editor-in-Chief of the company newspaper, Chairman of United Fund campaign; I revised the affirmative action program for the year, which was extremely detailed, and had to be approved by a federal representative. I made sure we complied with all rules and regulations. There had been a lot of talking and convincing upper management. I recruited and spoke at the Department of Social Services about getting good people off welfare and on jobs. I headed up the safety committee and planned all special events such as service award dinners, including picking out and ordering gifts. The agency hired another personal manager to help me, again saving money, and I did have a secretary who did most of the interviewing. I had a girl to handle insurance and credit union concerns. I enjoyed the job immensely and found great satisfaction in knowing I was handling it well.

On the way home, I often stopped at my friend's home, who had an attached beauty salon. She was always still working but let me use her beautiful and peaceful living room to quietly sit alone for a few minutes with a glass of wine. The wine seemed to help along with the pills. I just hated to go home to my husband Ronald, and then felt guilty, reminding myself that I had children there, too and they needed me. It seemed as though I had to prime or conditioned myself in order to go home. When I got home I kissed my husband and children hello. I acted happy and gay. Sometimes there weren't times I could because of my headaches. I didn't dare act oppressed or dissatisfied or I would have to answer a lot of Ronald's questions - questions that I could not give an honest answer to without a fight. I felt I had no choice but to go I'm pretending.

After about two years at work when I still had not received a raise and felt I was being treated wrong, because I was a woman, I quit. I was feeling more and more guilty about working. Maybe Dad was right. I should be at home. It seemed my job involved more of my mind then I wanted it to. When I was at home my mind was on my job. I felt guilty about that too. I wanted to be with the children to enjoy them. It wasn't fair to them. Maybe if I just stayed at home and felt better, and maybe just maybe, my feelings would change toward Ronald. I wanted to love him and respond but I just didn't. I couldn't give Ronald what he wanted.

After quitting work, I got more depressed. I really tried hard for a while cleaning, preparing special meals, redecorating, listening to the stories on TV at lunchtime. For a while it was new and okay but I had so much extra time left over. I didn't know what to do with myself when the children were in school. I got so restless and bored. I tried meeting my sisters for exercise classes. I even tried to get interested in church activities, but couldn't. Then I took a part-time job for a few weeks, teaching swimming lessons at the YMCA. I enjoyed it. The pay was low but it was fun and something to do for a while.

Ronald came home to tell me about this house.

"Veronica, all we need is so much money down," he said. It was $10,000. Mr. Moon said he would carry a second mortgage. Mr. Moon had shown him the house before I saw it.

"We can get it so easy", he said.

"What about the down payment?" I asked. We don't have it." "You could ask your father." He said.

"Oh no I never could just ask him," I said with fear in me.

Ronald kept saying that owning our own home would make us a family again. I had really built Ronald up to my father over the years. It was like saying "see Dad, you were wrong about him he did amount to something."

The more I thought of it, the more I thought it was a good way to get Dad's approval. Dad thought it was wonderful that Betty and Dawn had a home and kept it. They were good homemakers. I knew I could be also. Maybe if I had my own home, I'd try harder. I had already quit my job as a corporate personnel director a few months before. Dad seemed so pleased finally that I was going to settle down and be a housewife and a mother without a career. So I called him.

"Dad this is Veronica." My mouth was dry and my chest hurting. "You always said if I ever needed your help to call." "Yes", he said. "Shoot."

"Dad, we want to buy a house. Something we can invest your money into and cannot lose it as we are now renting." I was trying to say all the right things.

"I think that's a good idea. What do you have in mind?"

"A house, I said. The owner will carry a second mortgage. It's a beautiful home. It's only two years old, and now that I've quit my job I have plenty of time to care for it."

"I think buying a house is a wise decision." He said. How glad I was to say this.

"What can I do to help" Dad asked. Here was the big question. "Dad." The knot in my chest hurt worse. I could barely get the words out. Why do I have to do this?

"We need $10,000. I don't know where else to go."

The silence seemed to last forever, although I knew it was probably a few seconds.

"I want to hear more about the house and the details. I agree that I think it's a good idea. The children need a place where they feel a secure home to grow up in. You know I'm a firm believer in investing money. Can you afford it, now that you're not working? Can Ronald make the payments?" Dad asked.

"He says he can." was my reply.

"Good. The kids need you at home. You know I never felt you should have been working." He added.

If only he knew how much my work meant to me. I wanted to get his approval. I prayed for him to be proud of me and see that I would have been as good as any son. I had to show him I wasn't dumb, that I was intelligent. I had to make up for my poor grades in school that disappointed him and all he wanted was for me to be a housewife. How little I knew.

Dad agreed to lend us $10,000, and we were to pay it back hundred dollars a month.

The house was beautiful and we had plenty of room. The neighborhood was great and the children made friends quickly. The school bus picked them up right in front of our house. What more could we ask for?

Sadly, I can honestly say I never enjoyed the house. I was always worried about making the monthly payments and paying the hundred dollars a month back to Dad, which never happened during the time of being married. Ronald said the house was for me and told people he got it for me to make me happy.

When I took my magic pills, I could keep the house shining and beautiful, but I felt like a caged lion. Well, go out, I'd tell myself. Meet the neighbors; but I didn't want to go outdoors. I wanted out of my marriage! Out of this life! Out of me!

The phone was ringing. Damn phone. I hated it. I hated its intrusion. It always seemed to be interrupting. It could be Ronald. He already called that morning to see how I was.

"You had a bad night." He said. "You jerked all night and kept me awake."

"I'm sorry." I'd always say. It seems I got to the place I was always apologizing for feelings I couldn't help having.

"You were fighting me again in your sleep." He told me.

"I must have been dreaming." I said.

"Okay honey you can't help it." He said.

God, I felt guilty. The phone was still ringing. I didn't want to talk to anyone. I knew it couldn't be mom. She called at least once a day to see how I was feeling. I didn't want to hear her concern or how hard I was trying, not today. I didn't need her to constantly remind me of how lucky I was, making me feel more and more guilty. I'd feel guilty for having those thoughts or feeling like I didn't want to answer the phone, because it might be her. She loved me. She was concerned about me. Didn't I want her to be? We had gotten close over the last few years, too close. I told mom everything, so did Ronald. I didn't like that. He talked against her to me. He was jealous of my concern for her, yet he was always so nice to her and borrowed money from her and Dean.

I let the phone ring until it stopped. Anna came by that morning and rang the doorbell. Just say I haven't cleaned yet or picked up from the night before would be more appropriate. I didn't feel like getting out of bed to visit with her, or see anyone for that matter, so I didn't answer the door. I was keeping more and more to myself. I no longer went out shopping. I didn't feel like getting dressed up. I no longer visited my girlfriends.

What was bothering me so much was that we were so far behind on bills. That's another reason I hated answering the phone. It always seemed to be a bill collector. I was really getting upset. Ronald would say,

"Now don't you worry honey, I am taking care of it."

"But Ronald you told me you took care of it last week," I'd say, frustrated.

It's their fault. They have been all messed up. The phone would get turned off or the power. Ronald would always get it right back on.

"Where did you get the money?" I'd ask.

"I took care of it. Just leave it to me." He answered.

The worst part was the checks that were made out to my father's business in payment of the loan started coming back for nonsufficient funds. How can I explain this? It was a nightmare. Ronald assured me that he talked to my father and my father said not to worry, to catch them up when we could, but it seemed we never got caught up.

What must dad to be thinking? I wanted so badly for him to be proud of me. I knew he must have been frowning. I had all the ingredients here for a good life. Why wasn't it working? What was I doing wrong? What more did I want? Why could I not be satisfied with my life as it was? There were so many unanswered questions. I kept trying to think of the good things in my life, reminding myself that I should be thankful for what I had. It could be worse I thought, but the depression continued.

My life seemed so disorganized at home. I didn't understand how I could be so efficient and successful in business and not at home. Later it was explained to me when I was in therapy, but at this time in my life I felt like a failure. I felt like I was a mess. The house was a mess, the bills, my marriage, my whole life, and I felt trapped. I wanted to get out.

It got to the point when I went into the bedroom to go to bed with Ronald I actually could not breathe. I would get out of bed and open the windows even if it was cold outside. I just had to have air. Later, I found out that this could actually physically happen if you feel smothered by someone. When I went to bed, I hoped he didn't want to make love. If he did, it was easier to make love and pretend I enjoyed it, than to hurt his feelings and say I didn't want to. If I fantasized enough, I could physically enjoy it, but after awhile, even that was hard to do.

I told my psychiatrist that I could not sleep. If I told him that, I knew he would give me my magic sleeping capsules. They affected me in a way that I didn't mind doing things. I found this out one morning when I woke up and didn't want to face the day. I thought I'll take one so I could go back to sleep after the children left for school. I was surprised. I didn't get sleepy. I felt good. Kind of funny, but I liked it. Things didn't seem so bad and I wanted to clean the house. Yes much to my amazement, I did, and in no time flat. If I took one before going to bed, I didn't mind making love. In fact, I was even playful about it. I felt freer with my husband and didn't mind trying out different things. If we had an argument, I could take several and go to sleep. After a while though, I had to take more to get any results. My doctor told me that they had been taken off the market as many teenagers we're getting them and they found that they could be dangerous; still he could give them to me, when I promised I'd be careful and said how much better I felt. Of course, I had my tranquilizers too and my antidepressants.

When I ran out of medicine, it was awful especially when I could not reach my doctor. I could go for a while, but not for too many days.

As long as I took them I appeared normal and functioning so no one knew. When I didn't have them, I would feel panicky and my insides would be racing like a car in neutral at a stoplight. I was very edgy and cried easily. At that time I wouldn't let Ronald see me cry. In fact I wouldn't cry in front of anyone, but then I never really did. If I didn't have any medicine, I had to really fight to hold back the tears in front of others. I was having muscle spasms in my shoulders and of course my headaches would return.

The worst time was once when I just didn't have the money to get my pills and was trying to hold out until Ronald got paid. I was alone at home at the time. I had been hurting, but then it became unbearable. I tried pushing my head up against the bed headboard. Sometimes the pressure helped and sometimes I put my head into my hands and pushed as hard as I could. Before when I had these physical feelings they would last just a little while and then go away. That time nothing I did stopped the pain.

It felt like every nerve in my body was screaming, raw and tingling. I was jerking and could not stop. Ronald had told me I jerk a lot at night, and he could never wake me but this was the first time I saw myself jerking. My legs were drawing up to my chest and I had to kick them out again. I couldn't keep them still. I couldn't call our neighbor, and I wouldn't call a friend. I didn't want anyone to see me like that. I was scared and I felt like I was falling apart. I called my husband. He rushed me to our doctor friend. By that time I was throwing up. He gave me some of the same kind of medicine I was taking there at the office and he called my primary doctor himself. Once the medicine took affect I felt so much better and started to relax.

I remember thinking to myself, now I know why these kids that get hooked on drugs will do anything to get it. Their body has to have it. I thought to myself, if I had had to, I was to the point I would have broke into a store to get it. I was desperate.

My psychiatrist told me to never go that long again without my pills. I trusted him and never questioned his judgment, but I wanted and needed those pills. I was okay and felt even happy sometimes when I had them. Things didn't bother me, but the sad part was that I was slowly destroying myself. I was not really living. I was just existing. I was not facing up to what the problem really was and I didn't know why I couldn't.

It was a lot of my fault that I was in this situation. I had done such a good job of convincing everyone, mostly my family, how much Ronald changed since we went back together. And he kept his promise not to hit me again since the last time was so terrible.

It really scared him when he saw what damage he had done to me but it was really too late. I no longer loved him. I tried to. Many times I even convinced myself that I did love him. I wanted to believe it. He no longer hit or neglected me but rather showered me with attention. I had no privacy around him. I couldn't leave his side for a minute. He wanted to know where I was going even if it was just to the next room. He wanted all my attention. I tried to act like everything was all right. I was so concerned about the children's happiness. They were doing well in school and seemed happy. The only thing they knew was wrong was that mommy had bad headaches. I felt guilty over this. Little Tony, my curly headed middle child would bring me flowers he picked to help me feel better. He was so sweet. I kissed him and said, thank you honey. He would smile, and happily skip away. My youngest son Roy would want to play and I would always convince him that I would when my head stopped hurting. The guilt would get so bad, I couldn't handle it, so I would take more Milltown and go to sleep, hoping that when I woke, the headache would be gone, so I could play with him.

I knew I had to do something because of what was happening to me. I had to get out. Perhaps get a job. What about Dad, an inner voice would say.

I had told him I would not work anymore. I'd just have to explain that we need the money. Working before had always been my escape from this life. I was happy when working. I wasn't expected to be to be the perfect homemaker then and I was able to function. I would just have to work doubly hard so as not to neglect my children. I remember a few months before being offered a sales woman's job in an exclusive men's store and telling the man I couldn't take the job because I promised my father I wouldn't work after buying a new house. No wonder he had that look on his face. Was it shock or pity? Perhaps both. I was a grown woman with the family and I had to have my father's approval. Sad.

Anyway I called Dad. He wasn't pleased but I managed to convince him that we needed the money and I needed to get out of the house. It was just a part-time job.

"I'll be home for the children when they get home from school, and I'll have plenty of time for taking care of the house." I assured him.

Oh why did I feel I always had to explain to him? It was terribly frustrating, but I felt I owed it to him since he helped us in getting the house. I supported my argument with,

"My doctor says I need to have an outside interest."

"Join some clubs. Get involved in church work like Dawn." He said.

"We need the money Dad," I said.

"Well you know what you're doing," He concluded. The decision was made. Did he have to bring Dawn into our conversation? I thought angrily.

One thing I did know was that I had to get out of the house. I knew what was happening to me. Maybe if I had been happy with my life with Ronald and with myself, I could have been more content to stay at home and just do housework and cook, but I wasn't. I needed an outside interest before I withdrew completely.

More and more often I had caught myself just sitting and staring for long periods of time. I had told Dr. Albert this.

He said, "You need to go back to work."

I got a job right away in a woman's boutique selling cosmetics and other gifts. It was an elegant store and I loved working with pretty things. It was a fun job.

Another reason I had to go to work that I couldn't tell Dad was that I no longer had my magical sleeping pills. After a few accidents like falling on the slippery wax floor and banging my head and falling against a mirror and cutting my arm, Ronald suspected I was taking something. He found the green capsule and told Dr. Albert He warned me about them. He said they have been taken off the market because of young people using them as uppers. He only gave them to me because

I told him I couldn't sleep, which was true in the beginning. Then I found out that I didn't mind making love with Ronald if I took one before going to bed. He had no idea that I would take more if I wanted to shut off my mind from his constant late-night talking or that I would use them during the day to do housework. I had abused them. Now I no longer had them. All I had was my Milltown, headache tablets and antidepressants. Well, with the job I won't need them anyway. But I still needed the others more and more as my system got used to them.

I was not trying to change my situation, which was part of the problem. I was doing nothing to correct it. As long as I continued to live a life that was against every emotional need I had and was not getting, I was going against myself. To make things worse, there were things in my life that happened but I could not remember and did not understand, and feelings I did not understand. Subconsciously if something was wrong, whether I was aware of it or not, came out in one way or another. Unexplained headaches and a sick feeling inside most of the time for things I didn't understand occurred, and my chest hurt too. I really wasn't solving my problems by taking medication, and I was abusing pills. I was not taking my medications as prescribed.

Around that time another poem came to me. It explained how I felt inside and what my doctor said to me.

"My doctor to me is like an island. A solid piece of something I can hold onto and feel safe. I swim around this Island, venturing out further each time, looking for that solid piece of something I can hold onto and be happy with. When I leave this Island, I know each time how long I can swim on my own. Then return. I have found little islands and pleasures, some larger in my ventures, but each one is only intangible and soon sank or started to sink, so I returned to the island. I believe I have found my own island now in my family. It's not all happy there, but so far it hasn't sunk."

I had convinced myself that my family would be my happiness, that I would make it my happiness. It was something I knew I had. I would have to stop searching for that something when I didn't even know what it was that I wanted and needed so desperately.

Chapter 17

GOODBYE GRAM

IT WAS NOW 1974. I was 34 years old. This was the year my dear grandmother passed away.

In all the years I was married to Ronald I never complained to my grandmother about my marriage. For all she knew everything was okay. I just felt she had enough worries. She worried about mom a lot. I never really found out why. I didn't want to worry her so just never told her my problems. She knew I had some because she knew I went to psychiatrist, but didn't know why. Whenever she visited she would look at my concern and say,

"Veronica I'm worried about you. You have so much to do. You are working so hard and having the responsibilities at home too. I don't know how you do it."

I'd always reply, "I'm okay Gram. Please don't worry."

Whenever she came to visit which was about three times a year, it was extra special. She would call me as soon as they arrived at my aunt's where they always stayed. She always took me, my mom, my sister, and my aunt out for lunch; and I would always fix her hair. Gram was a pretty woman and always kept herself well. We always had that special closeness. I would sit beside her on the sofa, visiting with the rest of the family and hold her hand. Her hands were so warm and soft.

It was in July, I was giving my son Tony a birthday party when my mom said "Gram came home from the hospital today." I looked up startled from cutting the cake,

"What do you mean, came home from hospital? I didn't know she was in the hospital!" I asked my mother, as my heart stopped beating.

"You know she was there a few days learning how to give herself those shots for diabetes," she said.

"Mom, I don't know what you are talking about!" my mind was racing. My grandmother was in the hospital and I didn't know? I didn't send her a card or anything. She must've been terribly hurt to not hear from me. I was so upset.

"Veronica, I told you last week she was going." Mom said. "I don't remember." I replied. How could I have forgotten?

I didn't say anymore realizing I had been forgetting things lately. I couldn't remember mom telling me. Was my medicine beginning to affect my memory too? It might, but I didn't know it for sure.

As soon as the party was over I ran to my room and wrote grandma a letter. I had an urgent feeling. I had to get it off immediately. I told Gram in the letter how much I loved her and what she meant to me, that she had always been like a mother to me. Mom and I always joked about being more like sisters. We looked a lot alike and we wore the same clothes. She didn't look her age. I really thought of my grandmother like a mother. I told her how much all the times I spent with her meant and that I was so happy she had Gramps and found happiness with him. I went to the post office that night. I felt awful that she was in the hospital and I had not sent her anything and I didn't even remember being told she was going. Gram was the most important person in my life. I knew I needed her even though I never told her how much. It was just like I loved and needed my children to put it in a different way.

Always lived in fear of the day I would get a call telling me my grandmother died. If ever I got an unusual call like long distance at work from family, my first thought was that something had happened to Gram.

It was just a few days later, maybe, the call I feared came. Mom was crying. I knew something was wrong right away. I asked,

"Mom, is it Gram?" She said, "yes."

"Is she dead?" I asked, my heart in my throat.

"No", she answered. "She has had heart failure." "Why?" I asked.

"She had a little bleeding from her bottom. They wanted to take a scan and they gave her some kind of a dye. It caused her to have heart failure." she responded.

"Her blood pressure dropped very low. It doesn't look good. Your aunt and I are going to the hospital in New York. We are leaving tonight." She said.

"Mom, I am going too." The panic I felt was unbearable.

I didn't cry then. Mom was crying. I felt like I couldn't. As soon as I hung up, I sank to the floor crying in the corner of the room.

"Gram, Oh Grammie." I cried. I called her "Grammie" like I did when I was a little girl. My voice didn't even sound like mine. I kept saying,

"Grammie please don't go. Don't leave me please."

My girlfriend Holly was in the other room. She came out when she heard me. I looked at her and said,

"My grandmother is dying and I know she's dying." She had never seen me cry before and I couldn't stop. I didn't even care if she saw me cry.

"She can't go, she can't die." I wrapped my arms around my self rocking and crying,

"She can't die."

My friend said not to worry about the children that she would care for them. She helped me throw a few things into the suitcase. I couldn't think. Ronald came in with a man whose wife I had gone out with that night. He got so angry with me for going to the dance with him. We were going to go out with them that night. I had worked for this man many years ago and in engineering. He was the one my sister-in-law said I was having an affair with. We were all still friends. I looked at my old boss, and told him my grandmother was dying. He came over and put his arm around me. It felt good to cry on his shoulder. I don't know why I didn't want Ronald to comfort me, and he didn't. There, was too much there.

Before I saw mom and my aunt I told myself to be strong, that I had to comfort them. After all Gram was their mother and I was just her granddaughter. The ride was long and anxious. We hardly spoke the whole trip. All of us were lost in our own private thoughts. None of us knew if she was still alive, not wanting to take the time to stop and call.

I was remembering how just a few weeks before I was in Jersey with my sisters. We were better friends by then. I had wanted to see more of gram. She was at the event at my sister's. We had our usual family gathering and I had my usual sick feeling. I watched my sisters and brothers-in-law playing in the pool feeling free and having fun. Why can't I do that? Why am I so self-conscious around them? I was always quiet and reserved. My eyes stopped at my grandmother. I wanted to be near her. I love her but it seems there was so much unsaid and unanswered questions, like what did she think when I didn't go live with her and my sister went instead? There was so much I wanted to tell her. Did she feel like I just didn't want to share and confide in her? I hope not. I remember I got up from where I was sitting and went to sit next to her. On the way home, we stopped at her house to say goodbye. When we came in Gramps said,

"See I told you, the girls haven't forgotten about you." Obviously Gram did say something about not us coming sooner. I wanted to very much but I didn't want to ask my sister to take me to Grams. I didn't want to be any bother. How pathetically submissive I was.

"Gram," I said, putting my arms around her, "Did you think we weren't going to stop and say goodbye? She was embarrassed. We would never do that. You are the center of our family. Everything revolves around you. You are the most important person." I told her.

We kissed goodbye. As she hugged me I had the strangest feeling it was going to be the last time. It scared me, but I tried to push the thought and my feelings away.

Riding in the car just a few weeks later on the way to the hospital, my feelings came true. When we arrived at the hospital we went straight to the intensive care unit. Gram was conscious.

"What are you all doing here?" she asked. We had all discussed not letting her know how really concerned we were.

"We wanted to be here with you." I said to her. She looked at me and said,

"What about the children?"

"A friend has them, Gram." I answered.

"You shouldn't have gone to so much bother," she said with a frown.

I said lightly, "Do you think I'm not coming knowing you were in the hospital? They couldn't keep me away." Gram smiled and said,

"I must look a mess; my hair." She always worried about her hair.

"Gram your hair is fine. I'll fix it when you feel better." I said.

Gram was groggy and drifted off. I went looking for the doctor. The nurse said he'd be there, as soon as he could. When he arrived he told us he was concerned about the circulation in my grandmothers legs. It was not returning. When her blood pressure went so low it did damage to them. She was diabetic and the circulation was the problem. He said they would do all they could but it didn't look good. I went back in the room. She was sleeping with an oxygen mask. I held her cold hand. She opened her eyes and asked for some gum. I found a piece, broke it in half and gave it to her. In a few days, the circulation still hadn't returned. The doctor was very kind in telling us that her legs needed to be amputated. When he said this, my grandfather said she would rather die. My mother thought that was an awful thing for him to say, but knowing how independent my grandmother was he was probably right. The doctor added she was having kidney failure and he was afraid she wouldn't be able to take the operation. I said to him,

"If you operate she'll die and if you don't, she'll still die?" I asked with frustration.

"I'm sorry." He said.

My mother and aunt were crying. I couldn't. I went and I looked at her. A few days earlier she told me,

"I can't feel my legs."

"Well they're there," I told her.

Now I knew she was going to die. I had been praying for her, but I thought now it was time for her to go even if I wasn't ready to let go of her. I lifted the sheet. Her legs were cold and blue and there was an odor. I wanted to snatch those ugly things from my grandmother. To think that something so horrible could be happening to her was unbearable. I hurt so inside. Why could I not cry? I couldn't show any emotion.

My mother needed me and my grandfather needed me. Oh how my heart ached for my grandfather. They love each other so much. They were so close.

I went out to get Gramps. He said,

"Let's go get a cup coffee." He was trying to be brave for us. We sat at the counter and he started talking about her. He told me how much I meant to her.

"You know, he said, your grandmother never understood why it was Betty that came to live with her when she knew how much you wanted to. She told me you were often talked about back then."

It had been 17 years. I was right in feeling she always wondered why? I just didn't know how to tell her and she never asked.

"Oh Gramps, I wanted to so bad but I felt Mom needed me." Really mom didn't want me to go, and I couldn't let Gram know what was happening at home. It would've broken her heart." I didn't have to even tell him. He looked at me and said,

"She knew." I looked up with a start. She knew? How could she know? My head was spinning inside. All these years I worried about her finding out. So many times I covered for Mom. The times I couldn't tell my grandmother what was bothering me. I am glad she knew.

"Gramps," I was finally able to say "Gram knew about the men?" "Yes." He answered. She was worried about mom anyway.

"How long had she worried about mom?" She had always, for as long as I can remember," he said to me.

"Be a good girl and help your mom, she needs you." Was there much more than I knew about?

I went to my sisters. The next morning the phone rang. We both looked at each other and we knew the call that was coming. My sister answered the phone. I knew by her answers that my grandmother was gone. I can't describe how I felt. I ran to the bathroom, slid to the floor, quietly crying, "Grammy," that's all I could say. I wanted to scream. I felt so angry that she was gone. But I was at my sister's and didn't want to make a scene.

She came to the door and asked if I was all right. Yes, I answered.

We both quietly cried together.

"Betty, I'm going to do one last thing for gram. Something I know she would want." She looked at me questioningly.

"I'm going to fix her hair. She would want to look nice. She's with God. This is just her body here. You know how she always wanted to look good." I told her.

"Veronica, how can you do that?" she asked.

"I can and I will." I felt very strong and knew I could do it. My grandfather had long retired but he worked at this funeral home part-time when needed. I told him what I wanted to do. He said,

"Are you sure?"

"Yes" I answered.

He smiled and gave me a hug.

"You are a special girl, Veronica, your grandmother would like that very much." I felt so good when he said that. I talked my sister into going with me. She readily agreed. I told her again it was not Gram, but her body. Of course I had the help of my pills too, but I wasn't nearly groggy, as everyone else appeared to be. I was used to them; but they were kind of "out of it," they were crying so much. It hurt to see them crying so hard. I tried to comfort them.

When I got to the funeral home we went into the preparation room. Gram was lying on a table. Her legs were wrapped and she had a sheet covering her. There, were two men there. It didn't upset me when I saw her. I knew I had something to do and I was going to do it. I knew, in some ways I was really using my blocking technique again, as I did when my son was hurt. I used electric curlers, so it didn't take long to fix her hair really nice. I helped the man place her in the casket. Her body looked pretty. I felt good knowing that she was now out of this body with the decaying legs. Somehow, I knew her spirit was still alive and I could feel it. I know she was pleased with what I did and I was pleased with myself. I never broke down. It helped tremendously having my sister Betty there helping me. I went home telling myself, and pretended she was still alive and in New York, only sometimes I couldn't pretend too well.

After the funeral, I went around consoling everyone. I felt like screaming and screaming. I went to no one for comfort. No one thought of me. I had just lost the most important person in my life.

I cried a lot when I was alone. One day I threw myself on the bed. "Oh Gram I miss you so." I heard something and it was Ronald. He was in the bathroom. I didn't even know he was home. I got angry. I didn't want him seeing me cry like that. It was so personal. I resented him of course. He couldn't help that he was there. It wasn't his fault. It was just the way I felt that I couldn't explain. It wasn't until two years later, that the full realization hit me that she was really gone and then I let all my grief out. All the pain I felt. I cried hysterically in front of my therapist, Arielle. Arielle helped me so much and made it possible to be able to write this story.

Gram didn't get my letter in time, before she went to the hospital. She was already there, and my aunt read it to her. I hoped she understood and heard what I had to say.

There, were times after her death, I was concerned about Gramps, for I new how much he loved my grandmother. I'd call him. It seemed it always take him a while to answer the phone.

"Hello." He would say groggily.

"Gramps, it's Veronica. How are you?" I would say trying to sound cheerful.

""Hi, honey." I am ok." He'd respond.

But in his voice didn't sound okay.

Gramps had always been such a forceful man projecting loud and strong. Now he sounded so alone and down.

"What are you doing?" I'd ask.

"Just sitting here. I didn't even realize the house is dark. I guess I have to turn the furnace on. It is beginning to get cold here now," he stated. I could just picture him sitting in the dark, chilly house, not even aware of it, because he was lost in his thoughts, remembering and missing Gram. How I wished he could meet someone to share his life, so he wouldn't miss my grandmother so much. He was not a man to be left alone. He still was so full of life at 74.

"Don't worry about me dear, I'm doing just fine." He said before we hung up. I knew he wasn't doing, just fine and my heart ached for him.

I worried about my mother too. She was, or at least I thought she was close to her mother. Gram always seemed concerned about her, although I never understood why. Again the memory my grandmother saying to me, "be a good girl Veronica, your mother needs you." Those words burned into my mind and stayed there, until just two years ago. At the time, I felt concern for my mother and she wasn't showing much emotion after the death of Gram. I felt she was hiding it, not fully realizing. I was also guilty of it.

My mother's concern, as well as my aunts, was what would happen to the family business my real grandfather had built up. He had a gas service station, and the house. They wanted to know what was going to happen with it, right after Gram died; and were angry at Gramps for not saying something about it. Gramps told them at the time of his death, all property would be divided between his children and grandchildren. Gramps said he needed the income. He did however give my uncle the large home that my uncle and his family lived in. This was the family home my mother, aunt and uncle were raised in. My uncle could not work because of a serious accident.

Right after the funeral at the house with all the relatives they were already asking about what he was going to do with the property, he made the statement to Ronald,

"We just buried her today and already they are asking." Don my mother's husband, was upset at the funeral and then afterwards because he got rejected, and resented my mother spending so much time with her relatives. He proceeded to get drunk and made a big scene. I was so angry with him, when I got him alone I asked,

"How could you act this way today of all days? How I despised him.

At Thanksgiving, right after gram died, the family as usual went to New York for dinner at my sister's house. For the first time, Gram would not be there.

My sister told me at the dinner table, Gramps announced he was going to remarry. This shocked and displeased everyone, to put it mildly. I am told my aunt became hysterical.

My sister screamed at him,

"How can you do such a terrible thing?" My mother said,

"It hasn't even been a year. It hasn't even been a year since Mother died."

They came home quite upset and angry. Then they put more pressure on Gramps to do something about the inheritance that was coming. Gramps did tell them to take whatever they wanted after the funeral, as they did not live close by.

I was the only one who was happy to hear Gramps was going to remarry. Now I thought I don't have to worry about him. I know Gram would not have wanted him to stay alone in that big house, and manage his medicine. The rest of the family had very little to do with him. My mother and her man did not stop to see him and his new wife. The family mainly needed to discuss what would happen to the property. Now with him remarrying they were really worried. Gramps did die three years later and they were left with nothing. I felt if they had handled it the right way Gramps would have taken care of things like they wanted him to. He was not a man to be pushed and it hurt him that that was their first concern when their mother died. When he announced he was going to remarry, instead of being happy for him, they were upset that he would marry just months after Gram passed. They could not understand how much he needed companionship. The woman my grandfather married was a very dear lady who had just lost her spouse too. She and Gramps were very happy together and she took it hard when he died.

I went to visit her for the first time not long after my grandfather passed away. She and I still keep in touch with cards and letters. She told me my grandfather spoke very highly of me that made me feel very good. I'll always hate that I never told my grandmother why I didn't come to live with her, as we always planned. I wanted to do that more than anything else in the world. But back then I don't know if I could have even explained to her, because I didn't fully understand myself.

After my grandmother's death, I started taking even more pills. It seemed it took more now to make the pain I felt go away. I couldn't bear to feel the emptiness inside. I felt I had nothing left to hold on to. My precious pills helped me pretend that life was easier.

Chapter 18

ESCAPING THE HOUSE

THINGS LOOK BRIGHTER after I started my new job. I didn't have to be at work until 10 AM. Thanking me plenty of time to get the boys after school, and do what I wanted with the housework, and get myself ready. I took the right kind of job, as by now, living like a hermit I needed all the moral boosting I could get.

Selling skincare creams and make-ups and experimenting on my own face helped a lot. The job gave me a reason to dress up every morning. I also liked public contact ahead in many feel really good when I made up a customer's face and she was pleased and there, was a good sale.

When the shop wasn't busy, I get terribly bored, but not as bad as being home. I tried to keep busy cleaning and rearranging but sometimes I still wouldn't catch myself sitting on the back stool behind the see-through screen just staring into space. I think how long have I been sitting like this? I jumped up, shake my hand and get busy, even if it was just walking around. I was still fighting depression. Some mornings I can hardly move my body. It felt so heavy. I tired so easily. I decided I needed to make an appointment to see my doctor. It had been a few years and I was way overdue for a physical check up. I was eager to see Dr. Livingston again.

Sitting across from my doctor, the one who delivered my second child, I stared at him, as he reads the results of my check up. I had such a crush on him at one time. He was so kind to me when Tony was born. He stayed right there, with me, help me get through each painful contraction. I looked forward to his visits. I knew I was one of many patients who were secretly in love with him. I wonder if he ever suspected?

He looked up from reading the chart,

"Why has it been so long? You know if you should have this exam at least once a year." He was displeased but not as displays is when I had called him a few years ago asking for sleeping tablets.

"Time has gotten away from me so much as happened let me explain." He had told me years ago that he felt a good psychiatrist could help me overcome my depression and unhappiness. He knew of my marriage problems, but what really concerned him was I was 35 years old and crying over when my mother and when I was 16 years old.

After filling him in on all the developments over the period of time I did not see him he seemed relieved that I finally saw a psychiatrist but there, was concern on his face when I told him how long I have been see the other doctor and how long I haven't taken the medication. He was shocked I was taken so much.

"Veronica, there's something seriously wrong here. What has he done to actually help you other than prescribing you all this medication? I felt a little foolish when all I could say was

"Well I do feel better after talking to him'

I realized as I said it, that I haven't really changed or felt better about anything.

How often do you see him?" Dr. Livingston asked. I added "It has been four years" he shook his head frowning.

I'm very concerned about you. He looked at the medicine bottles I've given them.

"All this time and you still have headache and taking all this medicine." He stopped and looked at me.

"Are you still having an irregular periods? Is milk still in your breasts?" he asked.

"Yes has been there eight years now and I still only have periods three or four times a year."

"Veronica I want you to see another doctor. He is an endocrinologist, and a very good one." Perhaps he can find the answer. If he can't help you, he will know somebody who can. This hospital is known for finding answers to complicated cases. This is going on much too long already. You can't continue to live like this. I'm surprised you have done as well as you have."

How grateful I felt towards him for just saying that as he handed me the doctors name and telephone number on a piece of paper.

"I'm sorry about what happened a few years ago when you hung up the telephone on me. I can see now why you would be upset, as you have been my doctor for so many years. I wasn't even sure you would see me when I called. Thanks"

He smiled and said,

"Let's forget it."

I had an appointment to see my psychiatrist soon after the visit and told him about my appointment to see an endocrinologist.

"Why?" he asked me frowning.

"My gynecologist thinks it would be a good idea," I said. I went over my conversation with Dr. Livingston to Doctor Albert. I could see he did not like it. I was disappointed in his reaction and doubted him for the first time.

It was after this visit that he started limiting my medication. This meant I could not take the dosage my body had become accustomed to. He had known I was taking more than I should and he never said anything when I would run out of medication early, He would always prescribe me more but now he would not. Panic filled me at the thought of running out of medicine and not been able to get any.

"You'll have to make that last." Dr. Albert calmly said to me. After that, I couldn't reach him by phone. I had no choice but to try, but how?

It wasn't long before I had my appointment with the endocrinologist, but it was long enough for me to have gotten pretty desperate. I was having some really bad times. It's hard to explain these bad times. Perhaps I should say bad feelings. It was just a terribly scary feeling I couldn't explain. I would just start crying with fear. Sometimes it would happen at work, but I always managed to control it to the point where no one noticed.

I tried to limit my pills until I could get a refill but there were times when Ronald, the pressure and who knows what all really got to me. I tried to keep to myself. I tried to appear calm but at times even my speech wasn't right. My words came out jumbled up. It was embarrassing and I would try to joke it off. I wouldn't let Ronald see me cry, but there were times I just had to scream at him to leave me alone, which only made him worse. I couldn't pretend to be loving and to keep the pressure off of me without taking the medication my system was used to getting. If I took what I needed, I ran out before time for my prescription refill.

This happened once at work. I was to see Dr. Albert the following Monday. I was trying to make it till I saw him. It was Saturday and I had been out of medication for a day or two. I had already begged the pharmacist to just give me a few.

"Veronica, I just can't. I wish I could."

I knew he meant it. I had always found it embarrassing to keep getting medicine from him. Did he not appreciate my business? I'm sure he did. It was just that I was so dependent on those pills. He knew my desperation.

He said, "I could never understand why your doctor kept giving you so much over such a long period of time, but it wasn't my place to question him."

After leaving the drugstore, I had to get to work. My body was already beginning to tell me I needed the medication. Ronald said I jumped and jerked all night. At work I kept from crying as long as I could. I had tried to reach Dr. Albert. I just couldn't wait until Monday. All I could get was his answering service. I left a message for him to call. I waited and waited. No call came. The owner of the shop came in and she was using the phone. I became so desperate I went across the mall to use another merchant's phone, which I didn't even know, to call the doctor. I was getting to the point where I was shaking and could hardly even talk straight. I felt so humiliated. I finally got Dr. Albert and he told the druggist to give me a few.

I was now sitting in the office with a new doctor, the endocrinologist. He asked what was troubling me? I let it all out, starting with having to depend so much on pills to function. I hated it.

God knows how I hated it. Just talking about it started me on the road to recovery. He was stunned that I was taking so many different medications for such a long period of time, with no good results. I still had the headaches.

"What else is troubling you," he asked.

I must have talked an hour, but he patiently listened. I was desperate and knew it. When I finished talking he said,

"Veronica I feel you need help and the service of one of the top psychoanalyst in the country and he's right here. It may be a while until he can see you. He's terribly busy, but it's obvious that the doctor you have been seeing hasn't helped you. We' will take all necessary tests to see if your problems are physical to be on the safe side, but I strongly doubt we'll find anything.

"The first thing we have to concentrate on is getting you off all that medication. You will have to be hospitalized. It will take some time getting off of it. I'll try to make an appointment for you to see the specialist I have in mind. He's going to want to talk with you before he can take you on as a patient. I'll have my nurse call you when an appointment can be made. If you hear no more from me than you'll know your physical test came out okay."

A few days later, I received a phone call that I had an appointment to see Dr. Dressler who was called simply Dr. "D".

I had not been able to keep my appointment with Dr. Albert my psychiatrist as he was ill but he did renew my prescription. I told the nurse that he had told me to keep him informed as to my visit at Hospital. She told me I could see him the following week. It was my last visit with him. It was strange to say the least. I sat there, looking at him and feeling like I owed him an apology for having an appointment with another doctor. (How pathetic I was.) This man who I told my innermost thoughts to, shared problems with, and gave so much money to, and I still felt like I owed him something. I'll never forget my first visit with Dr. Albert and his first question to me was, "Did I experience the sibling rivalry?" I looked at him puzzled. What was he talking about? A sibling. What's a sibling? He changed his question.

"Did you ever feel one or both parents preferred your brother or sister to you?"

I answered him as honestly as I knew how to at that moment explaining what I was aware of.

"I don't think Mom or Dad really loved one more than the other."

"Did you have fights?"

"Yes but that's normal, isn't it?" What did this have to do with now I thought? Wouldn't it have been easy for him if I could have just opened my soul and given him all the suppressed and hidden emotions and thoughts deep inside that even I did not know. I thought to myself, I bet this is the usual, difficult question that all psychiatrists asked. It somehow just seemed too simple. No, all psychiatrists do not start out that way or even ask that question.

The clearing of his throat brought me back to where I was, in his office and he was saying.

"Who is this now, the doctor you'll be seeing at the hospital?" I told him. It was obvious he was uncomfortable.

"Of course, I have always felt it is good to have a second opinion," he responded.

Why couldn't I have spoken up and said, something like, "Well, dammit, why couldn't you have said something years ago?" But instead I sat there quietly and said something like,

"You have helped me so much and I appreciate your time." You paid for his time dummy, I told myself angrily. What was wrong with me? Why was I feeling guilty?"

He stood up and said

"Well keep me posted on how things go." You say they are going to put you in the hospital?" When?"

I don't know. I have to see Dr. "D" first.

"Let me know how you are doing?" As if he really cared. He cared, but he cared for himself. He knew he never helped me and also took my money. But most people wouldn't have been as gullible as I was. All I knew was he was someone I could go and talk to about anything, and it was okay. No matter what, I could talk about it. Feelings I was aware of, but not understanding why I had them.

This was the important thing, but back then, I didn't know that. I could not tell him why I had headaches most of my life. Why I was depressed, why I was so tired, why I always hot a sick feeling in my stomach at family get-togethers, why I was afraid of men on a personal level but not in business, why whenever I brought something to the house I'd think of Dad visiting and wonder if he would think it was nice. Why I still had bad dreams concerning my sister, why I couldn't talk about what happened after Dad left home without crying, why I couldn't cry in front of people and even show anger to them, and the rare times I did, I over-reacted by screaming and running to my room, woods or any place I could hide. Why I felt so controlled by my mother, why I couldn't ever say no to her, why I couldn't leave my husband when I wanted to be free of him so much, why I resented him so, when he claimed he loved me. Why, oh why did I feel so guilty and afraid, and of what? What was wrong with me? My body couldn't even function normally as a woman. (I didn't have monthly periods.)

I was a mess, with no answers.

All my "whys" and what caused these feelings, I did not know, but I was about to meet a man who would help me find out all the whys and make these fears disappear by understanding. He wants to help me find what caused these feelings in me and I wanted deal with them without tranquilizers.

I sat anxiously in the waiting room for the receptionist to tell me Dr. "D" would see me. So much went through my head, what does he look like, is he old? Is he kind? Will he be understanding and care about me? I have so much to say and to talk about. Will he listen? Will he give me time? He was so important to me. He didn't know how long I had waited to see someone finally to talk to, someone to help me. He was going to save me. I love him already. I wanted to be special to him too, for him to really care and help me. I made him so important before I even saw him. I had waited so long.

"Mrs. Knight, The doctor will see you now." The palms of my hand were sweating. How will I start, where do I begin? How much will he want to know? I can't explain all my feelings. I just know I'm afraid, so afraid and I don't know of what. What can I say to him for him to know how important this is to me, my seeing him. All these questions went through my mind as I walked into his office. It was a small dark office with a lot of shelved books. Dr. "D" was sitting behind his desk. He was a big man with glasses. I guessed him to be around 60 years of age. He didn't smile and seemed very serious. He was looking at papers on his desk. He looked over his eyeglasses and said,

"Sit down Mrs. Knight. Now what seems to be the problem?"

How can one sentence contain so much I wondered? I started talking and talking hoping I was saying the right things. Hoping he wouldn't reject me. He would nod from time to time, and say,

"Go on."

I didn't get much response from him. I kept waiting for him to make a comment or answer me when I talked. He would just barely look at me saying to my questions,

"What do you think?" or "we'll see."

He seemed so distant, was I reaching him? Doesn't he understand how much I needed him? After I finished talking, he said he would take me as a patient but there was a long waiting list. I had to wait for his receptionist to call me. It might be a wait of two or three months. Two or three months? Didn't he know how desperate I was? In my state of mind, I didn't realize I was just one of many individuals who needed to see Dr." B". I wasn't the only one with problems. I had to wait my turn until they called me, but all I could think was, doesn't he know how long I've already waited to see him?

I should have been gratefully contented to see him. Because of this man and with the help of his assistant, Arielle, I was going to be able to understand myself, my feelings, and how to deal with them and how to make changes in my life for the better.

Every day I waited for the phone to ring.

How I welcomed the phone call that day from Dr. "D"'s secretary. I wanted to get away so badly, then more than ever. Ronald was losing his job. The plant he worked at was closing. I didn't want to be with him every day all the time. I dreaded when he came home. Why did I despise him so? I still had to wait a while after the phone call to go to the hospital- a few weeks. Ronald was out of work. He applied for food stamps. I was so embarrassed. I couldn't make myself go to the store. I was surprised when he came home with groceries, better than we would normally buy, expensive cuts of meats, and a lot of desserts and cereals.

Ronald was able to get a job on his own, painting the neighbors homes, so this brought in some money, in addition to his unemployment and my small paycheck. He continued to apply for food stamps and got them somehow. Our power and water was cut off several times, but he always managed to get them put back on. He was offered to transfer to another town with the same company, but did not want it. He didn't want to move so refused the job. There were no jobs available at that time in our town. He stayed out of work for a year. The job he was offered paid less than he was used to making, and he said he rather draw unemployment. I hated him being home so much. I felt guilty for it. God how I wanted to get away.

Finally the day came for me to leave for the hospital. I was told I would not stay right in the hospital, but rather at the Hilton Hotel, across the street from the hospital. Two floors of the hotel belong to the hospital, and there was a nurses station right there. I was told I would take my meals there too, which I was not expecting. It's sounded too good to be true. It sounded like a vacation. I felt good knowing the insurance from Ronald's place of employment would take care of the majority of my expenses, since it was still in affect. At least I didn't have to feel guilty about this I told myself.

I thought of the boys, my children, the day I left. I was glad their father was able to care for them since he was still not working and they were out of school. It was then July. I felt relieved I didn't have to worry about them. Somehow it all seemed it was meant to happen that way. I said a silent prayer that when I came back home I wouldn't feel so depressed. I would be better able to care for the house and the boys. I will be an awesome mother I happily thought. But somewhere deep inside I heard a voice telling me that my problems will be the same at home, nothing will have changed there. For an instant, I felt afraid. How was I going to handle it without my precious pills, my medicine?

Am I doing the right thing? My need to get away was greater than any second thoughts I might have.

"Now honey you call me if you need anything," Ron's voice broke through my private thoughts.

"I will," I answered. I was thinking of the children. I loved them so much yet I felt so inadequate as a mother. I wanted to take more of a part in their school activities, their ball games, and their lives. I felt like I owed them so much. I tried so hard to give them a happy life. They didn't know how bad things were between their father and I. I wanted them to think everything was all right. I didn't want them to feel anxious as a child. I worried about them so much. They seemed happy. They accepted my explanation as to why I was going to the hospital, to find out what was causing my headaches. It worried me that their father would let them think that something was wrong with me. What do they think? They only saw the good side of their father. They only knew that I cooking meals, kept house, and listened to their prayers and kissed them good night. What else was I to them? Did I play with them enough? Were they given enough attention? When I come home from the hospital, I'll try to make it up to them, I told myself. But right now I was glad to be getting away.

"We'll miss you." Ronald's statement brought me back to the present.

"I'll miss you all too, but I know I'll feel better when I come home. Do you think the boys will be all right? I worry about them," I said.

"Now don't you worry about a thing. We'll get along just fine."

He was being so nice I was feeling guilty again. I wanted to get away so badly. I wanted to hide from him. I couldn't return his feelings. I didn't love him, yet I felt like I should, that I should be grateful. I welcomed the sight of the hotel where I was to stay for the next six weeks.

Chapter 19

MY HOSPITAL ESCAPE

THE HOTEL WAS nice and I liked the fact all I had to do was walk across the street to the hospital. I was wondering why I wasn't staying in the hospital. Later it was explained to me that the hospital was full and they mostly took the patients that needed closer supervision. This made me feel pretty good. At least I'm not so far gone that I needed to be hospitalized and watched closely. Maybe there was hope for me yet. Also, it wasn't as expensive in that hotel as it was in the hospital, and it was much nicer.

After checking in at the desk I was told to go to the nurses' station on the floor I was assigned. The nurses were very nice. While I was sitting there, one of the patients came in to get medicine. She looks normal I thought. She was even dressed in street clothes. She did look a little unsure of herself. She smiled at me and asked if I was a patient too. We introduced ourselves and she asked me to meet with her and some other patients for dinner upstairs in the restaurant. After taking my temperature and blood pressure and marking it on the chart, the nurse showed me to my room. It was a regular hotel room, really nice. She told me I was not to leave the hotel without permission first, from my doctor. Whenever I came back into the hotel, I was to sign in at the nurses' station. I was asked to do this even if I was just going upstairs to eat or go outside to swim in the pool at the hotel. They needed to know where I was at all times. If I wanted to go to town or any other place other than the hospital I had to ask permission. This didn't sound bad at all. All I had to do was ask permission, sign in and out. Really I didn't want to go anywhere at that time. I just wanted to go to my room, close the door, stay there.

I said goodbye to my husband. He said he would come back the next day. I didn't want him to, but said all right and told him not to worry about me. I was going to be just fine. I couldn't be anything but nice to him when he was being so nice to me. I had to pretend, and all the time.

When I lay down in the bed in the quiet room, I thought since one of the reasons I was there, was to come off the medicine I had become addicted to, I shouldn't take anymore of it. I didn't take any that day. It was just the middle of the afternoon and already I was feeling my need for it. My head felt like it had things crawling all over it. My insides were screaming. I had the greatest desired to pull the drapes down off the windows. I felt angry but didn't know why.

I told myself that this is how it's going to be. I might as well get used to it. I have seen people going through withdrawal and it didn't look pleasant. I remembered how I felt in the past when I really got bad and how I responded. I knew from past experience my withdrawal was not going to be easy. At least here no one will see me. I won't have to pretend everything is all right I thought. I have the privacy of the room and if anyone did see how bad I was feeling it was all right. I'm a patient. I started crying. it was getting worse. Why did I feel like tearing up the room when I was glad to be there? I just didn't understand myself. Well I'm not going to worry. I'll be taken care of here. These people will understand. I started tossing in my bed. I needed a pill so badly. My head started hurting. Oh no, I can't take that too. I felt desperate as I went to the nurses' station finally after what seemed a long time.

"Please do you have something for headache? I feel so terrible." She looked concerned.

"I didn't take my medicine."

"Do you have any in your purse?"

"Yes."

"Why didn't you take any today?

Then I told her I thought that was why I came here, to get off the medicine.

"That's not how it's done," she stated.

"Take one right away. You are not to change anything until your doctor tells you to. You will see him at ten o'clock in the morning. Now go lay down, and I'll check on you in a little while to see how you're feeling."

I left feeling pretty stupid. Why did I feel I was to stop taking them as soon as I got to the hospital? How would he do it, I wondered. How was withdrawal done? I thought I was supposed to go cold turkey. I had seen too much television. I was to find out the next morning when I saw the doctor.

Within half an hour I felt much better. It seemed I could almost feel the medicine working right away. How much of it was psychological? I wondered. I had heard my husband tell me for so many years, it's all in your head, there was nothing wrong and it was my overactive imagination. He would only say this sarcastically criticizing. Ronald thought all my problems were because my father and mother and he had nothing to do with it. Many times I believed it was about my parents, just to get the pressure off me. Well, now I didn't have to worry about that. At least for a while I wouldn't have to be with Ronald.

After knocking gently the nurse let herself into my room.

"How are you feeling? Better?" she asked. The girl I met at the nurses' station with her.

"I believe you've met Bonnie. She said you two were going to have dinner together."

I got up from the bed. I felt better, only weak. I was looking forward to supper. Finally Bonnie told me we would be meeting some other patients of Dr. "D's for supper.

As we walked to the restaurant, Bonnie asked me questions about myself. She seemed very curious. She explained to me that this was her second time back in the hospital. She wasn't complaining, she seemed somewhat resigned to it. She went on to tell me how she lost two of her children, that she had remarried, and saw her children only once in a while. Bonnie was a small woman in her early 30s. She had short light brown hair with a small face and large sad eyes. Although she talked quietly, she talked a lot. It seemed to me she liked being there. We got on the elevator and pushed the button to the top floor, which was the restaurant. I was curious to meet the others.

The restaurant was tastefully done and quite nice. This is like a regular resort I thought. It all seemed too good to be true. I was away from home on my own. Well almost. I felt so happy to be away from all the ugliness, then immediately felt guilty for feeling that way. But if I had a choice, I'd rather feel guilty, than go back. I was not aware of what lay ahead of me in the weeks and months to come or what serious work I had to do for myself.

As we approached the table, all heads turned in our direction. They were anxious to see the new patient. They already knew how much I would become part of their lives in the next few weeks. Bonnie introduced me.

"This is Judy, Robin, Tad, and this is Tads wife, she is visiting for the day." Judy smiled and said, "Hello." She was a big woman around 35 with pretty blue eyes and short hair. I liked her right away. She was outgoing and had a nice voice. Rob was short, plain looking and wore dark framed glasses. I guessed him to be about 42 years old. He had short dark hair and was a bit stocky. He barely smiled but nodded hello. He seemed very timid and had almost a desperate look in his eyes. Later I was to find out that Dr. Albert had been his doctor too. Ted looked interesting. He smiled and said hello and introduced us to his wife by name. He was a dark nice-looking man around 30. They were already eating. We sat down and ordered. Everyone seemed to get along so well.

I did notice when Bonnie talked, she mostly talked about her problems. I noticed the reaction of the others. They were polite but always changed the subject. I can see that it made them uncomfortable. they just didn't want to talk about their problems at the table, or at least the same ones all the time. I later found out they had heard enough of it during group and they had enough of it all day long. To come back to the hotel after being in therapy at the hospital, and talking about their problems wasn't a welcome thing to do.

The group explained to me at the dinner table, that the hotel had many of the hospital's patients there, as well as guests. Individuals came for psychiatric help but also for physical health. I was told that a lot of the patients who came to the hospital with physical complaints found out their problems stemmed from emotional problems they were not aware of or were afraid to admit. There were also many there who came once a year for a world-famous diet. They returned each year, having gained a lot of their weight back, but considered their stay there a retreat. Of course these individuals did not have to visit the hospital daily or undergo therapy. To them it was a vacation away from home and responsibilities. In a way that's how I felt too. Not that I was on vacation, vacations are supposed to be fun. I felt afraid, unsure and very vulnerable. But I did feel relieved that for a while, I was not responsible for anything or anyone one but myself. I just didn't feel capable. I was tired.

Judy and Bonnie asked me if I would like to walk over to the hospital and see the grounds and also to see where I would meet for private therapy and for group therapy. They wanted to show me the rest of the facilities that would be my home for the next few weeks. They told me that Dr. "D" likes us to spend as much time as possible over at the hospital with the other patients, when we are not in therapy.

As we were leaving the hotel and approaching the lobby, Bonnie asked me if I knew they had a pool at the hotel. She seemed excited as she led me towards the outside pool. It was glassed over with a dome; people could swim during the winter. There was a sauna also. Alongside the pool was a beautiful brick terrace with red geraniums planted along the wall. It was quite nice. I love to swim and lay in the sun and thought I would spend a lot of time there. As it turned out, I didn't. By the time I finished at the hospital everyday, I was tired and just wanted to go to the privacy of my darkroom with the door closed and locked. The pool only looked inviting that first day.

We walked across the street to the hospital. It was a hot July day, the kind of day when your clothes stick to your body. I hated the way my clothes always seemed wet, especially under my arms. I knew a lot of this was nervousness and always tried to keep my arms down so I could hide it. The slight breeze helped some as we walked along the beautifully curved sidewalk, which was built around the massive old oak trees. I love to watch the wind gently blow their leaves. I felt peaceful walking over, looking at the old hospital showing the grounds with the university. There was something majestic about it all. The hospital and the university buildings were made of rock, with large old rock houses with green ivy climbing all over the walls. I loved the architecture and the smell of the old boxwood bushes they had surrounding the buildings.

Behind these walls, I will find my answers, I thought. I already felt somewhat protected. They are going to help me. They will understand what I'm feeling inside, without me trying to explain. When I listen to Judy talk she is bodiless now, very quiet compared to before. Judy seemed okay. I wondered what her problem could be. Did we hide our problems so well? Judy was her second time back in the hospital for treatment. She had left too early last time against the doctor's wishes.

"Don't be too anxious to go home." Her voice broke through my thoughts.

"Wait until Dr. "D" says you are ready. He's a good doctor. You're lucky to have him. I saw him a lot at first," she continued.

"Now I mostly see one of his associates who works with him. I like her very much. Who will you see most of the time?" She added.

I told her I didn't know, that I just knew I was to see him in the morning.

"Well I'm glad to be back here and I'm in no hurry to leave," Judy said firmly.

It can't be that bad I thought if she wants to stay now. I felt better. Bonnie said, "I don't want to go home either."

My thoughts were confirmed. I was right. She does like it here. Why? I thought, but then I guess I knew part of the answer. Here, you don't have to deal with the outside problems and responsibilities. Bonnie seemed really sad and even rejected. I tried to keep her in the conversation. I noticed Bonnie didn't really seem to hear anything that was said to her. When she did talk, it was always the same subject. How can anyone help her, if she doesn't listen? I wondered.

We rode the elevator to the third floor. Ashley got off the elevator. Judy pointed to the right,

"That's the Myers Ward. That's one place you don't want to go. That's where the more serious cases are. They don't have many privileges there."

I looked down the hall of Myers Ward and did not see anyone except a few nurses in the hall, and a doctor at the nurses' desk looking over a chart. We walked down the hall in the other direction and around the corner into a small room where I was to spend many hours. The room had a small glassed in office with several doctors, nurses and day workers inside talking. It looked like they were having a meeting. In the room were several couches, card tables, a piano, radio and a record player with earphones on a young man's head. There was also a television and people were watching some soap opera. Oh, that would help them a lot, I thought a bit sarcastically. As if they didn't have enough problems. I hated the way I was rationalizing. It seemed I never had a concrete answer to anything. There always seemed to be a "but" or a "maybe." It seems I always had to justify everything in order for it to be acceptable. I hated this part of myself. It wore me out.

I noticed some of the patients were playing cards. Now that is a positive. They're not so far gone that they can't think. I felt encouraged. I didn't know what I was expecting, but I liked seeing them playing cards. Later I found out that a person can be extremely intelligent and do well in their business life or for that matter, be able to take care of a lot of things, but there could be a personal area in their life that they just couldn't handle. That was the reason for this, and that is why we are here at the hospital to find out why, to understand it and learn how to handle it. My eyes searched the small room, taking in everyone and what they were doing. Some were reading books or magazines, and some were just sitting and talking. Most of the people looked very serious. Some of the patients were dressed, talking and smiling. Some were in their robes, simply sitting and staring at the floor, looking like they were waiting for someone to take them by the hand and lead them someplace. They were the patients that required closer supervision, the ones that had to stay in the hospital instead of the hotel. I felt fortunate.

The patients looked up as we entered the small room. Some were glad to see us. I wondered if they felt encouraged knowing we were patients too? Some had no expression at all. Do they resent us coming into their room? I wondered. The ones playing cards asked us if we would like to join them. Judy said that we would tomorrow; we were just there to see the place. She introduced me and they were friendly and said hello. No one said welcome. That would not be appropriate, but I knew they accepted me. A couple of people came out of the nurses' station. Judy introduced me to them. They were training for their degree in psychology, and worked with the patients, under the direction of the doctors and the nurses. They were both young girls. I liked them right away, although I felt a bit reserved. How much would they come into my life? I was not sure if I wanted them to, not knowing at the time, that how much they did was up to me.

After being introduced to them, they went into the room and joined the patients in conversation. I heard one of them ask,

"How many are going on the hike with me tomorrow morning?" A few hands raised. The patients seemed glad to have their company. Judy said this was the room we were to come to every morning at 10:00 AM sharp and wait until our doctor called us to see him. Also when we weren't in private therapy or group therapy, they liked for us to spend as much time as possible in the room with the other patients, so they would be able to observe us to see how were responding to therapy and to the individuals around us. She explained that they liked us to participate as much as we could in activities with other patients. I didn't like that very much. I really didn't want to. I wanted to be in my room, alone. The idea of being watched and observed didn't appeal to me. I felt it was intruding on my privacy. Damn it, Veronica that's part of your problem, isn't it? Haven't you been private too long? I told myself angrily. I was there to be helped, wasn't I? I had to play by their rules. I had to do whatever they said, although they never said you have to play cards, or you have to go on a hike. Really all they did was encourage it, and of course to participate was healthy. This was by no means a game. But at that time, I had mixed emotions, and could not see its value. I just felt mostly angry and wished I could let it out on someone or even just figure out, how to let it out.

We walked down the hall to a large room that had about 10 to 12 large chairs and a couch in it arranged in a circle, at one end of the room. At the other end were a kitchen and a pool table. A couple were playing pool. They looked up as we walked in and said hi. The black one was very friendly and open. I liked him right away. Judy introduced us. John was the black and a psychologist. He was medium height and had a small frame with small facial features and very short hair. He had the whitest teeth and a big smile. The other young man was white and very withdrawn. He wanted to quit playing, but John said

"No we're not finished yet. I want to see if you can beat me." John waved goodbye to us and said

"See you tomorrow" and continued playing."

Judy said this was the room we would meet in for group therapy every day. I looked around the room, especially at the chairs and wondered what takes place in this room? Are we attacked and ripped apart? I see this in the movies on TV of group therapy sessions. I asked myself these questions and was afraid to ask Judy. I'll find out starting tomorrow I thought. My chest hurt and my mouth was dry thinking of tomorrow.

I lay in my bed that night hearing the hum of the air conditioner and feeling the coolness of the air blowing on my body. I was glad to be alone. I didn't feel smothered lying in bed as I did at home next to my husband. No, I thought, I'm not going to think of home. I will just think of tomorrow. I was full of anticipation and nervous about seeing Dr. "D". I want my first session with him to go well. I hope that he would remember me and care about me. I started to cry softly. I was afraid, yet I still felt somewhat protected. He will take care of me I thought. I hoped he would be gentle I prayed, as I felt the welcomed sleep overcoming me where everything seemed faraway.

There, was a knock at the door. I was confused. Where was I? Then I realized I was not home but at the hotel. I was still sitting in my bed trying to wake up when the door opened.

"Mrs. Knight, its time to get up," said the nurse.

"Thank you," I said as she softly closed the door. The room was still dark but I could see the bright light edging the drapes that it was daylight. It seemed as if I had just gone to bed. I felt relieved to find I was not at home, and the day was planned for me. I just had to go along with it and be there. What was "there?" I wondered. I was soon to find out.

I showered, dressed and reported to the nurses' station. Some other patients when they are getting their morning medication.

"We don't have anything new yet Mrs. Knight. Your doctor will call it over later. Report back here after the group therapy. We will give you your meds.

I thought I was coming off the medicine. Why would they prescribe me more I asked her?

"Your doctor will explain it to you when you see him." And I wondered why they had to talk in such a patient tone. I felt any questions I asked bothered her.

I looked forward to breakfast as I rode the elevator upstairs. I was hungry. I liked the idea that I could order anything I wanted and I didn't have to pay for it. The insurance was taking care of it. What a really good feeling. I didn't have to worry about money. I didn't need any. And the phone wouldn't be ringing every so often with someone at the other end saying Mrs. Knight when will you be taking care of this bill? I didn't have to handle money problems not for a while anyway. I needed to get stronger. The elevator stopped, and the door opened. I could smell the bacon cooking from the kitchen. I walked in and looked around the room until I found a familiar face. I saw Judy and Rob eating at a table. Judy motioned for me to join them. Rob look up and nodded hello. Do any of them talk I wondered.

"Bonnie and Ted already left, they're over at the hospital" Julie said. After enjoying our blueberry pancakes, bacon and eggs we went over to the hospital. On the walk over I tried to get some response from Rob without much success.

Jan and Bonnie were in the room when we walked in. Ted smiled big and said,

"Let's play some cards."

Judy and I said okay and sat down. Bonnie said she didn't want to and Rob shook his head and said no. A man who heard us said he would like to play with us. I notice he kept looking at me, and made me feel uncomfortable, but also felt flattered. I noticed a young blond girl there trying to get his attention. I have the impression that they had become close friends. I noticed him turn silently looking at me. I knew she was seeing me. She kept trying to get Ted to go for a walk out on the terrace that was just down the hallway. He didn't want to go and said he wanted to play cards. She got up and left the room angrily.

"Are we are going to be in a group?" I asked. Bonnie said, "All but Ted." I looked at Ted and he said,

"For some reason I just never attend." Judy went on to say,

"Dr. "D" determines who goes to group and who doesn't."

For some reason I felt glad Ted wasn't going to be there. I felt uncomfortable around him and didn't know what at that time exactly why.

Judy said,

"Ted is leaving us Friday."

"That's right I go home Friday," He said very sadly.

I wanted to know why. I thought he had a very pretty wife. He had two children he told us. What could be his problem? I guess I would find out. I could definitely tell he didn't respond to any of his wife's comments when I met her in the night before. He acted like he wished she wasn't there. He was very quiet then, although friendly. Now he was talking more and asking me questions about myself. I knew he was attracted to me. I really didn't know him. He was nice looking, but that never really attracted me to a man before. The only thing I could think of was that he was lonely and unhappy and I was too. We had very common experience that seemed enough at the time. I felt sorry for him. I was thinking how I would feel if I had to go home now. I felt a little excitement knowing he was attracted to me. I didn't feel so intimidated by him as I always did by the men in the outside world. Now it was the outside world and here. I am safer here, I thought.

A nurse stuck her head inside the door and said,

"Ted, the doctor will see you now." She was tall and pretty and had such a nice friendly voice.

"I was here first." Bonnie said. The nurse spoke kindly but firmly and said smiling, "you're next." Bonnie looked disappointed.

"That's Arielle, Dr. "D's associate, you'll like her a lot." Judy said.

"I had her for a while with Dr. "D", but now I see another assistant with Dr." D". She's nice too."

I didn't think at the time that I would like to see an assistant as well as the doctor. Somehow I would feel cheated. How uninformed I was. You really have the direct help from both. As it turned out, I came to love this assistant. Arielle became one of the most important people in my life, who helped me tremendously through our years under Dr." D's direction.

The wait was long. I hated to wait for something so important. Ted came back and left without saying much of anything. I was surprised at the change in him as he was quiet now with a frown on his face. Then Bonnie left eager to see him. She really wanted to go. She had come over early thinking she might be first. Will I feel like her in time, anxious to see the doctor? But then all I could think of what was I going to say. It will be easier if he just asks me questions I thought.

"Mrs. Knight." the voice broke through my thoughts. Well this is it. It's my turn. I was so nervous as I followed a woman named Arielle down the hall. She was looking back at me, smiling as we walked.

"And how are you today? This is your first day here. How do you feel? She asked.

"Nervous," was all I could say. God I was scared. We walked into a small room. There he was sitting behind a large desk.

"Good morning Mrs. Knight. How are you feeling today?" "Scared."

He chuckled a little and said,

"Scared. What's there to be scared of?" he smiled slightly. "I don't bite."

I smiled weakly, feeling foolish. What was I scared of? All I could think of was of being hurt. My chest hurt so. My hands were wet with perspiration.

"I don't know what to say," I managed to get out of my dry mouth. "Well just say anything that comes to your mind."

I looked at the woman named Arielle. She had a pad and pencil in her lap. I felt uncomfortable.

"This is Arielle my assistant. She will be working with you also." Arielle smiled. I felt better. Why was it so hard to talk? Dr. "D" said,

"Do you realize what you have been doing to yourself? Do you realize what your husband could do if he wanted to?"

"But he doesn't know how much medicine I've been taking. He doesn't know what all I do. He only knows what I tell him and I tell him what he wants to hear," I said quickly. Dr." D" appeared angry.

"Do you think you're facing reality young lady?"

I tried to explain to him how I had been feeling. How I had to act like I did in front of my husband.

"You are destroying yourself. All I can say is you have been very fortunate. You have had somebody upstairs looking after you. You have not been behaving as a responsible adult."

I tried to defend myself without much success. I couldn't make him understand. He was talking about reality. What was reality? It really shook me up and made me think when I left him about what he said. His voice softened after a while.

"I know you have been unhappy Mrs. Knight. It's up to you what you do with the rest of your life. I'll try to help you all I can. It's going to take awhile. We have to have your cooperation in every way. I don't want to hear excuses or any rationalizations for your behavior. You've got to start thinking differently."

After leaving the office, it was time for lunch. I wanted to be alone to think over my visit with Dr. "D".

Did it go okay? Was he disappointed in me? Oh dammit why did it matter so much what he thought. Then I knew I was afraid he'd stop seeing me if he didn't like me. I was glad I didn't see the others when I came out. They probably went back to the hotel or maybe they were in the day room. I didn't check. I walked down to the cafeteria to eat. I wasn't very hungry. I kept thinking about my visit with the doctor and then I had group therapy next. Well, I'll just be quiet in there. I didn't have to join in, I thought. It would be interesting to just hear the others talk. I'll just listen to them I told myself. I want to get off "Me" for the day.

After eating I walked back to the day room to go with the others to group. They were not there. I was told they had already gone into the room. I didn't realize they went that early. I walked down the hall to where we had been the day before. I was surprised to see most of the chairs filled already. I had wanted to sit next to Judy and Rob. I found an empty chair and sat down.

"You'll have to come early if you want to sit in a favorite chair," Judy said. The chairs were different sizes and shapes. Most of them were large and comfortable. Some were not. I can see why one would want to come early. I will too, in the future. Somehow it seemed if you have a good chair, in a good spot, you would be more comfortable. I wanted one in the corner of the room, but that was taken. I had to sit on the side with my back to the open window and road. I never did like that kind of seating. I liked the wall behind me. Anyway, I had no choice. I hate the way everyone looked at me with curious eyes. It was better after Judy introduced me to some of them. Everyone was quiet and sullen. In walked Dr. Lee a Chinese doctor. He was small with dark features and wore glasses.

"Good afternoon everyone." He said with a slight smile.

He wore a white jacket over his suit. Two others came in with him. His assistants, I thought. One was a young dark-haired girl. I recognized her from the day room and I had met her at the day before. The other one, as soon as he walked in the door, I felt intimidated. He too wore a white jacket over a dress shirt and pants. He was extremely nice looking with grey- black hair just over his ears and a neatly groomed beard. I disliked him immediately. He's too good looking I thought. I just know he's conceited the way he looks so sure of himself. I found right then I didn't like him. I'll not let him get to me. He looks so superior. I felt like he was my enemy right away. I don't know why I felt that way at the time, for later my feelings were to change towards him dramatically.

"I see we have someone new in the group." Dr. Lee said looking at me.

"Would you like to tell the group your name and a little about yourself?"

Everyone was looking at me. I didn't want to talk, but I had to at least respond to his question.

"My Name is Veronica Knight," I choked out.

It was so hard to talk. I felt like my voice was far away as if someone else were talking. Everyone was very interested. I told myself of course they are dummy. You think they want to share themselves with a stranger? It's only fair you tell them something of yourself. All I could get out was my name and that I came there to get off medications that I have become addicted to that another doctor put me on. Somehow it seemed if I added, a doctor put me on or prescribed for me, it didn't seem so bad. Not like I was all to blame. How foolish of me to think that by saying that it made it appear that I was not responsible. But it seemed easier to blame the doctor I trusted. They were waiting for me to go on to tell the more.

"Well I've had headaches since I was a child but no doctor has been successful in finding out a reason. I spent two weeks in a hospital in 1972 taking all kinds of tests and they all came out okay. I didn't have a tumor or anything like that. I hope to find out the why of my headaches while I'm here."

I looked at Dr. Lee, like is that enough? Do I have to say anymore? He got my message and said,

"Well, we hope you do too Mrs. Knight." He turned his attention to the group,

"How about each of you telling your name, and the reason why you're here briefly, so Mrs. Knight will feel more comfortable."

I looked at the man who walked in with Dr. Lee. He was sitting quietly puffing on his pipe. He introduced himself as Neal. Dr. Lee said, "Neal is my assistant and will be working with you all also."

Good I thought it's his first day too. That makes us equal for today anyway. I felt so strongly towards him and I just met him.

One by one the people in the group gave their names and why they were there. Bonnie said she was hoping to get well so she could get her children back.

"Why did you lose them Bonnie?" Dr. Lee asked.

"Because my ex-husband said I'm sick and it's his fault. I just did what he told me with those men and I was drunk. He made me drink until I was drunk."

"What men, Bonnie?"

"I don't want to talk about it." Bonnie said with tears in her eyes. "Okay Bonnie you let us know when you do want to talk about it." It was now Rob's turn. He told his name. I felt sorry for him. He looked like he hated to be there, and wanted to run.

"Don't you want to tell us a little about yourself, Rob?" Rob shook his head no.

"Tomorrow," he did say.

Dr. Lee was not going to let go so easy.

"You're a dentist aren't you, Rob?"

A dentist? Rob's a dentist, I thought.

"Are you in practice now Rob?" Dr. Lee asked

"Yes." Rob nodded. But I closed up to come here." I stared at him. He's a practicing dentist. How could he be? Was he different away from this place?

"Do you live alone Rob?"

"No, I live with my mother," he answered.

"What about your father. Where is he?"

"He, He's dead." Rob was shaking. He answered very quickly. It was obvious he wanted them to get off him.

"How do you feel about your father?" Neal asked him.

Oh, why don't you leave him alone can't you see he doesn't want to talk, I wanted to say to him. Anyone could tell it was very painful for him to talk.

"Not today. I don't want to talk."

"Okay Rob," Dr. Lee said. "Another day."

Another woman, a woman in her 60's said she came because she could not talk at times, that her voice just went away. Even now as she talked her voice sounded very weak and would break, fading. Dr. Lee asked her why she was in the group. She said they couldn't find anything wrong with her, that all stemmed from her emotional problems.

"And what are they?" asked Neal.

"I don't know for sure." She's looked so confused. Dr. Lee said to her,

"You lost most of your family that you cared for. Didn't you?" Your mother, your father, and now you're alone."

"I have sisters and brothers," she said weakly.

"Do you ever see them?"

"No they don't care about me. I have no one." "Why didn't you marry?' Dr. Lee asked.

"I couldn't," she said. There was Mother and Father." Her voice was getting fainter.

I can't talk." She barely managed to get out.

"That's your problem, isn't it Mrs. Vincent? You can't talk about your life without your voice going away. Doesn't that tell you a lot, Mrs. Vincent? You never lived your life for yourself. Now everyone is gone," he said more kindly but firmly so she would understand the reality of it.

Was this necessary? It seemed so cruel?

She started to cry, but muffled her sobs in a handkerchief she held in her hand.

"And what about you Alice? What happened to you?" Dr. Lee asked.

"I don't like myself," she said. Alice was curled up on the couch with a book in her lap.

"I'm not worthy to be a mother or anything." "Why do you feel this way?" Neal asked.

My husband is a minister of our church and a good one and I do love him and I don't know why. We had a party one night. I drink too much and went to bed with a member of the Parish. I know it was wrong. I know that was sinful and I have to pay for it."

"Does your husband know?" asked Neal.

"What do you think?" she responded. I think he will forgive me, and that he'll never forget.

"Ask the group what they think." Neal said.

She looked at the group looking very ashamed.

"We talked about this before." Dr. Lee's said. Perhaps the group can help you. Does anyone have a suggestion?"

I wanted to speak again. Dr. Lee went to the beginning of the group and asked each one, yes or no should she tell her husband? Most of them said no. I said no too. I felt she punished herself enough, that she was just human, and it was a human thing she did, if she didn't love her husband, and was unhappy. To tell him would just make it worse. I really felt this way. She said she was sorry that it happened, and she didn't love the other man.

Chances are, by the way she was feeling it wasn't going to happen again. Anyway that's how I felt and wanted her to know. For a moment she seemed relieved, but then she said she didn't know what to do. She felt she had to be punished.

"Don't you think you've punished yourself enough already Alice?" She just shook her head that she didn't know.

"I just don't want to go back there. I have no life to myself," she said now more angrily.

"He spends all his time with the members of the church. All I have is the children. Everybody wants something from me. I'm tired of it all, and feel guilty for feeling that way."

"Well, we will talk more about it later Alice." Dr. Lee stated.

"Now Bess, you have been here a long time haven't you?" Bess was a small petite, blond girl. She too was curled up on the couch. She had a large blanket wrapped around her. She looked to be a young teenager.

"A year." Bess answered. "I've been here a year."

"Why so long, Bess?" asked Dr. Lee. He already knew the answer. He just wanted to hear what Bess had to say.

"I can't seem to gain weight."

"How old are you, Bess?" asked Neal.

"Twenty-two." She answered.

Twenty-two? She looked like a twelve year old, except she was tall. Her hair was long and straight in a ponytail. She wore no make up. Her face was small with light features. She could be pretty, I thought if she put on some makeup and gained some weight.

Dr. Lee asked, "What is the problem Bess? Why can't you put on weight?"

"Well, I have anorexia. That's when you can't eat and if you do, you throw up and you don't put any weight on."

She almost seemed glad she had it, I thought. "You're afraid to put weight on aren't you?" She nodded yes.

"You don't want to grow up do you, Bess?" "NO!" she cried. "I don't." She was angry.

"Don't you make yourself throw up?" Bess wouldn't answer.

"Well, let's see now. If you don't eat, you won't put on weight. If you do eat you will get better and you can leave the hospital. You don't want to leave do you?"

Bess was staring at him angrily. He looked innocent and explained. "Bess has an illness called anorexia nervosa. She is suffering from malnutrition. Because Bess does not eat normally, her body does not mature as should a woman of her age."

We heard she did not even have a monthly period, as a woman her age would normally have. I don't have a monthly period. Does that mean I'm not normal, I thought. Once I went eight months without a period. I usually had one about three or maybe four times a year. That's all. No doctor could find out why. (I did later.)

"Bess has a fear of growing up, Dr. Lee explained to us. She wants to stay a child."

"Why Bess? Why don't you want to grow up?"

He even talks to her as if she were a child, I thought. Bess looks scared.

"I just don't. That's all I'm going to say." She said in a baby voice. I couldn't believe she was twenty-two years old.

"Okay let us know when you decide to talk about it," Dr. Lee said as he turned his attention to someone else.

"Now its your turn, Judy. You've come a long way haven't you?" Judy looked more serious than ever. Her blue eyes look straight at him. She's used to him I thought. She's not afraid of him.

"How are you feeling about going home this weekend?" He asked her.

"I don't know." she responded. My husband always gets mad if I get upset."

"What upsets you?" he asked.

"I can't stand arguing and it drives me crazy if I hear it." At that statement we all laughed. Even Judy found it funny.

"It's good to see you laugh." He told her. "What do you do when the arguing starts?"

"Go to my room and I don't want to come out. I want to come back here."

"You don't have to face that here do you?" he asked her.

How do you feel now being out of Myers?" (Judy was in the Myers Ward?) I would never have believed it.

"Why did you try to kill yourself?"

"I was just tired of it." Judy answered.

"Was it worth what you had to go through, Judy?"

"No, it was awful. It was terrible when they pumped my stomach; but the worst part was being in Myers. I have no privacy and was watched all the time." I wasn't going to do anything else, but they wouldn't believe me. It was worse than jail. They all look at you like you're nuts and I'm not nuts.

Dr. Lee smiled.

"No I don't believe you are, but at the time you were not yourself, and you weren't thinking rationally as you are now. They were only concerned for your welfare."

"Well," Dr. Lee's said looking at his watch,

"This is all we have time for today. So we will meet again tomorrow at the same time," he said getting up from his chair. I sat there for a moment trying to take it all in. Today was just the beginning. We only scratched the surface of some people's problems, but they went much deeper than that.

I was to spend over a year in this room every day for the first six weeks, then twice a week thereafter. In this room, I learned a great deal about myself that I was not aware of. I experienced some of the most painful emotions, even though the instances that caused them had happened years before. I was to relive those experiences and feel those emotions for the first time, the emotions that I held inside of myself for so long, some since I was a small child. It's amazing how group therapy works, how one can relate to what another person is talking about or experiencing, how it touches your inner soul, your subconscious.

In this room I learned how to really experience and feel the emotions of anger, jealousy, rejection and grief; and most important how to express them. Something I had a problem doing. In this room I learned some very important steps to better my life. No one person told me this, for when someone tells you, most of the time you'll reject it. You yourself have to realize it, to feel it, and to have insight. The doctors and the assistants professionally guide you along to help you.

Bonnie, Rob, Judy and I walked back together to the hotel, not one of us speaking about what went on in the group. It was a silent understanding that we wouldn't. Really we didn't want to. What went on in that room just stayed there. The whole time we were in the group sessions we never discussed outside that room what went on. We talked about other things beside our personal lives walking back to our hotel. After we arrived we all went to our room saying we would meet later for dinner.

I remembered that I was to check in with a nurse when I returned. I got up off the bed and walked to the nurses' station. Dr. "D" had told me that morning he was going to gradually take me off my medication, so I would not have too many discomforts with withdrawal. He said he was giving me some temporary medication to supplement for the other I would not be taking, and then gradually it would decrease. In time, I would be completely off the tranquilizers. He would leave me, perhaps on a mild antidepressant. We would have to wait to see how I responded. I was so glad to hear that. As I walked in, the nurse said,

"Mrs. Knight, you are to take some tests tomorrow that Dr. "D" ordered, so you will not see him in the morning, but report to group therapy at your normal time. You are to be at the hospital at 10 AM at this location." She handed me a slip of paper.

I was surprised. Dr. "D" didn't say anything about tests. I was disappointed I was not going to see him in the morning, but then I was curious as to what the tests were all about. I always enjoyed taking tests, although I was sure these tests would be much different than what I was used to. Do they really show you Rorschach ink smears, I wondered. I had seen this on television and the movies. That sounded very interesting.

I went back to my room and lay down to think about the day's happenings. There, was a knock on my door, only this time it didn't open as before when the nurse had let herself in. I was not anxious for any company. It was Ted. I was so surprised to see him, yet I felt a little bit of pleasure too.

He said, "I need to talk to someone. I feel I can talk to you. Will you please listen? Can I come in for just a minute?"

He looked so sad and upset about something. For some reason I felt sorry for him. I knew how it felt to be unhappy. I was always putting myself in the other person's place and treated them like I would want to be treated. I was taught this since childhood.

"Of course," I said. "Are you allowed to come in?"

"Yes, he said, smiling a little. I'm so upset Veronica. I have to talk to someone. You look, well, I felt looking at you in the restaurant, like I can talk to you."

"Can't you talk to someone else, or your doctor?" I was flattered he felt he could talk to me.

"No, and the doctor doesn't seem to understand. I'm not ready to go home, and he says I am. I don't want to go. He told me at first that I was going to leave Friday. Now he says I have to leave tomorrow. I just met you. I feel drawn to you."

He talked a while about his wife and his family. He lived in the country in a large house on farm. He wanted out and didn't know how to go about it. He had two small children and felt he wasn't much good to them as a father. He had been out of work for weeks with depression before he came to the hospital. He had been in therapy for several weeks. They're didn't seem to be anything wrong with him that I could tell. I felt he was just unhappy with his life situation and responsibilities and didn't know what to do about them.

I could relate to that. I kept the door open, still not sure whether or not it was all right for him to be in my room. I enjoyed him being there, but said he had better leave. I was afraid that we might get in trouble. He asked if he could kiss me goodbye. I had really wanted him to kiss me. I was nervous, but excited. He kissed me softly on the lips and held me for just a moment.

He really is lonely, I thought. I could be a dear friend to listen to him, but he is leaving tomorrow. He walked over to my desk and took a piece of paper and wrote a number on it.

"It's long distance, but please call me collect. I want to talk to you. I just met you and now I have to say goodbye. I wouldn't have approached you so soon but I had no choice. Please call." he asked.

I didn't want to hurt him. I felt needed.

"I'll call you." I told him.

"Promise?"

"Yes I promise," I said smiling.

He left and I lay back down on the bed. So much had happened today. How could so much have happened in one day? It was so different from being at home. I liked it. I looked at the clock and saw it was time to start getting ready for dinner. I was hungry now since I hadn't eaten lunch. I looked forward to eating with everyone, and sitting across the table from Ted, sharing a secret from the others.

Ted looked at me from across the table. He was so good looking I thought. It's a shame he was so unhappy. I just met him and he's leaving. I told myself, it's just as well. I didn't need this complication just coming into the hospital. I was here to concentrate on myself. This would only create another problem. I'm glad he's going, but right now, I'm glad he cared about me. He came by my room just long enough to say, "Please call," before he left.

I went to bed that night thinking about the day. Going over all the steps from the time I got up, it was an interesting day. I look forward to tomorrow. They wanted me to take a test. I liked that. They wanted to find out more about me. I felt happy. Someone really cares enough to listen. Dr. "D" said that I had been strong, and it was a wonder I was still functioning in the way that appeared normal. He added it was a miracle that I was functioning at all, and I was a very lucky lady.

I knew I had a lot to do with it. I was so determined not to let things get to me really badly. I was afraid of a breakdown. I just couldn't be weak. I knew it was a weakness taking the pills, but I needed them to survive. The pain, both physical and emotional was so great sometimes, and the fear I felt inside was so overwhelming. I needed something. I honestly couldn't stand it. It hurt so. It's a very frightening experience to be afraid but not to know of what. Just life.

There at the hospital, I felt the doctors and the staff understood me, and the patients knew too, for they have experienced similar feelings in one way or another. I liked being there. I felt comfortable, yet still afraid of what might be ahead.

"God, please let it be alright", I prayed just before falling asleep.

In the morning, I walked down the hall in the hospital looking for the room I was told to report to, in order to take the tests. I looked into a small room that had a number on the door that was on the slip of paper in my hand. My memory for recent details was not that good unless I made an extra effort to remember. I was reminded by the small incident that was probably the reason I didn't pass a State Real Estate Exam. I had been trying to get my license and had attended school, but had a hard time remembering figures. I should have known better. I'll try again when I leave the hospital, I told myself.

"Can I help you?" a young man who was sitting at a small table asked.

"I hope so. I am to take a test this morning. My name is Veronica Knight."

"Yes, Mrs. Knight, he said smiling, "Come in and sit down."

"My name is Jerry Wright." I will be giving you your test. First I would like to talk about you."

I wasn't expecting this, but I felt comfortable with him. I told him about the usual things, age, date of birth, place of birth, oldest of three children, mother and father divorced.

"What I really want to know is how you feel about things. Your life, your husband, children, your relatives, how you feel about being here and in general what you have been doing in your life."

I must have talked an hour. He seemed very interested and amused at times. He was easy to talk to and understanding. I was very honest with him and held nothing back. I told negative things as well as positive. Mostly negative I think.

He said I was an unusual woman because I like to do things that made people shake their heads in wonder. I don't know why. I guess I like to shock people and do what was least expected of me. I got pleasure from it. People said I looked so reserved and sophisticated. I could be, but basically I wasn't. I was very active and I had a lot of energy, until I started taking so many pills. I told him I loved life and wanted to experience as much as I could before I died. I told him about the poem I wrote when I was 28 years old. I sketched a picture of a tree for the first time when I was 18 for a doctor while staying at a hospital. It was important it was to me. I explained to him,

"Over the years I would sketch it frequently. Many times when I was just talking on the phone. I knew the sketch must mean something to me to keep drawing it over and over. Much later in life the words came to me one day at work, while sitting at my desk sketching it. I just started writing the words after talking to someone on the phone," I added.

"First I want to show you what the picture looks like." I took out a sheet of paper on the table and a pencil and started sketching it as I spoke.

"There, was one tree in the picture on the edge of very steep cliff. Some of the roots were sticking out of the wall of the cliff. In the background there is nothing but mountains, very steep mountains. Some reach up into the clouds. At the bottom of the mountains, there is a narrow stream. There is a moon in the sky with a cloud passing by it. The moon shares the sky with two birds in the distance. That's all there is in the drawing."

As I recited the poem to him, I found myself getting excited as I always did when I heard the words.

He was looking at what I had sketched he looked at me when I finished.

"That's beautiful," he said. I knew by the expression on his face, he meant it.

"Do you understand?" I asked. "Do you know what the picture means?" I was anxious for his reply. It was important to me.

"I think I know but I want you to explain it to me. The picture and the poem." he replied.

"First I want to explain what the poem means." I said.

"I am that tree. That's how I feel, at the edge of a cliff. It's scary. I am alone there and I am rooted to the ground, just as I am rooted in my marriage. I cannot move. When I talk about the limbs, they represent experiences. Although I feel stuck or rooted in my marriage, I have experiences of life and I want to have as many as possible. I have disappointments, in these friendships and experiences, but as I do, I am hurt, but grow stronger each time. I expect less from individuals. When I am disappointed I come back faster each time. When I was younger and less experienced, I hurt terribly each time I was disappointed, but as I grew older and wiser, I still trusted but not as much or as freely. When I was hurt, because of my past experience, it did not take me as long to bounce back. Just as the limbs of the trees grew stronger, so did I. Because of my past experiences, they cushioned my fall. As the tree sees the mountains in the distance, so did I. But I knew there was something beyond the mountains. There had to be more to life than I knew. I wanted to uproot myself and cross over those mountains to a new life even if I didn't know what it would be like. It had to be better. The tree is on the edge of the cliff, because that's how I felt, so near the edge I don't know why but it is scary," I went on.

"The time I was in the hospital with severe headaches, I told my sister, the pieces kept breaking off. She asked me what I meant.

I told her, "I can't keep holding onto the cliff. The dirt keeps breaking off in my hands. I kept grabbing trying to hold on. In reality, I want to hold on. I felt so close to just giving up, to falling in a black hole, and I was trying to hold onto reality. If I ever came close to breakdown it was then. At the end of the poem, I saw I would keep on trying. I won't give up. No matter how painful life is, I love it and somehow know it could be better."

"There, I told you what the poem and the drawing mean, all at the same time."

He was very quiet and just sat there, looking at me, which seemed like an eternity.

"What do you think?" I wanted a response.

"Yes, I could see something like that in the drawing. Your poem explains you well. It says a great deal. Have you ever had it published? Perhaps you can do it for the hospital. I feel a lot of patients could relate to it. Staff as well as patients."

I was pleased that he understood it. It was important to me to bring him and others to understand what I was trying to say.

"No it hasn't been published." I answered, feeling flattered that he asked.

"Perhaps you can leave it for the hospital for others to enjoy when you leave."

"I will. Thank you for saying so." I smiled at him.

"This is one of the tests you need to take. I'll call you when times up."

He left the typewritten pages with me. They were mostly questions like, "what would you do?" or "what do you think?" I zipped right through them and waited for him to return.

"Veronica this is all I have to give you. Someone else will give you the other part of your test. I'll take you to meet her."

I was disappointed he was not going to finish testing me. I liked him.

"Veronica this is Mrs. Harris. She is going to complete the test with you. It was a pleasure meeting you. I wish you luck and take good care of yourself."

I shook hands with him and thanked him.

Mrs. Harris was a middle-aged woman. She was friendly, but distant. I didn't like her as much. Well I'll just tell her what I know and go on. She's not really interested in me. I imagined to her, I was just another patient. We went into a smaller room than I was in before. There was a table and two chairs. Mrs. Harris said,

"Sit down Mrs. Knight. I have some pictures here I would like for you to look at and tell me what you think you see."

She pulled out some heavy white paper with ink blotches upon them.

I couldn't believe it. They really do show you ink blotches. I thought that was just in the movies, and now I was a part of it. I felt a little more important. She wants to know what I think. She's interested. Really I knew she was just doing her job and I was just another unknown but just the fact that she was waiting for my answer meant something to me.

"Mrs. Knight, tell me what you see in these ink blotches." A couple I saw very clearly,

"This one is a man, the shadow of a man, he is casting a large shadow that takes you over."

"Do you see anything else? She asked.

"No, that's all." I replied. She wrote down what I saw in the book.

"Now, what do you see in this?"

I looked at the card carefully.

"I see two women, standing facing one another. They are attached to one another, no they are not attached," I added.

"Are you sure they're not attached?" I didn't want them to be for some reason.

"No they're not. It just looks like it."

She showed me some others, but they were meaningless, a bat, a butterfly, etc. She didn't show me pictures with scenery and people.

"Now Mrs. Knight will you please tell me a story to go with each of these pictures. Tell me what you think is happening."

There was a picture of young girls standing by a tree, holding books in their arms. In the background was a farmhouse and a field being plowed by a man on a tractor.

"That's a young girl who wants to leave home. She knows there must be more to life. She's unhappy living there. She dreams of leaving and to go to school somewhere. She wants to better herself and feels sad that her family won't understand." I looked at Mrs. Harris.

"Does she leave?" she asked me.

"Yes." I said smiling.

"What do you see in this one?"

It startled me when I looked at it.

"That was easy." I said.

It was a woman sitting on the floor. She was crying. Her arms rested on the couch.

"Her grandmother just died. She is crying and very hurt. No one knows how bad she feels and she doesn't tell anyone. She cries alone.

Her grandmother was the most important person in her life and now she is gone." I said this without any emotion. It was just a fact.

Mrs. Harris looked at me for a while and then put the card down and wrote something again in her book. I wasn't feeling anything. I knew I saw myself in that picture. Why wasn't I feeling something?

The next picture had a man sitting on a couch looking very unhappy. There was a woman standing beside him with her hand on his shoulder.

"She is telling him it is going to be alright. He just lost his job she's comforting him." I said.

Mrs. Harris put the picture away and took out another. It was an office where there were desks. There was a woman pleading with a man.

"She wanted to just be friends with him. He wanted more. He wanted to have an affair. She was afraid of it. She was asking him to please not be mad, to just be friends with her. She is afraid of his anger and doesn't want to lose him as a friend," I said.

I didn't like that one. It was too recent. That's what I went through at work. I hated it. Why could not I just be a friend with the man at work that I liked? Why did they always expect more?

"Now Mrs. Knight tell me what you see here." It was a blank sheet of paper.

"Make up your picture."

I looked at the sheet. What did I see? What was my latest fantasy? "I see a hill. A mountaintop covered with green grass and little white, yellow and purple flowers. The sky is blue with white puffy clouds. There is a butterfly over the flowers. There is a man and woman sitting together on the grass. They are alone and smiling at one another."

"What are they doing there?" she asked.

They escaped from their everyday lives to be together. They're both married, but not to each other, and they are both unhappy in their lives. This day is theirs. No one knows they are together, and it is so special. They make love. They make love under the sky. It is beautiful I exclaimed.

"What happened later?" Mrs. Harris wanted to know.

I looked at her.

"They go home back to their own worlds. Nothing changes, but for the time, it was theirs and they're not sorry. They took something for themselves." I added very firmly. Everything else they did was for others and their family. This is all they had, the only happiness."

"Why don't they change their lives if they're not happy with them?" She wanted to know.

"They can't. It would hurt too many people. I have to think about others."

"Wouldn't you think this would hurt them, their spouses, if they knew?" I didn't like the question.

"Of course it would but they don't know. Why would it hurt more? Should they just tell them they want a divorce? They can't do that, and besides this is all they take for themselves that they want." They deserve some happiness don't they?" I asked impatiently.

"They're taking an awful big risk," she said.

I didn't know what she was talking about and didn't want to know. She was trying to mess up my fantasy, and I wouldn't let her.

"That's all I have Mrs. Knight. You may leave now." It jolted me I wasn't expecting to leave so suddenly. Did I say something I shouldn't have?" What did she think of me? Well, I'm not going to care. I will see her again, but Dr. "D" will know what I said. I hoped he would still see me. I hoped he would know I needed to see him. I was so afraid of him dropping me. I hope I did all right, I thought as I walked to the dayroom to see if any of the group was there. I felt like talking to someone. I didn't want to think of the morning and of the tests. I was so anxious to take them, now I know I wanted to forget them. I hoped I would hear something about them and that they turned out all right. What's all right? If they were all right you wouldn't be here dummy, I told myself.

It was my second day in group therapy and I felt apprehensive as I sat there waiting for the doctors to come in. I felt like talking now. I wanted to find out what this was all about. Dr. Lee, Neal, and Emily, the woman psychologist came into the room. Again, the sight of Neal bothered me. To me, he just seemed to be smug. Like he stood over us. I didn't like him being stronger than me. For some reason, the other doctors didn't bother me as he did. I talked about my marriage, my mother, when I was a teenager, my father, and just my whole life briefly.

"It's amazing how you talk about these things, things that are painful for you and you showed no emotion. You sound like a tape recorder all-in-one tone. How come you show no emotion?" Dr. Lee said.

I was surprised. I was just stating facts, things that happened. Why was I supposed to show emotion?

"Don't you feel anything?" He continued.

"Of course I feel things, I hurt." I answered.

He shrugged.

"Then why don't you show the emotion?" He asked in his strong accent.

I didn't understand him. Was I supposed to cry? I wasn't going to cry in front of all these people. Besides, I already did my crying before. It was over with.

"What do you think causes your headaches Veronica?" Neal asked me. I was surprised to hear his voice.

"I don't know."

"Don't you know that holding on to emotions causes headaches?" he said a bit sarcastically.

"I feel. I hurt." I said impatiently. What do they want blood I thought. I was getting angry. That's what he wants to do, make me angry. I'm not going to give him the satisfaction. I'll remain cool. I won't let him get to me.

"Do you enjoy the way your husband treats you? Do you like him having control over you? What do you do for yourself? What do you do for yourself?"

He must've read my records, I thought. "I do things for myself." I answered. "Like what?"

"I go to the beach with some girlfriends once a year." He laughed. "Oh you go to the beach once a year. Wow what a big deal. So, all year you look forward to that one weekend that you take for yourself."

I was getting mad, but determined not to show it.

"I can't think of myself all the time and I have children, a husband, responsibilities. I have to think of them. Besides my husband is not all bad. Sometimes I feel like I have no right to complain."

"I don't think you've complained enough. You must enjoy being a martyr." Neal said.

Now I was really mad, I calmly I said,

"I know what you are trying to do, and I'm not going to let you."

"What am I trying to do?" He asked me.

"You know I'm not going to tell you." I said through clenched teeth. I was not going to lose control. I'm not going to give him the satisfaction of it. He would love to see me cry, to see me angry. I hated him in that moment.

Dr. Lee stepped in. "I don't know why you won't answer Neal's question, Veronica. He is just trying to help you."

"I think he is being too hard." Bonnie spoke up.

"I would cry if you talk to me that way. I don't think he is being very nice."

Then Dr. Lee spoke to the whole group.

"It is important for you all to talk openly, to express your feelings. If you feel like crying, cry. If you are angry, don't be afraid to show it. We have seen everything here in this room. It's okay to say anything you want to. To act any way you want to. We are not going to turn you away. We will try to help you with your problem. That is why we are here."

I felt better after hearing Dr. Lee say that, but it didn't resolve my fear of Neal. What was I afraid, of falling apart? I heard an inner voice ask. I must not lose control, I said firmly to myself. No one would like me for what I am inside. I must be presentable to be accepted. How many times I told myself this. Dr. Lee said I could act any way I wanted to and it would be all right, but how? I didn't know how.

"How are you today Mrs. Knight?" Dr. "D" asked. "What's on your mind today? I hesitated.

"Go on." he said.

"I don't know what to do about something. It is bothering me so bad."

"What is it?" Arielle was looking at me too, waiting for me to answer. I was almost afraid to speak. My mouth was dry.

"Ted, one of your patients went home yesterday." "Yes, what about him?" He said almost impatiently.

"He came to my room to talk. He said he needed a friend was drawn to me and he kissed me but that was all. Honestly it scared me, but I liked it too. He asked me to call him, that he needed to hear from me and that I could call him collect at his home."

"You will do no such thing." He said loudly.

"I feel sorry for him he's lonely I know what it's like." I continued.

"You are not responsible for him. You know nothing about him. He's married and so are you and you both have problems you can't deal with already."

Then more gently he said,

"Mrs. Knight, that has been a great deal of your problems, feeling sorry for people and it has gotten you in trouble in the past. You have got to start thinking about what's good for you. You are responsible only for yourself, aside from your children and you have got to start thinking in these terms. Understand?" I felt better already.

"Yes". I answered him.

"Now, what happened at group yesterday?" He had already heard about it.

"I know the doctors are here to help us, Dr. "D", but Neal is so rude, unnecessarily rude. I don't think he should be so rough. I was able to take it okay, but some people won't be able to," I said feeling pleased with myself and strong.

"What did he say?" I told him.

"What do you think he was trying to do?"

"Break me down and I won't let him. He said I didn't talk with emotion and asked why I cannot talk about things without crying? I've cried. He wants to see me cry."

"What makes you think that?"

"I just know it. I can tell."

"You can tell no such thing. Besides what's wrong with crying? I cry." Dr. "D" said.

"You do?" I looked at him surprised.

"Sure I do." he answered.

"Well I just can't. I do, but not in front of people"

I was remembering how when I was little I was told not to cry. It made mom and dad angry. Then later when dad would spank me, I felt like I would not give him the satisfaction of crying. Why did I think he would be satisfied? I wouldn't let my friends or others see me cry, because I felt they would be glad they hurt me. I didn't want people to know me. I felt they would hurt me more if they saw that I was weak. Perhaps I would have been better off if I did let others know that I was hurt, but for some reason I had a fear of them thinking me week. I explained this to Dr. "D". I told him how I used to always go under the house to cry when I was a little girl. Later on in life I never let my sisters know how much they hurt me by making fun of me, or the things that I used to do as a child, like burning homemade dollhouses. It was so painful to me. I never let them know how it hurt. Women made fun of the way I would cook or clean. They were so organized, and I wasn't. I thought it was funny. Dad said he wanted me to be like them. Why did I have to work? Why could not I be a homemaker like my sisters? There was no pleasing him either. Even my mother hurt me when I was living at home as a teenager. Why could I not talk to her and tell her how I was feeling, how I needed her. I felt she didn't want to be bothered. I felt like such a failure in my personal life. I wasn't happy with me. How can I be successful in my job and not in my personal life, how can I be secure, and sure of myself there and not with my family?

"Because there you know what is expected of you," Dr. "D" answered. It's important for you to be yourself and for you to say and act like you feel. That way people know what to expect of you and you are what you are. In turn, they can like you or not and accept you as you are. It would make it a whole lot easier for you, instead of you playing a guessing game of what you think they might want of you, then trying to be that. What energy you must burn up." he told me.

Gosh, I thought. He made it sound so simple.

As soon as I got to my room, I called Ted. I know Dr. "D" said not to, but I had to call him to tell him I wasn't going to call anymore. Darn it. Why did I feel like I had to call him? Dr. "D" just talked to me about that?

"Hello." I heard Ted's voice at the other end of the line.

"Ted, this is Veronica."

"Hi," he said in a pleasant and surprised voice. Did he think I wouldn't call I wondered, realizing maybe I was wrong calling. I did feel silly telling him I called to say I wouldn't be calling anymore.

"Why not?"

Really, I wanted to say, what do we have to talk about? But instead I just said it was best and left it at that.

"I wish you well Ted, and hope you will be happy."

That's all I could think of to say. After hanging up, I knew Dr. "D" was right. I did waste a lot of energy and do a lot of things that were unnecessary. I'm so glad I had talked to him. I felt protected.

I woke up thinking about Tim, the man I had fallen in love with in 1967. Now it was eight years later. Through the years, he would call me from time to time. Just as I was getting over him, he would call, and I would feel excited all over again. Why had I felt like I loved him so back then? He was so important to me. I had felt "noble" in loving him and doing nothing about it, thinking and feeling we were putting our families first.

We told each other that no matter how much we loved each other, we had to think of our families. We both had small children. He was a deacon in the church. I was active in my church and sang in the choir. That made us good people, didn't it? We saw each other only a few times over the years, as we lived in different towns and he traveled to many states, but we told each other we would try not to see each other because of our families. That was the reason we only saw each other once or twice a year. The fact that he called every week for two years was enough for me. Did I sell myself short? How little I knew. I guess it was what I wanted to believe. I wondered now, did he really love me? I went through such hell because of him. Each time Tim told me he had to stop calling and seeing me, I would go to pieces. My mother had to give me a sleeping pill once just so I could stop crying. That was one time I couldn't stop crying. My husband accepted the explanation that I was depressed. Really, I don't think he cared enough to find out the real reason, and then I didn't care. I just wanted him to leave me alone.

There were times then, I would just leave my office job and drive around town. Once I found myself in a unfamiliar church crying in the restroom because there were workers in the chapel. I wanted some place to go where I could be alone. A church was all I could think of. When I came out of the restroom, the pastor saw me and asked if he could help me. I said no and went away. I couldn't talk to anyone. Later I went back and talked to him.

Now, that I was in the hospital. I thought of calling Tim. Did he care? I had to find out. He had come to see me a couple of years before. At that time he said he was getting a divorce. He wanted to know how things were with me. Because of my pride I told him I was very happy and things were going well. He told me he was thinking of marrying someone. I wished him well and he left. I still loved him, but would not let him know. He had hurt me so many times. Later, about a year before coming to the hospital, he had called me. He wanted to see me and talk. I invited him to my home during the day. I was being very brazen about it, to invite him to my home, but for some reason I just didn't worry about it. At this time, sitting at the kitchen table, he told me he wasn't very happy in his second marriage. I was surprised that he felt free to come and tell me this. I told him calmly that he knew what he was getting into when he married the young girl with two small children. I had no sympathy for him, but listened. Again I told him I was happy. He left kissing me on the cheek. I felt sad remembering how much I had loved him. Every fall season, as the leaves fell to the ground, and the fragrance of burning leaves filled the air, I would feel the familiar pain that I experienced that autumn day when he first said goodbye to me beside my car. He drove off leaving me begging and crying. It was then, that I went to my mother hysterically. It was like the end of the world to me. The pain was so great. Now I just looked at him at my door calmly remembering.

He had come to me to talk, when he had a problem, I thought. I needed a friend now. Would he care? I hoped he would care. I wanted to talk to him. I needed to know that he loved me. Why was it so important? I don't know, but it was. I didn't want to think he would just use me as I heard the term used often by others. I had to believe he loved me. I had to have gone through all that pain for something other than just a few meetings. He seemed like a fantasy love affair to me. A beautiful one, when I was with him, but was there all the pain for nothing? I had to know. I called him. The secretary answered the phone. Darn, I had hoped he would answer. Now, for some reason, I was afraid I wouldn't get him.

"Mr. Jones is on another extension, may I take a message and have him return the call?" I was afraid he wouldn't call back. I just had that feeling. It was a panicky feeling. I was about to have my unpleasant thoughts confirmed one way or another.

"Yes please tell him to call Veronica. I am at a hospital." I gave her my telephone number and room number.

"Please ask him to call me as soon as possible." I said before hanging up.

I sat there in the bed beside the phone expecting it to ring any moment. I was trembling and my blouse was wet with perspiration. My chest hurt and my head was hurting. Darn, why did I always get like this? I'm a wreck. I kept looking at the phone, just knowing it was about to ring. I waited and waited, the terror building within me. No, it can't be true that the phone was not ringing., He'll call, I told myself. He had another call and had to answer it. Someone came into the room and he had to talk to them. He'll call when they leave. He had to use the restroom before calling me. All kinds of excuses I thought of, until I ran out of them.

I sat there, numb, feeling nothing. I couldn't even cry. I felt empty. He wasn't going to call. He didn't care, not even that I was in the hospital. Is it true he wasn't the man I thought? Did he use me? I guess really I knew the answer, but I still wasn't ready for it, or was I? I called him didn't I? I tested him, as I had always been afraid to before. Well, I'm in the right place to find out, I thought. What was this empty, quiet feeling I had? Why wasn't I crying?

It was time for me to walk over to the hospital. I was to be there, at 10 o'clock. I had just 10 minutes. I waited for him to call as long as I could. It had been almost 2 hours. I hope they don't call me first, I thought. I didn't want to see Dr. "D". I felt awful and didn't know how to talk about it.

"Good morning Mrs. Knight how do you feel today?" Dr. "D" asked.

"I feel awful," was my reply.

"Well, let's talk about why you feel awful."

"I don't know what to say." I said looking at him. "Don't you have anything to talk about?" He asked. I looked at the floor saying,

"There is something, but I don't want to talk about that." He raised his voice saying,

Well, I'll tell you what Mrs. Knight when you do decide you want to talk about it, you let me know. Don't waste my time. There are other patients that do have things they want to talk about." I was stunned. I looked at him.

"Go on, go on out," he said firmly.

I wasn't unsure I heard him right. He was angry with me. I wasn't expecting this reaction from him. I ran crying from the room, to the nearest restroom in the hall. I locked the door when I got inside and just cried and cried. I hurt so badly. I couldn't believe what he said to me. Now what am I going to do? He's mad at me, and I need him. I felt terrible. I fixed my face the best I could when I stopped crying, but my eyes were all swollen. How can I go to group like this? Everyone will know I've been crying. I stayed in the bathroom as long as I could. I didn't want anyone to see me. I thought about group, about Neal. Oh no, I can't handle him today too. Dr. "D" was enough. I felt my chest starting to hurt. My head felt like it was going to burst. It started with my calling Tim and now it was really hurting. I needed some medicine for the pain, I thought. I'll have to ask for it. All I wanted to do was go back to my room and cry some more, but I didn't have time. One of the nurses gave me a pill for my headache. It didn't help much. I was so afraid of going to Group. I didn't want to see Neal. Now I was getting sick to my stomach and my shoulders were tightening up, as they did when I felt tense about something. I went to the bathroom and threw up. I felt a little better, but weak. I went on to Group thinking, I might as well get it over with. I was the first one there, dreading when Neal would come through the door.

One by one the other patients came in. Then I saw Dr. Lee and the woman psychologist. He closed the door behind him as he stepped into the room. Before he even sat down I asked,

"Where is Neal?"

As Dr. Lee sat down, he looked up at me surprised. "Why do you ask?" Do you want Neal to be here?"

"No" I said quickly, I don't."

"Neal had a meeting to attend. He won't be here today. Why don't you want him to be here?" Dr. Lee said patiently with slight smile.

It made me mad. He knew why, and darn him, he's enjoying it. I thought. I ignored his question. Instead I said,

"You mean I got all worked up over nothing, my headache and being sick." Dr. Lee looked amused.

"Does he do all that to you? Don't you like Neal?" "No, I don't."

"Why don't you?" Everyone was looking at me. I said exactly how I felt. It seemed I had no control over what I said. I was surprised at myself.

"I just don't need him today. He reminds me of a movie I saw recently."

"What's that?" he asked leaning in his chair towards me. He seemed very interested.

"Neal is like the shark in the movie I saw. I feel like he's lurking out there, in the water, waiting for me to make a wrong move, so he can attack me," I said very slowly and carefully so he could get my full meaning. That's exactly how I felt.

Dr. Lee laughed.

"Neal reminds you of a shark." He seemed to think it was funny.

"Why do you feel like that Veronica? Neal doesn't want to hurt you. He only is interested in your well-being." "Is it because of yesterday?"

"That too, but I felt like that from the beginning," I said.

"Do I remind you of a shark? Are you afraid of me?" Dr. Lee wanted to know.

"No, just Neal."

He sat back in his chair and looked up like he was really thinking about it.

"I wonder what this means that it is only Neal you feel this way towards."

"That's all I've got to say. I don't want to talk today. I don't feel well."

"Well Veronica, try to think of why you feel this way only towards Neal. Those are some pretty strong feelings you have."

Someone else in the group spoke up, and I just lost myself in my thoughts. I didn't want to be there, today. I had to think about Dr. "D" and what to do. I was glad when group was over. I dismissed Neal from my mind. Dr. "D" was more important. I had the whole weekend to go through. I can't see him until Monday. What am I going to do? How am I going to stand this anxiety I felt? I wished I could go to sleep and not wake up until Monday.

It was Friday and Ronald was going to be at the hotel tonight to pick me up. We were going to the beach for the weekend. I loved the beach so, and always welcomed any chance to go, but this time I didn't want to. I hated the thought of being there all weekend with my husband, trying to be loving, and not hurt his feelings. I just didn't feel like I had it in me to pretend this weekend like I normally did around him. I didn't even want to see him. All I could think about was Dr. "D". I've got to talk to him I thought. If I don't, he might let me go. That's what I'll do. I'll talk to him no matter how difficult it is. I can't have him mad at me. There, I made the decision. I felt better. I just wish I didn't have to wait until Monday. I wanted to tell him right away, but knew that was impossible. I had no choice but to wait. I would make it through the weekend, since I felt better about making the decision to talk to Dr. "D". I will have a good time, I said with determination, as if saying it would make it come true.

It was now 5 PM and time for me to get my medicine. I had been lying on the bed for two hours making my decision and preparing myself emotionally for my husband. I had just up made my decision when Dr. "D" arrived.

I was standing at the nurses' station with some other patients when Dr. "D" walked in to get a patient's chart. I looked up startled when I heard his gruff voice. I looked at him. He was like a god to me. I was so happy to see him. He didn't look my way although I was sure he saw me.

"Dr. "D"." I said happily. He looked up surprised.

"I'm going to talk to you Monday." I waited for his response.

I expected him to be happy about it as I was.

"So?" He said unconcerned, and looked back at the chart. He started talking to the nurse as if I never said anything. I stood there, shocked. "So" he had said, "so." The word went over and over in my mind. No he couldn't have, I thought, but he did. I knew he did. The terror I felt was unbelievable. I felt it mounting in me as if I would explode. I felt shattered. He doesn't care. He doesn't care. I mean nothing to him. The words kept going over in my head as I ran down the hall to my room. I threw myself on the bed sobbing as hard as I could ever remember. It was uncontrollable. To me "so" meant "so what" or "who cares?" or what's the big deal? It meant nothing to him that I had decided to talk to him. Did he realize that it was a big decision for me to make? It was hard for me to talk to him, to trust him. I am made up my mind to trust him completely to tell him everything, but he doesn't care my inner voice said again.

What made you think he wouldn't care Veronica, I asked myself? Who are you? You're not a big deal. He is going to stop seeing you now. I just know it. I made him mad. What am I going to do?

There, was a knock at the door. Oh no I thought. I don't want anyone to see me like this. I hope they didn't hear me crying. I had been crying so loud. It was my husband.

"Ready to go?" He asked enthusiastically, as if everything in the world was okay.

"No, I'm not ready. I can't go. I feel awful." I explained what was wrong.

"Oh Veronica it will do you good to go. You can forget all about it. You know how you love the beach." He dismissed my feeling bad.

"All the arrangements have been made and Mary's watching the boys. I looked at him. He was really excited about going. Why couldn't he have been like this years ago, when it really did matter. Now it's too late I thought.

"I need to take something for my head first. It hurts awful." I felt sick to my stomach. It had been a terrible day. Maybe it would be good going to the beach. Maybe the weekend will go by faster, but what was I going to say to Dr. "D" when I saw him Monday? I'll worry about that later, I thought; but all the way down to the beach, that's all I could think about, what he said. How can one little word means so much I asked myself.

"So," was the worst thing he could have said.

On the way down to the beach my head hurt so much I laid on the backseat of the car. The pill the nurse gave me wasn't working. My husband had to keep stopping for me to throw up, until I just had the dry heaves. I felt so nauseated and my head was hurting so. Wasn't there, any relief? I have taken all the medicine I could, and it wasn't helping. I couldn't wait to get the beach so I could lie in bed. Maybe my head would stop hurting then. By the time we got there I couldn't lay still in the bed. My head was screaming. I felt like it was going to burst wide open. I kept crying and crying. I couldn't stop. The pain was unbelievable. It had never hurt like this. How could a person take so much pain? I couldn't stand any light to hit my eyes. Even the sound of my husband's voice seems too loud.

"I can't stand it." I screamed. "I can't take it anymore. Please take me back." I cried. It was unbearable. For once he didn't try to change my mind. The ride back seemed long. I knew he was driving as fast as he could. I remember him telling me from time to time what town we were in. The drive back usually takes 5 ½ hours. I couldn't stand it that long, I thought. I couldn't lie still. I kept tossing and turning in

the back of the car. Everything was spinning around. I'm going to die. I know I'm going to die. I must be having a cerebral hemorrhage. Nothing else could hurt this much. Oh why did Dr. "D" do this to me? I thought. How can anybody be so cruel? I really blamed him in my state of mind, only I found out much later, I did it to myself. I had only myself to blame. When we reached the hospital, the nurse gave me a shot as soon as I got into bed. The rest of the weekend I don't remember. I was just so glad to be back. I couldn't even think of how I messed up the weekend for my husband. Later, I did feel bad about that.

Chapter 20

COMING OUT

"TIME TO WAKE up Mrs. Knight," the nurse said as she came into my room. She didn't just knock and go on this time. She came in and opened the drapes.

"You had a lost weekend. How do you feel?" She asked cheerfully. I was sitting up, dazed, realized it must be Monday, as the memories of the beach trip came into my mind. Did it really happen? It was a nightmare. I was alive! How did I live through it? The last thing I remember was getting the shot.

"I brought your medicine for you to take, but be sure to stop by the nurse's station for your blood pressure," she said as she walked out the door.

I felt quiet. It was all over, like it never happened. Today, I see Dr. "D". Reality hit me. I now felt calm. How can I let him know what all I went through because of what he said to me? It was bad enough that he told me to get out of the office, I thought now, feeling angry instead of hurt, as I had felt on Friday.

I was walking down the hall of the hospital when I saw Neal coming towards me. He was smiling. There was no avoiding him.

"Remind you of a shark, do I?"

He was standing right in front of me. I felt embarrassed. He found it amusing. Was he glad I was afraid of him? Darn. I didn't want him to know that. He must be feeling great satisfaction, I thought.

"Yes you do," I answered.

"Well, we'll talk about that at another time. You looked worried when I first saw you. Something troubling you?" He really seemed interested. I was surprised he was taking the time to talk to me. I felt flattered that he seemed concerned that something was troubling me. Because of this, I told him what happened over the weekend and what Dr. "D" said.

"Boy, I bet you're mad aren't you?" he asked. Now that he mentioned it, I was.

"What are you going to do?" He wanted to know.

"I don't know for sure." I said.

"I bet you're really pissed." I was surprised he used that word, pissed, but that was how I felt and told him, "yes."

"Well, are you going to tell Dr. "D" how you feel?" He seemed angry too, like I had a reason to be angry. I felt myself getting angrier.

"I can't tell him that. I've never used that word."

"Well, what's wrong with it?" If you're pissed, you're pissed!" He said very strongly.

By now I couldn't wait to see Dr. "D".

"Yes, I'm going to tell him that's exactly what I feel, because I am pissed," I said with great determination.

By the time Arielle came to get me I was really worked up. I couldn't wait to get to the office. Arielle stayed in the office with us.

"Well, Mrs. Knight did you have a nice weekend?" he asked pleasantly. I couldn't believe it. He sounded just like nothing happened. That showed how much it affected him.

"No, I didn't." I'm pissed." I almost spat the words out. I was surprised at my anger. How did I have the courage all of a sudden to talk like this?

"You didn't? What seems to be the problem?" He was remaining so calm. It didn't bother him that I was so upset.

"You know what the problem is. You know what you said to me. So! How could you say that? How could you be so cruel? I was going to talk to you about something that was very important to me, and hard to talk about. I had decided, and I wanted you to know, and all you could say to me was, "so."

"What was I supposed to say?" He asked with the questionable look on his face, like he hadn't done anything wrong.

"I wanted you to care, but you didn't. You said "so," like, so what?" Darn him. Why was he making me say this? He knows what he did. He meant to do it. I was really crying now. I was screaming at him.

"I liked you. I trusted you. You were important to me, and I'm just another patient. You don't care. You men are all alike. You are just like my father. I hate you for not caring." I was surprised at what I was saying. I was surprised that he didn't seem shocked when I said, "I'm pissed." It was like he was used to hearing the word pissed. He was just calmly sitting there.

Now he leaned towards me and said very loud and firmly.

"I am not your father. I am your doctor. You cannot think of me as your father."

I was surprised. I said that I wasn't aware that I had been thinking that and besides that, I love my father. He just called me last week. Everything was fine then. Why did I say that? I know I used to feel that way, but I don't know. What was wrong?

"I told you before Mrs. Knight, that you had to talk to me. I do care about your problem, and I'm here to help you."

"You could let me go like you did with Ted. He didn't want to go home. You have control over everything just like Dad."

Again, I was surprised I said that, but he wasn't.

"I'm not going to let you go. You will leave when you feel you are ready. Now what was it that you couldn't talk about on Friday?"

Gosh, I had forgotten about it, and everything that had happened. It didn't seem so important now, I told him, without showing any emotion. He got angry. Oh no, I thought. Here he goes again. What was so bad about calling Tim?

"You are not to call anyone or do anything that I do not know about outside this hospital. You're not responsible for what you do right now. Do you understand? No more phone calls."

I couldn't understand why he was angry, but I liked him saying I wasn't responsible. I felt it was going to be nice, not being responsible. He is going to take care of me. I felt better again.

As I was leaving, Arielle smiled and said,

"You did good." I really felt good I actually showed anger, but I cried too. I even used the word "pissed." I was really proud of myself.

Now if I can only get away with it and he would not reject me. He said he wouldn't, but I wasn't sure. I'll just have to not get so upset, in the future when I show anger, I thought. I walked down the hall thinking, it's still hard to believe I acted that way. Did he do it on purpose to make me angry? Is that what Dr. "D" wanted to do? I convinced myself that he did do it on purpose, and I was supposed to act that way. He never did tell me, and through the years I have always wondered.

As I walked toward group therapy, I felt peaceful. I even felt better towards Neal. I knew now he had egged me on when I talked to him earlier. He wanted me to tell Dr. "D" how I felt. I felt softer towards him, but I still didn't trust. He was still in control and I couldn't let him be in complete control. I couldn't ever let him see me angry. Today I'll be quiet. I already had my emotional session for the day, and I didn't want any more. I felt the headache coming on and asked for a pill. I wanted to catch it very early before it started hurting badly again.

At group I was quiet, kept to myself. Dr. Neal focused his attention on me. I told him I didn't want to talk; I had showed my emotion for the day.

"Oh now, you can only show emotion once a day?" he said, shaking his head up and down and smiling.

Why did he always find everything so amusing? He didn't bring up the subject of Jaws and I was grateful for that. Later on when someone was talking about his or her husband, I found myself agreeing with her about something and told her I knew what it was like. Hearing her talking about it stirred up some angry feelings in me. What is this? I wondered.

Neal started talking about my husband again, and how I treated him like everything was okay, that maybe the woman that was talking felt like I did. Maybe she was a martyr too. I felt the anger again. Just when I started feeling good about him, he had to mess up.

"Tell Neal how you feel about what he said Veronica." Dr. Lee said.

"No I'm not. I'm not getting upset today," was my reply.

"If you are mad and don't show it, if you keep it inside you will get a headache," he told me. I answered quickly.

"No, I won't."

"Oh now you know when you are going to get a headache and when you're not," he said sarcastically.

"I won't get a headache because I already took something for it," I said smiling. He started laughing.

"Now I've heard everything. First you decided not to show emotion today, because you already showed it once, and now you tell me you take a pill before you get a headache, so you will not get one." I'd say you're pretty much in control of things aren't you?"

I didn't answer. He was making fun of me. The rest of the time I stayed quiet. I felt so good when I came in there, now I didn't.

After group I walked back to the hotel with the others. Most of the time I enjoyed being with them, as I felt we all have something in common, and I didn't have to pretend with them. They didn't expect anything out of me, but now I wanted to be alone. When I told the others, they understood. I didn't have to explain. I went to my room and lay down; I wanted to reflect on the day.

I felt so tired, but yet peace filled me that I didn't quite understand. Arielle had said I did well. What did that mean exactly? I had always been afraid to show much anger before. I didn't like the way I exploded and it seemed the more I let out the angrier I got. I must have had more in me than I expected. How much more was I hiding from myself?

Dr. "D" told me at one of my sessions, that burning my homemade dollhouses was my way of expressing anger, when I was a child. The fact that I always saved my paper dolls was a good sign. I felt so bad when they accidentally burned, because I was that doll. I wanted someone to come save me as I always saved my doll. I wanted someone to take me away from what I knew. When he told me this, it made sense to me. I did make myself the doll. I did pretend that it was me. I always liked to pretend that I was small, so small that I could hide in the blades of grass. It would be like a jungle. When I was much older, I used to wish I couldn't make myself small and hide, as I did when I was a child. I was talking once in therapy and when asked how did I feel when I was scared or depressed my answer was, that I wanted to make myself small and hide.

"Like you did when you were a child?" Arielle asked.

"Yes." I answered as the memories flooded back to me. I loved the small cars that I played with and the little rain puddles. The puddles became lakes. I could sail my small boat in them with my paper doll inside. It was real to me. I didn't know that setting fire to my dollhouses and a couple of times to a field was a way of expressing anger. I didn't realize or recognize the anger I had inside of me, and what was I angry about as a child? When I was older I knew I was daring, not afraid of danger. I did everything hard and fast in sports, even in driving a car. These too, were ways of letting anger out. Whenever I was upset, I would drive the car very fast. I had control over it. I took chances with my life. I saw now what I didn't before, how angry I must've been. I knew of occasions that I felt this way, but how many times did I not recognize it? I didn't know I was still angry with Dad. I loved him. Things were okay now, so why did I lash out at Dr. "D" comparing him to Dad? I found out later, it was because I made him so important to me, as I did my father. I wanted from him what I wanted from my father as a child. When he became angry with me, I felt he was rejecting me, as I felt my Dad had. I felt like I had to be good, or he wouldn't love me. I didn't realize at the time I felt this way, I just knew he was important and I feared him also. This didn't make sense to me. How can you love someone and fear them also? Later I found out what you fear, is the rejection or fear of being rejected. I was to learn one of the reasons I feared my father every time I saw him as an adult, was because when I was a child, I used to dread him coming home from work, because it meant a spanking for me. My mother told me that I was not a good girl. I had remembered my father telling me that, when he gave the doll to my sister. I was convinced I was not a good girl; therefore I was not worthy of being loved. I tried so hard to be good, to get their approval.

Now that I was an adult, I knew my father would not spank me, but I had become so used to fearing him as a child, that subconsciously the fear was still there. Many years later I also found out on my own, with Dr. "D"'s guidance, that the reason I didn't like my mother to kiss me good night, was because I wanted to stay mad at her for telling my father on me. In my childlike mind, I couldn't stay mad at her if she kissed me. I would feel guilty, so I must have deserved the spanking. She must have loved me, or why did she kiss me good night? This realization came to me one day, while preparing a meal.

I was so excited and happy about finally understanding it; I called Arielle to tell her. She had already known the answer; it was for me to put it together for myself. In therapy, you were not given all the answers. Mostly you have to find out for yourself, and with time you do come to an understanding and acceptance. It is such a good feeling when the pieces finally come together, and make sense. Once you understand why you felt a certain way and act a certain way you can go about correcting it to where you are comfortable and happy with your decisions. I once read a line in a poem that stands out in my mind. I was trying to apply it whenever I had a decision to make. It goes like this.

"When faced with the decision, make that decision as wisely as possible, then forget it.

The moment of absolute certainty never arrives."

There was a knock at the door. I looked towards the window. It was getting dark. How long had I been laying here? There was so much to think about. It was Judy.

"Are you going to eat with us tonight?" Are you okay?"

"Yes thank you. I just wanted to be alone. I had things to think about," I told her.

"You don't have to explain to me. I understand." I liked Judy. I couldn't imagine her trying to take her life. She seemed so okay.

How many of us are there that walk around everyday putting on a façade? I wonder how many people are out there in the world that needs to be here getting help?

It's not something to be ashamed of, as many think. At least we admit we have a problem, I thought a bit angrily. I hated people that acted like they had it all over others, but then I wondered was a lot of it my imagination? Could I be wrong about Neal?

I had been talking to Dr. "D" and Arielle about my sister. I saw Arielle sometimes now too. I was seeing Dr. "D" about twice a week. I would see Arielle all the other days. I liked Arielle very much. And could really talk to her better than I could Dr. "D". I wasn't afraid of her, and she seemed to understand me more as a woman. I felt secure though in knowing Dr. "D" still was interested, because he was talking to Arielle daily about our sessions. I had told Arielle how I was still, after 20 years, having daydreams about my sister. I kept reliving what happened when we were teenagers. Bessie told a lie on Ronald and me when we were teenagers to my mother. She said she heard me ask Ronald to sleep with me. Mom wouldn't have cared, but it really hurt me when she said this. It also bothered me terribly when she acted like she didn't know me at school. I felt terrible when she went to live with my grandmother. I didn't understand why I was always so uncomfortable around her, even when we were adults and had made up. We were close when my grandmother died, or at least I thought we were. Why did I still feel she did not like me? Why did it matter so much? I couldn't get rid of the bad feelings or the bad dreams I had had all these years.

As I walked into the room to see Arielle and Dr. "D", he said "Mrs. Knight we're going to try something different today. I'm going to give you some sodium amythol. It's like sodium pentothal, the truth serum. I'll use a little hypnosis on you too. It won't hurt a bit. As a matter of fact you'll feel good and relaxed."

I wasn't scared, but interested. I wanted to know how it worked. "Now just lie down on this table and relax. This will just take a few seconds, and you'll start to feel the effects," he said as he came towards me with the needle.

He was being very nice and gentler with me than he had been in the past, I thought. He was right, it did feel good, as a matter of fact, and I loved it. I could get used to this real fast, I thought as I felt the relaxing drug enter my bloodstream. It wouldn't do for me to be a person used to receive drugs other than medicine. I liked that feeling too much. It was so pleasant. I wished it could last and last.

"Now Mrs. Knight start counting backwards from one hundred."

I did until the effort was just too much and it interfered with the good feeling I was having.

"Mrs. Knight, do you hear me?"

"Yes." I could barely answer.

"You will hear everything I say and remember it when you wake up." His voice seemed in another world, far away, yet it came through so clearly, very distinctly. I had no resistance. I felt very vulnerable.

"What do you remember when you were just a little girl and your parents brought a new baby home?"

"I don't remember anything" was my reply. He continued. "How did you feel when your sister was born?"

The questions startled me for an instant. I couldn't answer. I kept thinking of his question. How did I feel when she was born?

Deep inside me, so deep from I don't know where something was building up. What was happening to me? I thought. I can't control it. It was a wave swelling up to break on the shore. I have never felt this before. It kept getting larger and larger. It was overwhelming, and then suddenly, I felt like a child. I felt tears running down my cheeks as I started to sob gently at first, then I heard myself crying like a two-year-old child. It was pitiful and very sad. My inner mind thought, I can't believe this is happening; that I'm actually doing this. Why can't I control it? Where did it come from? I kept sobbing uncontrollably. I heard Dr. D say softly.

"Just what I thought. You will open your eyes and wake up Mrs. Knight."

Suddenly, I was awake just as I was before I laid down. It was all over. I knew what happened, because my cheeks were wet and he told me I would remember. He didn't say anything else other than,

"That's all for today. Arielle will see you tomorrow."

I walked out feeling in awe of what happened. I didn't know I had those feelings way back then. Is that why I feel like I do towards my sister? My father did tell me once, that I used to take my sister's bottle away from her when she was an infant. They would find me in the closet drinking the bottle. I was eighteen months old then. Did I feel like the new baby had taken my place? Did I feel rejected way back then? He gave me something else to think about.

"Let's talk about your mother Veronica," Arielle said. I found myself being uncomfortable at her statement and wondered why, without saying so.

I took a deep breath and said,

"What do you want to know? Mom and I are very close", I added quickly.

"We are more like sisters than mother and daughter. She was just 16 when I was born."

"How do you feel about that?" She asked.

"What do you mean?"

"I mean about her being more of a sister than a mother."

"I'm proud of Mom. She's pretty. Many people have asked if we were sisters."

"That's not answering my question." Arielle said firmly.

"How do you feel about her being more of a sister that a mother?" she repeated.

I thought a while before answering and said very quietly and hesitantly,

"I really wanted her for a mother more, but I felt like my grandmother was more my mother. I could talk to her and feel comforted by her. It's not Mom's fault though. She was so young and had four children one right after the other. She did the best she could. I felt of her as a mother as far as giving her respect though. I never talked back. We have had only one argument as far as I can remember. It was when I was 16 and upset about those men coming to the house, the time that she slapped me. I told you about it. Remember?"

"Yes, I remember." Arielle responded.

"Tell me some more about your mother. Why do you feel you were close?"

"I told Mom everything. She knows about my whole life. I felt closer to her if I told her. She seemed interested."

"If I go on a vacation, I always call her during the day. She wants to know what I am doing."

"Didn't she seem interested if you talked about other things?"

"Not as much. It seemed hard to reach Mom sometimes. She always kissed us and said goodbye when we left her house. She calls me every day from work." I answered.

"What does kissing you goodbye each time you leave her house reminds you of?"

"It's reminds me of when I was a little child and she kissed me good night when I went to bed."

"Why didn't I like that Arielle? Why didn't I want her to kiss me good night? I never understood that."

"I don't know for sure." She answered. "I want you to think about that from time to time." Someday the answer will come to you, and you'll understand more of what was going on with you. I don't think you have ever really understood your feelings and that is what we are going to work on. What else do you remember?"

"I only remember mom hitting me one other time and that was when I was in first grade. I remember her saying "This is not a birthday spanking."

"We were in the large house that we lived in, in East Orange New York. We were in the toy or playroom. I can't remember what it was about. I do remember something about artificial fruit being on the dining room table and thinking it was real. I might have tried to eat some of it. I know I never wanted to make my mother angry. I was afraid to," I said, looking at her questioningly. I felt the old fear as I said this. I still have the childlike habit of holding my hands together in front of me when I was nervous as I was doing now.

"Why are you afraid?" Arielle asked. "Think hard now." It was hard for me to speak.

"I don't know for sure." I answered hesitantly as I kept thinking.

"I remember when I was three or four, I was on the back porch with my mother by the back door." I found myself being drawn away from Arielle. The sensation was like that which I experienced when I was in the hospital undergoing tests, and my husband would come to visit and get angry with me. I felt the sensation of being "pulled away", like I was on an amusement ride.

"What's wrong?" Arielle asked.

"I don't know. I feel funny."

"How do you feel? Describe it to me." Arielle asked.

I told her how I felt.

"Tell me exactly what you remember."

"Arielle, all I can remember is that something terrible happened. I think my mother got terribly mad at me for something. Ever since then, I've been afraid of her anger. I can't think of it anymore." I feel dizzy." I said.

"The fact that you are feeling like you are, is your body's way of telling you something very important." Anytime you have this sensation of being pulled away when you're talking to someone, pay close attention to what is being said, and try to figure out why you are feeling this way. Something is touching on your subconscious. Emotions, especially suppressed emotions, have a way of affecting us physically."

"Now try to remember what happened that day," Arielle told me.

I looked down at the floor and thought for a while.

"Think very hard."

"I'm trying," I told her, still feeling dizzy. I started crying after a while.

"I can't remember Arielle. I can't remember." It scares me and I don't know why." I just cried feeling so frustrated.

"Okay." Arielle said kindly. We'll go on to something else. Just the fact that you do remember something happening and your response is a positive step. That's good," she said smiling.

"I would like for us to talk more about your mother." Arielle said.

"What else is there to talk about?" I said a bit impatiently, feeling like I didn't want to.

"That's all I can remember."

"No, that's not what I mean. She said, "Would you go on to another subject, in regards to your mother. I know you don't want to talk about her. Why? Why are you hesitant? You say you both were close," Arielle added.

"Yes." I answered, looking at her, not understanding why I didn't want to talk anymore.

Arielle pressed on saying,

"Veronica, I think your mother and your husband have a lot in common."

"No, they don't," I firmly said. "How can you say that?"

I just think they do. They are a lot alike. They both make you feel guilty. They both have control over you."

"I don't feel guilty about Mom. I feel sorry for her. I know she's not happy, and I want her to be happy."

Arielle said very patiently,

"You feel guilty if you don't do everything you can for her or tell her everything. You feel guilty for feelings that are normal and natural. For instance, when you wanted to go visit your father in Florida you felt guilty. You wanted to live there. You felt your mother needed you. You've felt guilty for wanting to live with your grandmother. It was perfectly normal for you to be mad at your mother without feeling guilty every time, but you didn't even allow yourself that. Tell me what you will show anger about."

I'm mad at her because I had to quit school because the talk about her got so bad. I was very embarrassed, but yet I understood she was having such a bad time. She was not herself.

Arielle said quietly and slowly,

"You can reason out something, so it makes sense and you cannot understand it, but it's perfectly normal to be angry at the same time, and you couldn't or felt you weren't allowed to express how you felt at the time." As a matter of fact, I don't believe you ever have. Have you?"

"No I haven't. I never told her." I didn't want to hurt her."

Haven't you been hurt? Who knows how much you have been hurt?"

"I told the doctor once." Suddenly I felt like I've been cheated.

"I want you to pretend that I'm your mother. Tell me what you would like to say to her." Arielle said.

"That's silly I can't do that," I said, feeling embarrassed.

"Try." I put my head down and thought of my grandmother and how much I wanted to say to her but couldn't. I looked at Arielle.

"You always worry Gram. She was always worried about you. She told me to be a good girl for you, but you didn't care about me. You never did."

I was surprised at what I was saying and with the anger that I was saying it. It just came out. I continued crying and yelling.

"I could never talk to Gram like I wanted to, because of you. I didn't want to worry her anymore. I needed her. I needed someone." I stopped. I didn't like what I was saying. The words just came out. How could I have been feeling this way, and not know it? It scared me.

"I don't want to say anymore." I told Arielle.

"That's a lot of emotion you have there." she said looking at me to answer.

"I didn't know I felt that way." I suddenly had my composure like it never happened.

"I don't like what I said."

"I know it must be scary. I think you have a lot of feelings you don't want to admit, because you're afraid of feeling guilty about them. You have reason to be angry, Veronica. It's nothing to be ashamed of. Well, our time is up. So, I'll see you tomorrow," she said with a smile.

"You're doing good." Arielle added.

This is good? I thought walking down the hall. It scared me. What am I going to do with it? I asked myself, not sure I wanted to know the answer.

I was sitting in group therapy listening to the others talk. There was a new woman who I had never seen. I guessed her to be in her 50s. She was a very attractive woman. Beautiful, I thought when she smiled, which seemed to be most of the time. What was so unusual was that when she smiled, her eyes looked so sad especially when she talked. I saw her in the dayroom the day before, and she got my attention right away because the room seemed to light up when she walked in. Now she was talking, and she had my full attention. I couldn't believe she was a patient. I thought her to be a member of the day staff. She had said her name was Mavis.

"I came to try to find out what has been causing my headaches," she said with a slight smile.

"What do you think has been causing them?" asked Neal.

I don't know. They are getting worse. I can hardly bare them at times, and I don't want to take medicine, but it seems aspirin doesn't work."

"Do you think it might be psychological?" asked Dr. Lee.

Dr. "D" seems to think so," Marvis said still smiling.

"Do you have any problems at home?" she was asked.

"Not really. My husband does drink sometimes, and I worry so about him hurting himself when he does, but that's all."

"What do you do if he drinks?" Neal asked.

I just care for him. I love him and I wish he wouldn't, but it just seems he can't help himself. I left him once; I kept going back home to check on him to see if he was all right. I was afraid he might set the house on fire. He smokes, and sometimes he passes out. It worries me so. I stay there, until I think he will be all right. Mavis said.

"It sounds to me like you never really left him, if you go back home every day and babysit him. Sounds like you're more of a mother then a wife to him." Neal said to her.

I looked at her for her reaction. That kind of a statement made me mad. She just smiled a little with those big sad eyes and said,

"Yes it does sound like it doesn't it. I don't know what else to do. I don't want him to hurt himself. I love him. I know he loves me, but he just won't stop. He's a good worker when he's sober, and he's a good man."

"How do you feel about babysitting him? Don't you need to lean on him some?" asked Neal.

"That would be nice, but I can't when he needs me so."

"How much longer do you want to do this, the rest of your life?" "I hope not. I don't want to," she answered.

Sounds like he has it made. I don't see why he would want to change," Neal added.

"I hope things change while were here," said Mavis.

"Is he seeing the doctor too?" Dr. Lee asked.

"No, just me. He is staying here in town to be with me."

"From what you tell us, it sounds like he should be taking therapy too. Why isn't he?" asked Dr. Lee.

"I just can't get him to. He's trying though, he is," she said still smiling.

What is she smiling about? She should be crying and I thought. Now I see what Neal means about some of us having martyr complexes.

I had resented him saying that to me, as I didn't see myself as a martyr, but wasn't I being one? What was I changing at home? Nothing. I was keeping up the façade to my husband, to outsiders that everything was fine. I have even been fooling myself at times. I'm not much different from Mavis in what I haven't been doing, but I really couldn't see it before. I could see that the way she was handling her situation, nothing was going to improve.

Mavis had even convinced herself that she didn't have that much of a problem. She just had headaches. I can understand why. It must be terribly lonely for her, I thought. She really was being more of a mother to him. She didn't really have a man she could lean on, or even count on, except when he was sober, and she said she still loves him. How could she be so understanding? Didn't I always make excuses for my husband? I had been reluctant to talk about him in therapy, or even with Dr. "D" and Arielle. I didn't want to face my situation either. I was just like Mavis; I was seeing my own denial now.

Judy and the others told me I acted differently when my husband came to visit, that I was much quieter and looked very sad. They asked me how I could take the way he was always teasing me and making fun of me. They said he was always putting me down. I never really paid that much attention to it until then. I knew he did it a lot in the past, but I just kind of blocked it out. I guess I just got used it. When they told me, it reminded me of others telling me the same thing, but it had been a long time ago. We didn't have many friends that we associated with. My girlfriends picked up on his dislike of them, and felt uncomfortable around him. Really he didn't like for me to have friends. I did, but saw them at work or during the day when I could. I mostly just stayed home at night the last few years. The first few years I played cards with some women in the card club. I belonged to a women's sorority that I enjoyed very much, but even that became embarrassing. He did not want to attend any of the socials. I finally ran out of excuses and quit.

I had told Dr. "D" but I didn't want to see my husband at hospital anymore. I dreaded his visits, and always got a headache before he arrived. When he was there, with me, he acted so loving. I felt guilty if I did say anything negative about him in group therapy, or to Arielle or Dr. "D". He was not pleased when I asked him not to visit as often, and as usual I felt very guilty and made up some reason as to why it would be best if he limited his visits. He finally agreed and I felt relieved. Now I won't have to worry as much about him visiting and my having to pretend to be the loving wife. It was becoming more difficult to pretend, now that I was at the hospital.

I was having a session with Arielle one day, when there was a knock on the door.

"Come in." Said Arielle

It was John Lovell, one of the male psychologists at the hospital. "Excuse me," he said, "but I have to leave for a few days and I

have something here that I want to give you Veronica. I feel that you would like to have it and appreciate it."

It was a sheet of paper folded up. I was puzzled about what it was, but decided to read it later, as my time with Arielle was very valuable to me.

Arielle seemed to recognize it and looked as though she approved of him giving it to me. After our session, I walked out onto the porch deck and read it. It was beautiful to me, and said so much of what I felt for so long. It was a psalm entitled "Please hear what I'm not saying." It's reads as follows:

> *Don't be fooled by me. Don't be fooled by the face I wear. For I wear a mask: I wear a thousand masks, and none of them are me.*
>
> *Pretending is an art that's second nature with me, but don't be fooled, for gods sake don't be fooled.*
>
> *I give you the impression that I am secure; that all is sunny and unruffled with me, within as well as without, that confidence is my name and coolness is my game.*

That the water is calm and I'm in command. That I need no one, but don't believe me please.

My surface may seem smooth, but my surface is a mask, my ever-varying and ever-concealing mask.

Beneath lies no smugness, no complacency, beneath dwells the real me in confusion, in fear, and aloneness.

But I have hidden this. I don't want anybody to know it. I panic at the thought of my weakness and fear of being exposed.

That's why I frantically create a mask to hide behind, a non-chalant, sophisticated façade, to help me pretend; to shield me from the glance know that knows

But such a glance is precisely my salvation. My only salvation, and I know it. That is if it's followed by acceptance, if it's followed by love. Is it the only thing that can liberate me from myself? From my own self- built prison walls, from the barriers that I so painstakingly erect. It's the only thing that will assure me of what I can assure myself, that I am really worth something.

But I don't tell you this. I don't dare. I am afraid to. I'm afraid your glance will not be followed by acceptance and love. I'm afraid you'll think less of me, that you'll laugh, and your laugh will kill me. I'm afraid that deep down, I'm nothing, that I'm just no good, and that you will see this and reject me.

So I play my game, my desperate pretending games, with a façade of assurance without, and a trembling child within.

And so the parade of masks. And my life becomes a front. I idly chatter to you in the suave tones of surface talk. I tell you everything that's really nothing, And nothing that's everything, of what's crying within me.

So when I'm going through my routine, do not be fooled by what I'm saying. Please listen carefully and try to hear what I'm not saying, what I'd like to say, what for survival I need to say, I can't say.

I dislike hiding, honestly. I dislike the superficial game I'm playing.

The superficial phony game.

I'd really like to be genuine and spontaneous, and me, but you've got to help me.

You've got to hold out your hand, even when that's the last thing I seem to want or need. Only you can call me into aliveness. Each time you're kind, and gentle, and encouraging, each time you try to understand because you really care, my heart begins to grow wings. Very small wings, very feeble wings, but wings.

With your sensitivity and sympathy, and your power of understanding, you can breathe life into me. I want you to know that. I want you to know how important you are to me, how you can be a creator of the person that is me if you choose to.

You alone can break down the wall, which I tremble behind. You can remove the mask; you alone can release me from my shadow world of panic and uncertainty, from my lonely prison.

So do not pass me by. Please do not pass me by. It will not be easy for you. A long conviction of worthlessness builds strong walls. The nearer you approach me the blinder I may strike back.

It's rational, but despite what the books say about man, I am irrational. I fight against the very things that I cry out for. But I am told that love is stronger than strong walls, and in this lays my hope. Please try to beat down those walls with firm hands but with gentle hands for a child is very sensitive.

Who am I, you may wonder? I am someone you know very well. For I am me, and perhaps, maybe I am you.

I finished reading the poem and sat there, with tears in my eyes. I was not the only one who has felt this way. Someone wrote this, but I didn't know who as there was no author named. It was beautiful. It was sad. I had never read anything so profound and honest. I was glad that I was able to say that I had been feeling this way far too long and that now some of my thinking was beginning to change. I didn't want to pretend anymore. I wanted to be loved for the real me, for what I was inside, the part of me that I had hidden for too long.

Several weeks had passed now, and I was feeling more comfortable in group, when before I kept myself guarded. I talked a great deal and I thought I was participating as I should, but Dr. Lee and Neal did not seem satisfied. What did they want from me?

"You talk about sad things that have happened in your life when I ask you Veronica, but you still talk like you are on a tape recorder. If I did not look at you and know that you are here, I would think a tape recorder was brilliantly played. Dr. Lee said to me.

"You talk with no emotion. Where is your emotion?" Neal wanted to know.

I was feeling frustrated.

"What do you want? Do you want me to get mad? Why should I? It happened a long time ago."

"Don't you feel anything?"

"Of course I do. I have feelings. I feel a lot. Just because I don't show it does not mean that I don't feel. Why should I show anger now? I don't understand it," I said a bit angrily.

"It's not normal not to show feelings, to talk all in one tone about things that affected you so deeply." he answered.

"Wouldn't it be something if I went around showing emotion all the time. You don't show anger in my family. No one does. If your feelings get hurt or if you are mad, you just keep it to yourself. No one likes unpleasantness. If I tell my sisters, my brother-in-law, my mother, my father or the people I work with every time my feelings were hurt or when I was angry, no one would like me," I said.

"Is that what you're afraid of Veronica? That they will not love you anymore, that they'll reject you," he asked.

"I don't know Dr. Lee. I just know the few times I have shown anger to my parents, there was a bad scene. I don't want that. I don't want to make them angry. I'm afraid of it." I answered.

"Just because a person gets angry at you, doesn't mean that they're going to stop loving you. You scold your children don't you? You get angry with them. Do you stop loving them?" I was surprised.

"No." I answered. "I never thought of that before. I am angry at them at the time for whatever they did, but I don't stop loving them."

Dr. Lee smiled and said, "Then why do you think that others stop caring for you if you show anger at them?"

I thought about it and said,

"I don't know. I've just always felt that way. We weren't allowed to fight as children or even argue. Mom and Dad would get mad. I've just never heard my mother and aunt argue or even disagree. Not even my grandmother. I can't stand to hear people fighting. I feel sick to my stomach. Once I heard my mother and her boyfriend arguing. They're married now. I started crying and asking them to stop. That is why I would always run away from my husband when he would start yelling at me. I can't stand it. That is when he would hit me because I would try to get away from him. I would run out into the woods like I did when I was small, to get away from it. He would try to stop me sometimes and that is when our really bad fights started. He wanted me to stay. I don't want to talk about it anymore."

"There, you go again. That sounds familiar," said Neal. She'd rather hold it inside and get headaches. She likes her life just as it is."

Damn him, he's at it again, I thought.

You must just like coming here to group Veronica so you can help others with their problems, so you can babysit them too. It looks like you don't want to work on your own problems."

I was getting really mad.

"It's easier, isn't it to help someone else out. That way you get off yourself," he continued.

I said through gritted teeth,

"All right Neal, leave me alone."

"Well, when are you going to work on yourself? You know the time is slipping by and before you know it will be time to go home," he said.

"I have been talking about myself." What more do you want? You're just not satisfied until you break someone down," I said feeling near the edge not knowing how much longer I could hold my temper with him. It had been building for some time.

"Well, I guess you'll just go back home playing mama and the life you like. You must like it, or why don't you change it?"

"I can't. It's easy for you to say. You're not involved. I can't hurt everyone. I have children to think of," I shouted.

"What kind of a mother can you be with headaches all the time?"

"That's enough Neal."

"What do you tell your children when they need your attention and you're not feeling well?" he pushed.

That did it. I screamed as loud as I could.

"Get off me. I told you I don't want anymore. Leave me alone." I had a coffee cup in my hand. I threw it across the room and kept screaming, which seemed like forever. The scream came from me, and it seemed it was coming from somewhere else far away. I hated him. Why did he have to keep on? Now look what happened. I'm screaming and I can't believe it's me.

When I came to my senses, I realized how I must look. I was horrified that I behaved like this. I had actually lost control. He did it. I let him do it. How I hated him. I ran from the room without looking at anyone. Where was I going to go? There is no place to go. I ran into the restroom expecting someone to come after me and not wanting them to. I was so embarrassed. How can I ever face them again? I looked at my face in the mirror. I hardly recognized myself. I looked so ugly. My face was swollen and I was still crying. I looked at the tears rolling down my face and thought how did this happen? Today started out okay. I was feeling all right when I went into group. I didn't mean for this to happen. That's what I get for leaving myself open. I should've kept quiet today. It's dangerous to talk.

I had to get hold of myself. I wanted to hide, but there was no place to go. There were no woods to hide in, no barn to go to. Things seemed different now that I had come to the hospital. More real. I knew what I had to do. My thinking had somewhat changed for the better. I had to go back into that room and face those people. But how could I, after the way I acted? What must they think of me? I must have looked so ugly. I had lost complete control. How could I have screamed like that? Well I hope they're satisfied, I thought. They wanted me to show emotion, but God did I have to do it like this? Neal had won. He broke me down, but I knew my thinking wasn't right, when I said it to myself. Everyone had said it was all right to show emotion, that people that cared wouldn't change their minds about me, just because I showed anger. How would the group feel? Would they hold it against me? Why should they? It wasn't against them. But how would they feel about me as a person? It must have been terrible what they saw in me. What was I going to do? I knew it soon as I said it, what I had to do. It was necessary. I had to go back and face them. I had to go back into that room. I couldn't hide it anymore. It was one of the hardest decisions I had ever made in my life. I washed my face with cold water, and told myself it was all right if I didn't look good. That's to be expected after crying. The group wouldn't care what I looked like.

I walked across the hall and opened the door to where the group was waiting. Everything was very quiet. They turned and looked at me when I entered the room. I couldn't look at them. I just said,

"I decided to come back." And went to my chair and sat down.

"The group is glad that you came back Veronica. You did the right thing." Neal said. The man beside me, who had just joined the group a few days before, took my hand and said, "I'm glad you came back too."

This surprised me as he was not friendly to anyone and always seemed so angry and mistrustful of everyone.

"Thank you." I said to him. The rest of the group started saying, "Me too."

"How do you feel about what the group has to say about your coming back?" asked Dr. Lee.

I smiled and said that I felt good about it and I was sorry for what I did.

"It is not necessary to apologize," Dr. Lee said. "As I said before you are all free to say anything you want to in here and express yourself in any manner you feel."

Neal looked at me and said,

"I'd say you had an awful lot of the emotion within that head of yours Veronica, that you have not been letting out. That was a lot of energy I saw you display. Just think what you could do with all that energy, if you were to apply it all to working on yourself, as you did today. It was good that you let me know how you felt. I was pressuring you. You are a strong woman Veronica, but sometimes it is working against you. More often than not," Neal added.

I looked at him. I wasn't angry now, and it surprised me.

As I walked away from the group, I felt calm as though it had never happened. I wanted to put it out of my mind, but knew I couldn't and shouldn't. It did happen, and it was good, so they told me. The group didn't seem to mind. Bonnie, Rob and Judy seemed the same. We walked across the street to our rooms with the usual chatter, about everything else but what happened in group.

It wasn't so bad after all I thought. But did I have to be so volatile? I'll have to try not to explode like that again. I can get mad without exploding, surely. I just let it build up for too long. I should have told Neal how I felt long before I did. I had waited too long. I let it build up. Is that what I did with my husband too? I knew the answer to that, as soon as I asked it of myself. Wouldn't it be nice I thought, if people could just say how they felt about things as it happened? Is that possible? Why couldn't I do it? Maybe someday I would be able to.

All my life I liked to paint. I guess I could be classified as a "mood painter." I had to be in the mood to paint well. When I was, it came easy. I never took art lessons. I believe it just comes naturally. I probably inherited it from my father, who is a good artist. I exhibited some of my paintings and art exhibits and painted on several occasions for individuals. I painted a bird dog in a wheat field for a contractor who poured my patio at home. My best paintings I have given to friends who admired them. Recently here at the hospital, I was in the mood to paint again. It was nice having my room to paint in. I enjoyed the privacy and resented any intrusion when I was in the process of painting. It interrupted my train of thought. When I was painting, I never laid down the brush until I finished. It usually took me from 2 to 5 hours to complete a painting. I mostly painted ocean scenes and sailboats. I painted ships too, on occasion. Most of my oceans were stormy, as that was how I felt, stormy inside. If I felt calm I would paint the water come with the sunset. Many people would come to my room to see my paintings, the nurses, the patients, and also the hotel staff. I did a painting for Arielle. It was my favorite. It had the waves crashing on the shore and rocks nearby. There were two seagulls in the foreground.

I tried painting one for Dr. "D", a ship, but I had much difficulty. I wanted it to be right, to be perfect. Every sail, just so, every rope and line in order. It came out stiff, not natural, but it was the best I could do. Everything was in order, but I didn't like it. Arielle and I talked about the difference.

"Veronica I can't believe the same person painted these two paintings. If I did not know better, I would think they were painted by two different people with two different personalities. Why are they so different?"

"I don't know Arielle. Yours came so easy. It didn't even take long to paint, about two hours and it's my favorite. I tried much harder with Dr. "D"'s and it took me a very long time. I wanted it all to be "just right" but it doesn't look as well as the others."

"What does that tell you? Can you see any connection in that and how you feel about Dr. "D"? Now think about it for a minute," Arielle said. I thought and then answered.

With you I can talk easier. Maybe that has something to do with it. Your painting came easy. I felt freer. That's it. I feel freer with you. I can talk to you easier. For Dr. "D" it has to be right."

"Why do you say that?" she asked.

"That's just how I feel. I wanted that picture to be perfect, but it was so hard to do."

"Just like you want to be perfect for him". I was surprised until I thought about it.

"But I want to be right with him. I want my therapy to go right," I said a bit frustrated.

"Don't you know there isn't any one right way to have therapy, as far as how you are to act? You are supposed to just be yourself. If there was any time that you should be yourself, it is now with Dr. "D". You are again associating him with your father. You always wanted it to be just so, or rather right, for your father, to get his attention and approval, and when you felt like you didn't get it, you rebelled in every way you could to get his attention, but even then it was negative. To you, that was better than nothing. His spankings were better than nothing. At least you were getting his attention. Now don't you see you're doing it all over again with Dr. "D", or at least you're trying to. He's not going to let you, and you find it frustrating. It would have been better if your painting for him had been free and if you could have done it without worrying about it being right or perfect as you wanted to be. No one's right all the time or for that matter perfect. I'm not and no one expects you to be," she added

You're right Arielle I see it now. I don't want to feel this way about Dr. "D". I want to feel comfortable with him.

"Like you would like to feel with your father, but never have. Maybe someday you will. You will learn when you have a better insight to your problem in this area." Arielle said.

A knock at the door brought me back to where I was, and away from my reflection on my conversation with Arielle about the painting. It was Bonnie.

"I just wanted to see if you're ready to eat supper?" she asked. "Yes, just let me put my paints up." I was wishing I had more time

to paint as I was in the mood, but I didn't want to eat alone. I felt more comfortable with the others, even though I mostly sat and listened to them talk. Mostly Judy and Bonnie talked. Rob still quietly sat there. He seemed to enjoy being with us, but he never had anything much to say. I thought him to be strange. It wasn't that he was just shy. I've seen shyness before. Even when he didn't speak, he acted so afraid. He would never really answer any questions about himself. I found it very hard to believe that he was a practicing dentist. I knew he had to be different away from this place. We were all nice though and always included him in our dinners and walks, and sometimes sitting around talking.

A few days had passed since my experience in group when I ran from the room. I was sitting there with the others, but not in the same chair I was the day it happened. I guess I was being superstitious. I felt if I didn't sit back in the same chair, I wouldn't have another bad day. Most of us had our favorite chairs and would try to get there early so we could sit in the same chair. I sat in the same chair I the felt the most comfortable in emotionally. It depended on where they were placed in the room. The man that had been so nice to me that day always sat in the same chair. For days now he had been very quiet, where as before, when he first came to group, he had been loud and angry sounding. None of us knew why as he never talked about what was actually bothering him. I appreciated his kindness that day in taking my hand and telling me he was glad I came back, but didn't give it another thought after telling him thank you. In group therapy, I wasn't open and friendly although I wasn't unfriendly either. It just seemed in group therapy, you didn't have to be sociable.

Today, however he was not being quiet, and he was angrier than ever

"What seems to be the problem, Bill? Dr. Lee asked him.

"I think this is a bit of hogwash. I don't know why I waste my time coming here. I don't believe in it," he shouted.

"Everyone is a phony. You can't trust anyone. No one really cares about you. It's no different in here then on the outside. I've had enough of this shit," he added.

"Why do you feel that way?" Dr. Lee asked as if he was a bit surprised but acting his usual calm self.

"I just do. You can't be nice to anyone without them shitting on you. That's life."

"Do you feel anyone in here has mistreated you? If you do, let it out," said Neal.

"Yeah, I do feel that way, as a matter of fact, it happened," Bill said angrily.

"Tell us what happened." Neal said.

"Oh what's the use. I don't care. I don't like any of you. I am sick of this bullshit."

"Well, we can't help you with the problem if you don't tell us what it is." Dr. Lee told him.

"Take for example, her," he shouted, pointing at me. I was shocked. Oh here it comes, was my first impression. I talked too much the other day, and now he is disgusted with me. He didn't really mean what he said to me, I thought.

"I was nice to her. I really cared about what she was feeling, and for the first time, in a long time, I let my feelings show. That was something unusual for me. And how does she treat me since I told her what I did? Look at her. She is sitting on the other side of the room. She hasn't sat next to me since that day." He looked at me and shouted.

"What are you afraid of? That I am going to touch you again? Well, believe me you don't have to worry."

I was shocked. I hadn't expected this.

"Oh no." I said immediately. Neal raised his hand for me to be quiet. He looked at Bill and said.

"Is that what you think? That Veronica doesn't want to sit next to you because you showed your feelings the other day? Do you feel like she rejected you?"

"Well, look at her! What do you think? Bill asked.

Neal looked at me.

"Veronica what do you have to say about this." "He's wrong." I looked at Bill and said,

"Bill, you're wrong, so wrong. Why did you stay quiet all this time thinking that? Why didn't you tell me how you felt and what you were thinking? I appreciated so much what you did the other day. Maybe I should have told you more than just thank you. But I was so embarrassed. I didn't sit back in that chair because I felt like if I didn't, I wouldn't have such a bad scene again. I was being superstitious. I know its silly, but I was afraid to sit in that chair again. It had nothing to do with you. Honest."

He looked at me as if he didn't know whether or not to believe me. "Please believe me. I am telling you the truth." If you had sat anywhere else, I would have sat next to you."

He didn't say anything. I didn't know what he was thinking. I didn't know whether he believed me or not. I knew how much it must have hurt him to think I rejected him after he showed he cared what I was going through. I know what it is like to hurt like that, and he was now blaming me for hurting him. I wasn't even aware of it.

When I thought about it, I can see why he felt that way. I did change chairs right after he had held my hand and showed empathy. I felt really bad about how he took it.

How many times have I done the same thing? I asked myself.

"I just realized something." I said aloud before the group after thinking about it.

"I've done the same thing Bill has done. I must have done it many times, believing I was being rejected. Maybe I wasn't. I never told the person. If Bill didn't tell me today, we wouldn't have known what he was feeling. He would have gone on believing I rejected him, when really I didn't. Its only because he said something, I can tell him what actually happened, the reality of it. I wonder how many times I have put myself through pain, blaming someone else, when really I was to blame, when in reality they didn't mean it the way I took it. I didn't realize it until just now, seeing what Bill has done. He put himself through agony because he took something wrong. I could have been wrong about people too.

Maybe my bother-in-law didn't reject my baby years ago, as I had thought. Our children are grown adults now, but when they were babies, he was overly protective of his child. He didn't want our babies in the same playpen or even to play with the same toys. I felt like he thought his baby was better than mine or that my baby would give his child germs or something bad. It really hurt me back then and I carried those bad feelings for a very long time. It was his first child as it was my second. I wish I had said some thing a long time ago to let him know how I felt, then maybe he could have told me what he was truly thinking without me having to think the worst."

"That's just one case. There, have been many others." I said with great wonder. I felt good about the insight, but bad about all the years I had done just that, let my imagination run away from me."

Dr. Lee addressed the group.

"Veronica just realized something that is of great importance to all of us as well as to her. How many of us have done that? Felt rejected, when in reality, we never bothered to find out the real reason behind the action. We let our imaginations rule us. If you don't speak and let people know how you feel or you don't ask questions, how are we going to find out the real reason for anything?"

Bill never came back after that day. I don't know what happened to him. I felt bad that he left and sorry he had to have that experience for me to learn a great lesson about myself. I really liked him and wished he had stayed and worked out his problem. I hope he left believing me in why I didn't sit in the chair next to him.

I was having a session with Arielle and she was asking me how I felt about our role-playing the other day. My pretending she was my mother. I told her I felt silly at first and was surprised at how I talked with such passion and anger. I didn't mean to say what I did, but must have meant what I said, or why did those words come out of me?

"I believe you have had those feelings for a long time. You just have not been aware of them," Arielle stated.

I started talking about my grandmother. I told Arielle about my summer vacations as a child and how I wanted to live with her someday. I told her about Gram being in the hospital dying and how I felt. I went on about fixing her hair after she died, and not being afraid. I told myself her spirit was still alive and this was just her body that I was taking care of.

"And how do you feel now?" She wanted to know.

"What do you mean?" I said, not being sure I wanted to know. "I mean about your grandmother being gone."

I didn't want to hear it. I didn't like her saying that. It sounded so final.

"I don't think about it. I mean I know she is gone." My voice sounded like someone else's. I felt far away again. I continued.

"But I can still talk to her. She hears me. I pretend she is still alive. I didn't see her that much since she was in New York and me in South Carolina. I just pretend she is still alive." I was contradicting myself and knew it, but that's what I did sometimes.

"I don't want to think of it, Arielle. It hurts too much. She was very important to me. I love her." I felt tears coming to my eyes.

"But she is gone Veronica. You can't pretend that she is not. You won't see her again," she said gently.

I screamed.

"I don't want to hear that. Arielle, don't say that." I was feeling very panicky.

"But it's true. Your grandmother has passed."

"No." I screamed. Then the reality of it came rushing to me.

"You have to let it out Veronica. You didn't when she died. You put up a front and acted strong for everybody else, when you were really hurting inside. You didn't want to admit it to yourself, so you went home pretending she was still alive, even though you knew she was really dead. You never really accepted your grandmothers death," Arielle told me.

I was sobbing terribly and couldn't control it. The reality of it all came rushing up into my face like ice water. She was gone. I needed her and she was gone. How it hurt.

"Go ahead and feel the pain, Veronica. That's part of living. It's normal to feel hurt. You should allow yourself to feel it. In time, it won't hurt so much when you accept it. Remember the good things about your grandmother and how happy you were with her."

I looked at Arielle through my tears.

"But Arielle, she was everything to me. I didn't want to lose her," I said still sobbing.

"Death is a form of rejection, you are losing the one you love, but not in the same way you are familiar with rejection. Both kinds hurt. In this case it couldn't be helped. Death is a part of living. We have to learn how to accept it, and feel the pain," she added, kindly.

"Is this necessary?" I asked her.

"Yes, it is necessary. You can't deny yourself the pain of life. It's not normal. If you didn't feel it, it would be abnormal. For you to pretend and not face reality is unhealthy," she said.

I looked at her face trying to understand. I trusted her so. She must know what she is talking about. It is just that it is all very new to me. I didn't like to feel pain. I always took a pill when it got unbearable. She was telling me to feel it. That it is healthy to learn to cope with it. Oh, how I wished I could. I wanted to.

After talking to Arielle and facing the reality that my grandmother was really gone for good, and that I would never see her again, I felt a quiet kind of sadness, but I felt a calmness and peace I didn't understand. It had been so scary to face it. I remember the fear I had when Arielle started talking about my grandmother's death. I didn't want to hear it; now the fear was gone. I had accepted it. I knew she was gone, but I still felt I could talk to her and maybe, just maybe, her spirit could hear me. The thought that I might see her again, even if it were not on earth, comforted me, and I held on to it.

I was sitting in group listening to this young girl talk about one of the jobs she had babysitting. I looked at her rethinking how hard it was to believe she was as young as she was. She looked and seemed much older than 22 years old. She said she started drinking when she was 11 or 12. She was an alcoholic. I didn't know that alcohol could make one age so much. She seemed awfully hard. But I liked her. She had a rough life and came up the hard way. Her father was an alcoholic too. Something she said, I don't know for sure what, touched on me for I was feeling very sad, and was fighting back from crying. I didn't want anyone to notice, as I had kept pretty quiet since I had those two emotional sessions in group. I wanted the attention off of me and focused on somebody else. I was beginning to feel like I did with Dr. "D" that day, when he gave me sodium amythol. Something was building up in me and I did not understand it. Why did I have tears in my eyes? It was getting larger and larger. I looked around the room to see if anyone was noticing my panic, as I didn't want them to. No one was paying me attention but Neal. I caught his eye. Did he see the panic in me? I hoped not. I didn't want him on me again. Damn I want to stop, but no, it was still there getting greater and greater. I couldn't ignore it.

"Does anyone have anything they want to say?" Neal asked the group.

Damn, he did notice. Well I'll just stop. I tried to. I tried to think of other things, but it wouldn't go away. By now tears are running down my cheeks, and I couldn't stop them. What's happening to me? I thought. I couldn't control myself. Why I am I crying? By now I started quietly sobbing. I put my head into my hands. I couldn't look at anybody. Suddenly they all seemed far away. I heard Dr. Lee's voice ask me what I was remembering? I didn't answer. I wasn't remembering anything. I didn't know why I was crying.

"Something Ann said that bothered you?" Darleen asked.

How I wish it were that simple. I didn't know what she said that bothered me, nothing as far as I knew. Then why was I crying? I seemed so far away from them.

"How old do you feel?" asked Ellie, the new young psychologist.

I heard my voice answer.

"Eight years old." Why did I say that?

"What are you feeling?" she added.

I knew I felt frustrated. I was crying harder now.

"I can't watch them. I can't I'm scared." I cried in the child's voice. "Who can't you watch? Why are you scared?" Ellie asked. Why does her voice seem far away?

"My brother and sisters, I said. I'll get a spanking. I can't watch them." I heard myself saying. I spoke in a childlike voice. All of a sudden I realized where I was. I was in group therapy. The reality of it hit me hard. What have I done? Again I did it. I started crying harder. I curled up in the big chair I was sitting in and buried my face in my arms. I kept saying,

I'm sorry. I'm sorry. I'm sorry. I felt so ashamed. God how could I act like that?

"Veronica, Veronica." I heard my name being said. Veronica look at me."

It's Dad. It's Dad's voice. It sounded far away again.

"Veronica, look in the group." No, it's not Dad. It's Neal, I told to myself. It sounded just like Dad, I thought.

"Veronica, look up." Neal said again.

"I can't. I can't. I'm so ashamed. I'm sorry." I cried.

"Veronica", Neal said firmer. "You have nothing to be ashamed of and nothing to be sorry for." I liked the sound of his voice. Suddenly

I trusted him. I looked up at Neal's face. It made everything seem more real, Neal, the people in the room, and where I was. I slowly and carefully looked at the faces of everyone in the room. I was afraid I'd see disgust on them. I was surprised to see kind faces. Faces that smiled at me or looked concerned. They care, I thought. A couple of women were crying. They still like me. Why did I think they wouldn't? I finally looked back at Neal.

"What happened?" I asked him.

"Something Ann said touched on your subconscious. You must have been feeling that way when you were eight years old and watching your brother and sisters. It finally came to the surface, the feelings you were suppressing all these years could be a part of what's causing those headaches," Neal said with a faint smile.

"Let's talk about what happened when you were eight years old."
"I had forgotten about it, but now I remember. Mom and Dad used to go out a lot. Sometimes we had a sitter, sometimes we didn't. I used to watch my younger brother and sisters. I was the oldest and was responsible. I had to set a good example. Dad often told me if they did something wrong like tear up the house, I would be scolded. I didn't want to make them mad at me. I didn't know if was that bad. I mean, I don't remember feeling like that, like the things that I said a little while ago, but I must've felt that way, or why would that have happened? I didn't mean for it to. I couldn't help it." I explained.

"That happens sometimes, Dr. Lee said. That's one way group therapy works." Someone can be talking about something and they can consciously or unconsciously remind us of something in the past and it can trigger our memory, as what happened to you Veronica. And In this case you did not remember it; it was subconscious. You didn't or felt like you couldn't let out your feelings then, but it did come out today."

Dr. Lee then explained to all of us that we have feelings and emotions even as a baby. He said,

"If that's hard to believe just watch a little puppy. Have you ever noticed how a dog acts if it is kicked or scolded? They cower, and if they are punished enough they become afraid of people. It takes time for them to regain trust in a person again. We as people, have our emotions even as small children, even before we can talk. We cried when we were hungry or uncomfortable, that's a baby's way of saying, I want attention. We are taught as adults, to behave as adults. It's sad that sometimes we are taught too early, when we still want to be children. Really all of us still have a bit of a child in us. I know I do. That's the fun part, but mostly we behave as adults who still have childlike feelings inside of us. If we have kept hurt feelings from the time we were children and they have not been resolved, they we will continue to affect our everyday lives, until we let them out and try to understand them. A lot times, if they are subconscious, they will affect us in the physical way, such as headaches, chest pains, and in many other ways. That's why it is important we learn to express ourselves at an early age one way or another."

"Well our time is up for today. I'll see you all again tomorrow," Dr. Lee said with a smile.

Chapter 21

THE SHARK IS GONE

I WALKED UP TO Neal after Dr. Lee turned to leave and said to him, "Neal, thank you for helping me out today. I appreciate your understanding. I don't think of you as a shark anymore."

Well that's nice to hear. I think I'm many things, but not a shark," he said lightly.

"I feel differently now towards you. I don't believe you were trying to hurt me anymore. I'm not afraid of you like I was before," I added.

"That's good to hear too," he said grinning.

I was beginning to get nervous, not knowing why, and quickly said goodbye.

I walked away feeling like I wanted to do something for him. I wanted to show my appreciation somehow. He understands how I feel, I told myself. That meant so much to me. I know. I'll paint him a picture. I think he would like that. I walked faster and towards the hotel. I was excited about starting the painting for Neal. I wanted to surprise him.

On the way back to the hotel, I welcomed the walk, taking my time because I wanted to think about what Dr. Lee had to say about how we feel as children, but sometimes we are too young to express how we felt. I found it also interesting, but yet to hard to believe what had taken place in-group that day, the way in which my feelings came out from the time I was eight years old. I really didn't remember feeling that way, until the very moment it came to me while I was in group therapy.

I thought about the little puppy feeling rejected. I remember always feeling sorry for the puppy left alone by the others, while looking at a litter, throughout the years. I realize now that I have been relating to that puppy or kitten. I'm sure my father and mother didn't mean to push me aside, and they may not have, but I felt that way. I had always felt like I was in the way as long as I can remember. I really don't know why I felt that way.

I thought of my youngest son Roy. I remembered once we were in the grocery store and passing by the baby food section.

I said to him, "That's what I used to feed you when you were a baby." He was then 10 years old.

"I know, he said. I remember." I laughed and said, "How can you remember? You were just a small baby."

I tussled his hair as he looked up at me seriously and said "I do remember Mommy. You fed me too fast."

I was startled as I remembered feeding him quickly because he always ate fast. Wanting to know what he would say next I asked casually,

"Well, why didn't you tell me," knowing full well the reason why he couldn't.

He said a bit frustrated.

"I couldn't talk. I was a baby."

I knew he was telling the truth and was stunned that he remembered. I remember thinking it must be frustrating for babies to express their feelings. I was to remember this conversation for the rest of my life.

Moving down the hall in the hotel I walked up behind Dr. "D" and Arielle. They did not see me and were laughing like two children. I stopped walking as I didn't want them to see me, and I wanted to watch them like this. This side of Dr. "D" was new to me. They were waiting for the elevator and had punched both buttons to two different elevators. Both elevators were coming down at the same time and both doors opened at the same time. They were both giggling and Dr. "D" said to Arielle,

"I'll race you to the top."

They both jumped into two different elevators and the doors closed. I could still hear their laughter. The incident reminded me of what Dr.

Lee had said in group therapy, about all of us having some child in us. I had just witnessed the child in Dr. "D", and it seemed to make him more human to me, not like such a god as I had always considered him. I liked seeing him act this way although I knew this was a personal side of him that I was not to know.

I got to my room. I started painting. I decided to paint Neal a sailboat, with just small waves of water. That night, the painting came easy. I was careful not to make the mistake I did with Dr. "D"'s painting. If it doesn't turn out like I like it, I'll just do another one, I told myself, so I wasn't worried about how it was going to look.

Surprisingly, the painting started to take shape as I wanted to. I felt very happy and excited as I painted. I couldn't wait to give it to him. I finished it after about three hours and decided to wait until the next day to apply the whitecaps to the waves. The paint would be good and dry then. I painted with acrylic. I didn't have the patience to wait for an oil painting to dry. I often wished I wasn't so impatient. I was impulsive and when I was excited about something, I had to get to it right away. Many times my impatience worked against me and I knew it.

Maybe someday I'll learn to be more patient, but for now, I want to get this painting to Neal, I said to myself. My giving the painting to him seemed very important to me.

The next day in group, I felt good as I went in and sat down. I had a secret, which included Neal. I was doing a painting for him, and no one knew it. I'll give it to him tomorrow I thought as I sat down and waited for him to come in. I looked forward to seeing him and I took extra time in getting ready. I wanted to look pretty and hoped that he would think so. I had thought of him most of the night. Gee, how my feelings have changed, I said to myself.

A new girl walked into the room. She was very pretty with long brown hair and a good suntan. She introduced herself as Susan said that she was from Florida. Darn, why did she have to come? Things were just starting to look good for me with Neal, I thought. I don't know what I was expecting from Neal. What I do know was that I wanted his attention, and now I felt like I wouldn't get it as much with this new pretty girl in the group. Neal was talking to her, asking her questions about herself. I actually felt jealous. I couldn't believe it. I was jealous of her. It was a very uncomfortable feeling that I didn't like.

Now, I'll have to finish that painting for sure, I told myself. After group, she tried to be nice to me and invited me to her room. I made up some excuse why I couldn't go, saying I had to get back to the hotel. I didn't want to be friendly, although I tried not to hurt her feelings. I didn't want to like her. I was afraid of losing Neal's attention. I knew it was wrong to feel this way, but it just seemed I couldn't help myself, and I hated the sick way I felt when Neal looked at her in group therapy. I would catch him staring at her. I didn't like it, and felt so helpless about what to do. I really couldn't do anything, but give him that painting and hoped he'd like it. I wanted him to like me so much. I wasn't unaware of how much I had grown to like him over the past two weeks, until Susan came. I was surprised that I had these jealous feelings.

I finished the painting that night, and was very proud of the way it turned out. I was eager to give it to Neal. I was wishing it were morning already. I used to always tell my children when they didn't want to go to bed, that if they would go to sleep, it would be morning quicker. I went to bed waiting for sleep to overcome me, as I thought of tomorrow.

It was morning. I felt happy and excited as I showered and then dressed. I carefully applied my makeup and fixed my hair, hoping Neal would notice. Suddenly, the days seemed to take new meaning. I hurriedly went to the nurses' station to get my meds, then upstairs to the restaurant carrying a bag with the painting in it.

I had a session with Arielle that morning. I told her about the painting and how I felt so differently about Neal. She seemed very interested and questioned me further about my feelings.

"I didn't like him at first, remember? I almost hated him," I told her. "Yes I do remember very well. You had some very negative feelings against him." she said shaking her head yes, smiling a bit and adding,

"What's happened to change your mind about him?"

"Arielle, I was all wrong about him. He really cares about my feelings. Yesterday, I was really upset, and he understood. He helped me to understand." I said excitedly.

"Yes, but that's his job. He's trained to understand." She reminded me. I didn't like hearing and that.

"Yes, I know". I felt my face frowning.

"I know I shouldn't care like I do. I don't want to. I was jealous of the new girl from Florida, and I didn't like that feeling. I'm not used to being jealous. I even felt some jealousy when I saw you the other day with a different patient, laughing." I was surprised that I added this.

Arielle looked surprised when I said, "You did?" Her eyes were wide.

"What did you think when you saw me with her?"

"I felt like you were friendly with all your patients, and you are to all your patients like you are to me. That I shouldn't feel like you like me especially, just because you act interested in me. Then I told myself quickly, I was wrong for feeling that way. Of course you have other patients. I guess I just wanted to feel special again," I said with a smile.

"Well, at least now you are recognizing your own feelings and thinking about them. That's good," Arielle said smiling, and then more seriously,

"Now, back to Neal."

Suddenly I felt foolish and didn't want to talk about him anymore, but she wouldn't leave it alone.

"What are you going to do about your feelings?" Arielle asked. "I don't know Arielle. It's not funny. It's serious how I'm feeling." "How are you feeling?" she asked.

"Frustrated. I feel frustrated," I said as I started to cry. "I don't know what to do." Not yet. I have to think about it. What can I do?" I asked, looking at her, waiting for an answer, like she could make everything all right.

"I think you should talk to the group about how you are feeling. I'm sure you're not the first person who has ever felt this way towards the doctor," Arielle suggested.

"No, I could never do that. I would be so embarrassed. How can you say that? Tell him in front of the whole group? In front of everybody?" I said very quickly, feeling extremely nervous.

"Arielle, promise me you won't tell anybody. Not even Dr. "D"." I pleaded.

"That's for you take care of. I still think it would be good for you to talk about how you feel in group," she said very seriously.

"It could make you feel better if you understood it."

"No, I'll take care of it, I don't want to talk about it anymore today Arielle, please."

"Okay. We'll leave it alone for now, but you're going to have to deal with it sooner or later."

I felt relieved as I walked away from her office. I got my mind off of the seriousness of it by thinking of giving the painting to Neal.

Anxiously waiting for him to enter the room, I could feel myself get all warm inside when I saw his face. He is so good-looking I thought. I was daydreaming about what it would be like to kiss him. What is he like away from here, I thought. I daydreamed about us being on a date. I tried not to look at him for fear I would catch his eye. I did a few times and felt embarrassed. I knew it was safe to look at him when he was talking to Susan. I kept wondering what he was thinking when he looked at her. I was miserable every time she had his attention. I knew I was being foolish and told myself so but it didn't stop me from feeling that way. Damn, what am I going to do? I was glad when 3 o'clock came. It was all over with. I didn't even pay attention today, as far as what went on in discussion. All I had on my mind was Neal and wanting the session to be over with. I waited for everyone to leave. I caught him as he started to turn to leave.

"Neal, I did something for you." He looked surprised as I brought the painting out from behind the couch. It was still in the bag. I didn't want the others to see it.

"It's to show my appreciation for you helping me, when I was having a bad time in here." I took the painting out.

"I did this especially for you. I hope you like it." I said quickly looking at his face for response. He looked surprised and smiled really big.

"Thank you. You did this for me? You painted this? It's really good. I'll put it right in my office now. Thank you Veronica."

He likes it, I thought. I can tell he likes it. I felt pleased and suddenly embarrassed. There was nothing else to say.

"I'm glad you like it. I was hoping you would. I'll see you tomorrow.

I said hurriedly as we walked out the door.

I couldn't keep a smile from my face as I walked down the hall. I didn't even try to catch the others who had started back. I wanted to walk alone and think about our brief conversation. I went over every word that was said, holding onto them, not wanting to forget anything he said. Damn. Why did this have to happen? I was better off not liking him. How can I be so happy one moment and then miserable and frustrated the next? Arielle said to talk about how I felt about Neal in group therapy to understand, but I could never do that. I couldn't let everybody know how I feel. They would laugh at me. Why did she say that, I wondered.

A few days had passed and as I was walking out of group one day I caught up with Neal.

"Neal have you hung your painting yet?" I asked. I am imagined it hanging on the wall in his office. I was terribly disappointed when he said.

"No I sure haven't. I just haven't had the time to go get a frame. I've been so busy recently."

"I'm not busy Neal. I have all this free time when I'm not seeing Dr. "D", Arielle or in group. I can go to the store and get you one. I'll be glad to. I want to"

"Okay if you really want to. Thank you." He went into his office and brought it back to the hall where I was waiting and handed it to me. I waited for him to give me the money for the frame but he did not. All he said was,

"I appreciate it." No mention of the money. I looked at him waiting, but all he said then was

"See you Monday." And left with a wave.

Oh no I thought. What am I going to do? I have no money and I have to get the frame. Then I realized today was Friday and I won't see him until Monday. I would get some money from my husband before Monday as I always saw him on the weekends, but all I could think about was, I have to get the frame today and get it back to Neal. I don't know why I was thinking like that, why it was so important, but I felt compelled to get that frame and get it back to him before 5 PM. He had to have it today. I just had two hours left. I hurried out of the building, feeling my heart beating very fast. I felt panicky. I felt like something else had taken over my body propelling me to go on. Get that frame. Get that frame was all I could think. I have just two hours to get it. I borrowed someone's car and drove to the shopping center, which wasn't far away. I knew what I was going to do. I was going to go into a store and get a frame. I didn't have any money, but that was not going to stop me. Nothing will stop me the way I felt. I had no fear. I imagined myself walking into the store, picking up the frame and walking out the door with it. I have to take my painting inside with me so I'll be sure to get the correct size I thought. I have never done this before and never thought how to do it. Normally, I would never have had the nerve to do it and I always considered myself honest. Even when I worked in the cosmetics store alone, I never even took a $.25 brush. Now I had no hesitation of taking something without paying for it. I didn't even try to figure it out. All I knew was I had to have that frame and get it back before 5 o'clock. I pulled the car in front of the store, got out and walked into the department store with my painting. I went to where the frames were on display. I kept looking straight at all the frames, until I found one I liked and that fit the painting. For some reason, I picked a very inexpensive one, even though I was not paying for it. Maybe somewhere unknown to me at the time, I would not think it is serious, my stealing, if it weren't expensive. I don't know. I picked up the frame and held it beside my painting and without looking around, I just walked right past the line waiting to be checked out and passed a woman at the cash register. As I walked out the door I thought I couldn't believe I'm doing this. I can't believe this is me. As I was walking across the parking lot to the car, I kept waiting for a voice to shout.

"Stop!" The walk seemed forever. I tried to walk normally and not run, although I felt like it. Suddenly I was very scared. My legs felt weak and I was trembling. As I fumbled for the keys, I noticed my hands were wet. So, I was nervous about this. God, I was scared. I drove away still trembling. No one saw me. It was so easy. I just picked it up and walked out. No one paid any attention to me. I was lucky, I told myself. It was after 4 o'clock. I didn't have much time. I couldn't park the car in the parking lot at the hospital because I didn't have any money for parking. I didn't even have any change. What a time for me to be broke. I'll have to park down the road at the park. It doesn't cost to park there; I'll just have to walk to the hospital. I have to hurry I told myself still very nervous. I got to the park and parked the car. I had to take the glass out of the frame. The staples were holding it in. I can't leave the glass there, I told myself as I slipped the backing off. I wasn't thinking straight. My hands couldn't stop shaking. I was trying to get the glass out without removing or bending the staples that held it in. I was hurrying so, trying to beat the clock. The glass broke as I tried to pry it out. I noticed people looking at me, as they got in their cars. I was standing in front of the car working on the hood.

I'll have to slow down. People must wonder why I am acting like this. I must look strange, standing here in the parking lot, frantically trying to remove glass from picture frame. I cut my hands taking the glass out, but didn't feel any pain. It was just another inconvenience to me that took more time to cleanup, so I wouldn't mess up the painting.

"Think Veronica, slow down I told myself firmly." "You're not thinking straight." I finally got the glass out of my painting in the frame. It took a while to bend all the staples with what was left of my fingernails.

"There, it looks nice. Now I have to get it to Neal." I told myself. I hurriedly locked the car doors and walked down across the street to the hospital. It seemed I had to wait for the traffic for such a long time so I could cross the street.

"Why do some people have to drive so slowly?" I said impatiently. The elevator seemed to take forever. It was 4:55. I practically ran down the hall to Neal's office. His door was closed and locked. It was dark inside. No, I thought he's got to be in there, I went through such trouble. I hurried to be here before five. I thought he would be there. I ran into his secretary's office, she was still there, typing. She looked up as I entered the room.

"Where's Neal?" I asked almost shouting. She looked at me surprised.

"He left early today. He won't be back until Monday." Dr. Lee is still here. Do you want to see him?" she asked. Suddenly I felt like I'd been hit in the stomach, and all of the air was out of me. I felt very tired. The rush was over. The storm had passed.

"No, no it's not important," I responded quietly.

I walked back towards the park feeling so strange. Why was it so important to get it to him today? I could have given it to him Monday, I asked myself. Why didn't he give me the money? I felt a little mad. I went through all this trouble today.

"He didn't know what you were going to do." An inner voice seemed to say. But he could've given me the money. Did he do it on purpose? Why would he? I thought about it and felt miserable. Friday night though, I was given some money. I wrote a short note to the manager of the store where I had taken the frame explaining that I had stolen it and that I was sorry. Along with a note, I enclosed the money to pay for the frame. I had called the store earlier to find out the managers' name. I felt better about paying for it, but confused as to why I had to have the frame that day. Why couldn't I have waited until I had some money to pay for it? Why was it is so important? Why did I feel that strong urgency? So many questions went through my mind that weekend. My husband came to see me, but I couldn't bring myself to tell him or anyone for that matter. I was too ashamed. I only knew for sure that nothing would have stopped me that day from taking it. I couldn't wait to talk to Arielle about it. She was the only one I trusted. I was beginning to realize more and more that I really did have a problem by the things I was experiencing here at the hospital. I guess I became more aware of my feelings and actions. I paid closer attention to them. And I knew for sure that it wasn't normal to go around lifting things from stores, even with having such a strong impulse. Just by having that urgent feeling told me something was wrong. I knew it wasn't normal.

Finally Monday arrived. I hurried to dress, eat and get over to the hospital, hoping that I wouldn't have to wait too long to see Arielle. Today I wasn't going to see Dr. "D". Somehow, it seemed easier telling Arielle. Really I wanted to talk about it. I wanted to understand it. It was finally my turn to see her. I had hardly sat down when I said,

"Arielle, I did a terrible thing. I couldn't help it. Nothing could have stopped me, and I don't know why I did it."

"Will you please tell me what you did?" she asked a bit frustrated by my opening sentence. I told her what happened and how I felt.

"Now do you understand why I felt you should have talked about your feelings in group or at least to Neal? I was afraid you might do something foolish but I didn't think you would do anything like that." She said with her eyes widening.

"Does Dr. "D" have to know? I sent the money to the manager at the store. I paid for it. It's been taking care of.

"Yes, I have to discuss it with Dr "D". We don't want something like this to happen again," she said.

"But Arielle, I would never do anything like that again. I was so scared walking back to the car." I said.

"You had good reason to be scared. Do you realize what they could have done with you if they caught you? It wouldn't have been very pleasant." All I can say is you're a very lucky lady they didn't," she said.

"Arielle I know it was wrong, but honestly I couldn't help it. I don't know what happened to me. I felt obsessed to get that frame."

"It's a good thing that you are here so we can work on what happened and understand it, so it won't ever happen again. After I talk to Dr. "D" tonight we will talk more about it tomorrow. Now we need to talk about your going home for the weekend. How do you feel about that?" What she said caught my breath.

"Oh Arielle do I have to"? What she was saying scared me. Arielle said very firmly,

"Well you're going to have to go sooner or later you know. It's part of your real life and here you're somewhat protected. You don't take

care of your problems here, you learn what the problems are, and how to take care of them." She kindly reminded me with a smile.

"I don't want to but I know I have to. I just hate the thought of having to start pretending all over again." I told her.

"Don't," she said matter of matter-of-factly. That's one of the things you did wrong. Don't pretend. Act as you feel," she said.

"Oh Arielle I can't." Ronald always acts so hurt and pitiful. I can't stand it. It has always seemed easier to let him think everything is all right.

"Do you want to go on pretending for the rest of your life?" she asked.

"No." was my reply. I don't. I don't love him, but I feel so guilty for not loving him. He's good to me in a lot of ways." My reply sounded weak even to me.

"What I mean is, he's as good to me as he knows how. It's just once in a while things get really bad. Especially if I let him know I'm unhappy and want a divorce. The argument starts, then I want to leave, and then we have a really big fight. I don't know what to do. It scares me how he might act if I really left him for good. I don't think he believes that I will. I have gone back to him twice when I did leave, but then I only did it because I felt sorry for him. I worry now how the boys will take it too. They are older now. How are wish I had stayed gone before when we were separated. They were small then. It didn't really matter to them. I have to think of them too."

I realized I was just rambling on, trying to convince Arielle why I couldn't show my honest feelings. I could see I wasn't convincing her. She just shook her head and said,

"It is just not good what you have been doing. You see where it has gotten you so far. Do you wish to continue this way," she asked softly.

"No." was all I could say. Then my time was up.

"Think about it Veronica. I'll see you again tomorrow and we'll discuss what happened Friday," she said as she walked me to the door.

I went out on the terrace to think about our session. They seemed to be getting more serious and complicated. Arielle gave me so much more to think about. I tried to imagine going home for the weekend. The thought scared me, but I knew I had to go. Okay, I'll try another approach with Ronald. Maybe I can get him to understand why we can't keep going on like we have been, I told myself.

I looked at my watch. I have 30 minutes before it was time for group therapy to start. I was anxious to give Neal the painting, now that it was framed. And for some reason, I wanted to get rid of it, as though giving it to him, and my not having it, would erase what I had been through to get the frame. I walked down the hall to Neal's office. Hopefully they would be preparing for group. How I wish I had originally waited until today to give the painting. It would have been so much better. I walked towards his office feeling very nervous. I slowly looked around the corner into his office. He was sitting behind his desk smoking a pipe and looking at some papers that were laid before him.

"Neal," I said very quietly. He looked up surprised as though he was deep thought. I felt a bit uncomfortable, feeling like an intruder. I quickly said,

"I've got your painting for you. It's framed."

He got up and came around the desk holding out his arm to take it saying.

"I hope it wasn't too much trouble."

"No not at all," I said lightly, thinking about all I had been through and a bit angry with him for not giving me the money. I suddenly wanted to get out of there, I was so nervous. Neal seemed very pleased. Smiling, he said, "Thank you very much. I'll hang it today right over my couch."

"You're welcome." I quickly turned around and left.

I went into group and waited until it was time for the others. I was hoping Neal wouldn't come in early. I really felt uncomfortable now, and I didn't understand it. I was relieved when the others started coming into the room. Neal came in last, after Dr. Lee. I couldn't look at him.

In group therapy, we were listening to Bonnie talk. It had been six weeks and Bonnie was still talking about the same thing, rejecting any help or advice from anyone. Most of the others had little to do with Bonnie, as they were tired of hearing her problem. It was the only thing she would talk about and she wasn't really trying in any way to change her situation. I was about the only one who was company to her, and even my patience was wearing thin. I have always been a sensitive person when it came to hurting someone else's feelings, to the point that I would hurt myself. This was one of my greatest faults. However, on this day, Bonnie was getting to me. She was talking, as she usually did, that her situation was hopeless and she wasn't willing to listen to anyone. Without meaning to, I just came out with "Bonnie, I believe." and stopped. There, was irritation in my voice to the point it surprised me.

It wasn't like me to come out with something like that. Neal jumped on it right away.

"Go on Veronica, finish what you were going to say," he urged. "No I can't. I'm sorry I interrupted."

"No it's all right. Go ahead and say it," he told me, as if he knew what I was going to say.

"I don't want to hurt her feelings," I said to him. Bonnie looked hurt already. She kept looking at me with those big eyes of hers.

"I like Bonnie, but she's getting to me. I'm sorry she isn't happy, and I wish I could help her, but I can't," I said.

"What is it you want to say to her? Say it. Tell Bonnie how you feel."

"Bonnie sometimes I feel like you just like it here, that you don't want to get better." There, I said it.

She looked very hurt and tears came to her eyes.

"How do you feel about what Veronica had to say to you?" Neal asked her.

"I'm very hurt. I thought she was my friend." Bonny said.

"Bonnie I am. I'll be the only one that will tell you. I don't want to hurt you. I like you, but you're getting to me. It's depressing what you talk about. We all have problems, but we are working on them. You don't seem to be, and it's all you will talk about. You get mad at everyone that tries to help you," I told her.

I don't know where my courage came from, as I have never told anyone anything deliberately to hurt them.

"Does anyone else feel this way toward Bonnie?" Dr. Lee asked the group.

Several said yes, that they felt the same way but didn't want to tell her. They just tried to avoid her. Bonnie was really hurt and started crying. We all felt bad about it but Dr. Lee said it was necessary for Bonnie to know how others around her felt about her and what she was doing, that she would not know how we felt unless we told her. The same applied to other individuals in our lives. If we didn't like something we had to tell them.

After group I tried to catch up with Bonnie to tell her I was sorry I hurt her, but that was how I felt, and I still wanted to be friends. She didn't say much. We walked together back to the hotel but she was distant. I had hoped she would understand, but she was not ready to. I spoke to Arielle about it the next day. She told me it was okay for me to say what I did. It would not be a problem for me unless I made it a problem. Now it was Bonnie's problem. It was up to Bonnie to handle it and whether or not she wanted to continue our friendship. Arielle said that it was good for me to get something off my chest that was bothering me and that I should try doing it more often. It wouldn't always solve the problem by my doing so, but at least it was a step in the right direction.

"Enough of that now. Let's talk about something else that's really important," Arielle said to me, putting the emphasis on the 'really.' I knew what she was getting to.

"You told him?" I said taking in a breath. I was not anxious all of a sudden to hear what Dr. "D" said. A part of me was still afraid he would give up on me.

"Yes." she answered. Then she said more slowly,

"Dr. "D" said what was really important about the whole incident, was that you realized what you did was wrong and you did later send the money to pay for it." Then she added,

"But that doesn't excuse what you did. You are very lucky you didn't get caught." This time she put the emphasis on the word 'very.'

"Arielle why did I do it?" I asked.

"Dr. "D" said it was important to you to have Neal's approval," she said.

"Neal's approval?" I exclaimed.

"Why would I go through all that just for his approval?" I couldn't believe it.

"Whether you realize it or not you made him a very important figure in your life right now, just like you made Dr. "D" and your father. Remember you said Neal sounded like your father at one time during group. And also to add to it, there is the way you feel about him, since you found out that he understands how you feel.

"That's very important to you. A woman wants to feel that some man understands her. You wanted to do something for him, but really it's for yourself. You wanted your painting on his office wall. That way he would be reminded of you, and he wouldn't forget you. You didn't want to wait for him to get the frame, for fear that he wouldn't. So you made sure it was taken care of, so he would hang the painting in his office. Right?"

"Yes you're right." I knew it was all true, as she put it into words. "You are going to have to solve this problem now Veronica. You are going to have to talk to Neal about it." Arielle said firmly. I knew she was right. I couldn't go on feeling so uncomfortable around him.

"Did you give him the painting yesterday?" she asked. "Yes," He said thank you. He said he would hang it then." "That must have pleased you." she said.

"Yes." I said smiling and satisfied, but feeling a bit ashamed.

"Did you ask him for the money for the frame? Did you ask him why he didn't give it to you in the first place?" she inquired.

I looked down at the floor ashamed because I hadn't had the nerve to ask him.

"No, I didn't. I'll ask him when I talk to him." I said.

"Good, I'm glad you decided to talk to him, the sooner the better. Now that you're ready to go home for a weekend, we think it is a good idea for you to go home this coming weekend," she told me.

"Alright I'll plan on it," I said adding," but I don't want to."

I walked away from that session feeling like I had so many things to think about. I can't handle Neal this week. I'll do it next week after I spend the weekend at home. That's enough to concentrate on for now I decided. I knew Arielle was right, and I wasn't going to change my mind about talking to him. I just couldn't do it now. It's too soon I told myself, promising that I would for sure next week. I felt satisfied that I had made a definite decision about it. Wondering if I felt relieved because I was postponing it.

I called my husband to tell him that I was coming home for the weekend. He was very pleased to hear that and said he would be there Friday to pick me up. Rob, the dentist, was to go home Friday and we thought we would have a little going away party at dinner in the restaurant Friday evening. I asked my husband to join us, as he would be there, about that time. We all talked about it after group that day and told Rob we would meet him at 5 o'clock in the restaurant. He said okay and we all went our separate ways to our rooms. My husband and I were in my room talking, when Judy called me on the phone from the restaurant and asked if I had seen Rob? I told her no, but he had asked me to call him at five before going to the restaurant. He said he was going to take a nap and wanted me to call and wake him up. I thought it was unusual, as he had never asked me to do that before. It was about 5 o'clock now and I told Judy I would call him. She told me she was worried so they went to ask the waiters from the restaurant. She was told that Rob had purchased five bottles of wine about two hours earlier that would have been right after group. I was surprised. and it was dangerous to drink with the medication Rob was on. Maybe two glasses of wine we were told would be all right, but not five bottles. Why would he purchase so much? He was to go home in the morning and he should have been happy. I told my husband what Judy had said and tried to call Rob, but there was no answer. Why would he ask me to call him, and then not be there? It didn't make sense. I kept trying to call. My fears increased. I looked at Ronald.

"We have to tell the nurse. I'm afraid something is wrong." We went to the nurse's station and told her. Immediately she went down the hall to Rob's room. She used her key to unlock the door.

"I need help," she told my husband as she walked into the room. "Stay with him while I call Dr. "D" Veronica stay outside." "He's not dressed," Ronald told me.

"Come with me," the nurse said to me.

"You'll need to tell Dr. "D" what you know."

She called Dr. "D". After she talked a few seconds she said to me, "Dr. "D" wants to talk to you. Tell him exactly what you heard."

I told him what Judy told me over the phone. He said for my husband and I to come over to the hospital in our car to the emergency room and that there would be someone there. He was calling over right away to notify them. I walked hurriedly back to the room with the nurse. I stood outside as a nurse and my husband dressed Rob and brought him around. As my husband came outside he said to me,

"There is a love note to you from Rob beside his bed." "What?" I said and in shock.

"Are you sure it was to me?" I couldn't believe it. Why would he write me a love note?

"He drank all the wine. All the bottles are empty," he added. He drank five bottles of wine. Why? And a love note to me? All these questions raced through my head as we helped Rob to the front door. The nurse went back upstairs after we reached the front door and she saw that we couldn't handle Rob by ourselves. He was so drunk and he was crying.

"Wait here with him while I get the car." my husband told me.

Rob started talking in a whimpering voice between sobs.

"I love you. I love you so much. Please don't leave me. I don't want to go home." He was hanging on me pleading.

I couldn't believe it. How could this happen? I was no more friendly to Rob then anyone else. I didn't encourage him anyway. I felt sorry for him and was friendly, the same as everyone else but that was all. I had no indication he felt this way.

"Please, please don't leave me." He kept saying over and over. I'm tried to quiet him by telling him it was going to be all right, that they were going to help him at the hospital.

"No don't leave me. I love you. Please don't leave me," he pleaded. We got him in the back seat of the car and he kept crying the whole time on the way over to the emergency room.

When we got him out of the car and stepped into the corridor of the hospital, he was holding my arm, begging me not to leave him. It took three attendants to pull him away. He was so pitiful. What happened to him? Rob seemed just fine before this happened. He was his usual patient self. I had felt that he didn't gain much by being at the hospital. I really didn't know, as I was just going by what progress I had seen while I was there with him. He never did talk to anyone in group. I don't think he was very cooperative. None of us ever had any indication of exactly what his problems were.

Ronald and I went back to the hotel to meet with the others as they're waiting for us to join them for dinner. I explain to them what happened. I didn't mention what Rob had said, as I didn't understand it. I never did see that love letter my husband told me about. The following Monday Dr. "D" seemed a bit angry about what had happened. He wasn't angry with me, as he told me not to worry about it that I wasn't responsible. Rob was still sent home the next day. I never did find out what happened for sure, and that was the end of it.

I had mixed feelings on the ride back home that evening. It seemed like a long time since I'd been home. I dreaded it in a way, but I was anxious to see my sons. I realized how much I had missed them. I had been so busy working on myself, I didn't think about them so much. I knew they were being taken care of and I felt relieved that I didn't have to worry about them for little while. I was always afraid of them getting hurt, or if they weren't home when it was getting dark. I wanted to always know where they were, and felt uncomfortable when I didn't see them for a long period time when they were outside playing with their friends. I loved them so much. They were very important to me. How can I ever hurt them by a divorce? They were at the age when divorce would really affect them, nine, eleven, and fifteen years of age. How the years have flown. Ronald didn't talk much about the incident that happened back at the hospital. He knew I wasn't interested in Rob other than just as an acquaintance, whom I had met there, at the hospital. Rob was there seeking help for his problems too. I didn't say much about either, as I didn't know what to say. I was still stunned by the whole incident. As we pulled into the driveway of my home, I could see that my flowers, the shrubs and trees had grown so much.

I felt that familiar knot in my stomach when I thought about going to bed that night. I was already thinking about it. No, I told myself, I'd put it out of my mind for now. I wanted to focus on the children. They came out of the house as we pulled up, the older one holding back a bit as he always did. I was happy to see them and could tell they were happy to see me. It seemed that they too had grown. We went inside the house and they were full of chatter about the recent happenings in their lives. I felt like a visitor though. It was a strange feeling being back in the house that had been home to me. I knew I was there, just for the weekend and I felt very uncomfortable. I didn't want to show it though. That night when we went to bed, I just closed my eyes and made up some fantasy when Ronald made love to me.

Over the weekend, it just confirmed my mixed feelings that I couldn't make a change, but I saw that I had to. I couldn't continue to go on the way I had the past years. I was anxious to go back to the hospital and felt guilty for wanting to, knowing I'd be leaving my children again.

As I kissed each one of them goodbye, I told them how much I loved them. All they knew was I was at the hospital because of my headaches. I had a headache the whole time I was home, but I was able to control it somewhat with a medication. I was by then, almost off of all the tranquilizers I had been taking for three years.

Chapter 22

FACING REALITY

I WAS GLAD TO get back to my room at the hotel. It was my haven. I didn't have to face being reminded of one of my major problems, my marriage. It was easier to be at the hospital than at home. I could see if I went home and didn't change anything, I would be right back where I started. I didn't want to be there. It was so very depressing and I hated having to take a pill every time I felt unhappy or panicky about my situation. I vowed I'd never get hooked on them again. I was learning what it was like to feel. It was extremely painful at the time but after it was over, I always felt more peaceful. At least I was learning how to deal with my feelings. To me that was a big step. The fear of facing or accepting a fact that is painful, I found out, was not as bad as I thought it would be. I had magnified much in my mind. The old saying, "there is nothing to fear but fear itself" is such a true saying. Right now, I fear a divorce and yet I wanted it. What I feared was what I might have to go through to accomplish it. I knew what my husband was capable of, or at least I thought I knew. What was to come was a more horrifying fear.

Upon returning back to the hospital from my weekend home, I talked about my fears to Arielle as soon as I saw her. I found my marriage very difficult to talk about. I just didn't see how I could make a change. Really I was afraid to. I felt so trapped.

"I think you should talk more about your family life in group Veronica. Perhaps the group can help you understand your feelings better. Why don't you share it with them?" Arielle asked.

"I guess I haven't shared much because I really felt embarrassed by it all. My reasons for staying in the marriage sounded so weak, even to myself," I added. "If I were on the outside and it was happening to someone else, I'd say she was stupid for staying in the situation."

Arielle smiled and said, "It's always easier to say that about someone else. But when you're involved it's a different story. You, and you alone have to make the decision about what's good for you." "When are you going to talk to Neal?" Arielle asked with a great seriousness.

"Today. I'll make myself talk to him today. I know I have to." "I'll be anxious to know how it goes."

I started to perspire already feeling the anticipation of it. Darn now my dress will be wet. It's bad enough having to talk to him without him seeing the wet spots under my arms. I would have to remember to keep my arms at my side. I went into the bathroom to freshen up and go over in my mind what I wanted to say to Neal. Should I wait until after the group? No, go now; get it over with, I told myself.

My legs felt so weak as I walked down the hall to Neal's office. I was terrified. How I dreaded it. My thoughts and feelings have always been so private and now I was going to tell him what I had been feeling and going through. I hoped he didn't think I was silly. I hoped he didn't laugh.

My chest was hurting as I approached his door. It was open. That meant he was inside. I stood outside for a moment and took a deep breath before I knocked on the door.

"Come in," he said.

I couldn't speak as I walked in. He looked a bit surprised. I hoped he was not thinking I was making a pest out of myself.

"What can I do for you Veronica?" I was surprised that I could hardly talk. My lips were sticking together. Suddenly my mouth went dry.

"Neal…..I…..have….a……problem." I was finally able to say. His smile faded and he looked serious.

"Do you want to talk about it?" he asked.

"Yes, I have to." I said unable to look at him. I was trembling and my hands were wet. I held them together in front of me as I always did, when I was nervous or scared of something.

"Sit down. Now what seems to be the problem?" I tried to speak again but hardly could.

"I can hardly talk. My mouth is so dry." I had never had such difficulty in speaking in my whole life. I was visibly shaking and couldn't stop.

"It can't be all that bad." Neal said. "Wait here. I'll get you some water."

While he was gone I seemed to calm down a little. When I drink the water it was easier to speak. I could talk a few words at a time, with each swallow. I started telling him about how I felt in the beginning about him, and how my feelings changed when he understood how I felt. He listened intently and quietly, not saying anything until I finished.

"I am trained to understand, Veronica." I looked at him. He must have known what I was thinking.

"That doesn't mean I don't care about your problem and what you are going through. I do. I'd like to see you happy and to the place that you can handle your problems without medication, and I believe you will in time." I was glad to hear him say that. He went on.

"What you are feeling is quite normal in a patient doctor relationship. Let's talk about it. I'll help you."

I was beginning to feel more at ease. I told him what I did to get the frame for my painting.

"Did you do it on purpose Neal?" I asked him.

"Do what?" He acted surprised.

"Not give me the money." Did you do it so I would say something?" He shook his head no. He was really surprised. I could tell it was genuine when he said,

"No I wouldn't do that. Look I'm sorry. You took me by surprise that day. I didn't have the money and just didn't say anything. I should have. I did offer to pay for it when you gave the painting back to me framed." You said never mind it wasn't that much. I let it go. I shouldn't have. It was my mistake not telling you in the beginning."

He had offered to pay for the frame when I returned it to him, but then I just wanted to forget the whole thing. It didn't seem important then. He had no idea I was going to take it from the store. It really was my fault. I did surprise him that day, offering to get the frame for him.

Even if he had told me he didn't have the money then, I don't think it would have made any difference. I shouldn't have been in such a hurry. I could see it very clearly now. Neal was so understanding listening to me. He helped me to talk. By the time I finished I was so grateful, but not to the point of feeling indebted as I did before. The feeling I had when I entered the room, and the way I'd been feeling about him was gone. I just liked and respected him, but with an understanding of it all. I felt good about it, and proud of myself for having talked to him about it. Arielle was so right. I did feel better. I should have done this a long time ago.

Neal shook my hand as I left and said,

"Veronica I appreciate your coming to talk to me and I appreciate how hard it was for you to do so."

"Thank you Neal and thank you for understanding and helping me to talk."

Then I laughingly said, "Look at my clothes," holding my wet dress away from my body.

"This proves how hard it was to come and talk to you." We both laughed as I turned to leave. I left feeling good that I could joke about my wet dress in addition to having talked with him. I couldn't wait to tell Arielle. I suddenly felt happy and that feeling stayed with me even when Neal came into the room for group therapy. I was surprised I was not embarrassed, as I had expected to be. I felt so different and I liked the feeling.

The next day I could see that Arielle was happy for me that I had talked to Neal and felt good about it.

"See there. It wasn't so bad was it? The world didn't come to an end, and you're still here," she said, smiling.

I was smiling back, pleased with myself.

Being at the hospital and undergoing psychotherapy opened my mind to a lot of things I couldn't see before. I didn't just think about my life and what it had been like, but my feelings. I was thinking a lot about my father and mother. I had made them both such important figures in my life. I had allowed my feelings to take over my actions. I realized that even though I was now an adult, I was acting like a child. I was listening to others in group talk about their fathers and mothers, and would think, they're still holding on, even as adults. Then I realized that I had been doing the same thing. I was talking to Arielle about my thoughts during one of our sessions.

"I'm glad you can finally see that," she said to me. "You never really cut the cord from your mother. You kept trying to get from her what you thought a mother should give. Your mother gave you all that she was capable of giving. You found out that even parents are human. We, as children, expect so much from them, but as we mature, we should let go and learn to be on our own."

I thought about what she said before I spoke.

"Yes, I see what you mean. I never really did let go. I was still trying to be a good girl, to get her approval. I have so many mixed feelings about her. I love and then I resent her. It's confusing."

"Remember what you learned a while ago? You can still love someone and yet have bad feelings towards them. You never told your mother how she hurt you. You carried hurt feelings around all these years."

"You know Arielle, I feel differently about Dad now too. I see him as a man, an individual, not a god. I love him and I respect him. I know now that he loves me."

"How do you know that?" She was smiling a little.

"He had to have loved me. I can remember many good things he did with me when I was a child. I don't know why I couldn't remember them before. All I can think of was how much I wanted him to hold me, and was hungry for attention as a child. But I'm not a child anymore and I can reason about things that I didn't understand before.

"Like what for instance?" she asked.

"Like about him showing love. Arielle, he wasn't shown love when he was a child." For a few days I stayed with Dad's mother. I couldn't stand it. I was 10 years old then. Also, my grandfather was not a loving man by nature. He might have feelings, but he didn't show them. If my father wasn't shown love as a child, how could he have shown it?

It must have been very hard for him," Arielle added.

"And he didn't know what you wanted a child."

As we talked, a greater realization came over me.

"No I never told him. In my childlike thinking, if he loved me, he would hug me." Dad supported all four of us when he and Mom broke up. No court told him he had to. It was something he wanted to do. He did it on his own. We didn't know where he was. I remember too, all the nights he played games with us when we were kids. How could I have forgotten that? All I could think of was, make him proud of me. I thought one day he would just come out and say, "Veronica I'm proud of you." I wanted that so much, but he didn't know. I never told him."

Arielle added.

"People don't know what you want from them unless you tell them." What she said made so much sense. It seems so simple, and yet I never thought of it. It was always so hard for me to talk to Dad. I always got nervous.

"I just have to learn to talk to him."

"That would be a beginning," Arielle said.

"Arielle you don't know how happy I feel realizing all this. I am starting to see things so much clearer. Thank you for listening and helping me."

"That's what I'm here." for she said and smiled. "I'm glad you're beginning to see things differently. That's a big step for you."

I was in group a few days later. Someone was talking about their life, something about change. I don't exactly remember what it was about, but it must have touched on my subconscious, for all of a sudden a thought came to my mind. A complete insight and understanding that this was My Life! I could do what I wanted with it. Without thinking I blurted out,

"Oh my gosh, I just realized something. And then I realized that I had interrupted whoever was talking. I stopped and apologized.

"No go on Veronica," Neal said smiling.

"What did you just realize?"

"This is MY life," I said putting the emphasis on the word my.

"That is something that is said all the time Veronica. Why is it today that it means something?"

I knew I was being dramatic and louder than usual, but I couldn't help it. I was so excited.

"I know. I heard it for many years. I have told it to other people. I've probably said it to others about myself. People always say something like, "it's my life, I'll do what I want to," or something like that, but it's true, and I never really realized it before. I've always done what was expected of me."

Neal interrupted. "What YOU thought was expected of you sometimes?"

"Yes," I said hurriedly, dismissing his remark I wanted to continue. "It really is my life. No one is making me do what I am doing. I am responsible for what I do."

Neal and Dr. Lee we're smiling. I realized I hit on something really important.

"What does that mean to you?" Dr. Lee asked.

"It means a lot. It means everything." I don't have to live anymore like I have been. I'm going to change it."

As I said this the reality of what that meant rushed to my face.

"Divorce". My happiness was short-lived, as I started to cry.

"Why are you crying Veronica?" I was surprised that I cried so easily. I didn't even think about it.

I knew what that meant. I knew what would happen. I would be blamed. Everyone thought that we were happy. I put up such a front. The children would be so hurt."

I cried. "What am I going to do?" I said, knowing what I was going to do.

"I have to get a divorce." I said, knowing it was true. The reality of it was extremely painful, and I felt the pain, reminding myself what Arielle had told me, it was necessary to feel pain, to ride with it, it would end. I didn't feel ashamed this time as I sobbed. The realization was overwhelming. Every thing was quiet in the room. They were letting me feel it. I was barely aware that Group was over. One of the patients came up to me. I heard Dr. Lee say that I needed to be alone. He was right. I stayed in the room for a while and just cried. I was surprised that it felt good to cry and I let it come. I felt calm when I left the room and very tired, but it was a good tired. I had made a decision and I was going to carry through. I guess I had known what I had to do for a long time, but I had never really accepted it until then. I didn't know what was ahead for me, and I was going to try not to think of it. I would just take one day at a time, I told myself.

I lay in my bed that night thinking about my whole life and what it had been like. The things I had wanted to do and never did. The opportunities I had given up by marrying so young. I remember telling my mother and her girl friend one day in the car as we were riding that Ronald and I were 'different' when they tried to tell me something about us being so young to be going steady. They said they had felt the same way when they were young and going with someone. They had kind of laughed and said, "You'll find out." I knew both of them were kind of bitter, for they both had had bad experiences in marriage and in relationships. Then I thought of all the people who tried to discourage me about marrying Ronald, saying that it would never work. My own father had told me this when I was just fifteen years old and going with him. "Veronica", he had said, "you are too young to go steady, and the boy that you are going with comes from a different background. You have nothing in common."

I had defended Ronald to him and to everyone else, saying he was different than the rest of his people. I was out to prove everyone wrong, and in doing so, I had made a mess of myself. My life appeared normal and good to everyone on the outside. Ronald had succeeded in his career and finished school and I had a good job. We had three beautiful sons, and a nicely decorated beautiful home. What could be wrong? Everything! I told myself. I just dreaded telling them so. I won't think about it now. I'll just have to take care of it. I was suddenly anxious to just get on with it. Now that I had made the decision, I wished it could be all over with. If only life were that easy. I was reminded of a saying my father had, "Good things don't come easy". I remembered asking Arielle why people stayed in bad situations if they were unhappy.

"Because they are familiar with it, change is frightening", she had told me. I had to give that a lot of thought over the years before I fully realized exactly what it meant. Now I understood it.

That night I also thought of how far I had come since coming to the hospital. I had come a long way and could see it. My whole idea of life had been wrong, but I still had much to learn and I was anxious to do so.

I had been at the hospital by then for about nine weeks when Arielle told me it was about time for me to start thinking about leaving and going home for good.

"Veronica, you have made a lot of progress, and Dr. "D" feels you are ready to leave. I'm telling you this now, so you can start thinking about it. You can plan on leaving in about a week. How you feel about it?"

When she said it, I took a deep breath. I knew the time would come when I would hear this. Really I was surprised I got to stay as long as I did. "I have mixed feelings about it, Arielle. A part of me wants to go and start putting into action some of the plans I have made, and then a part of me wants to stay here".

She smiled and said, "That's a normal reaction. You are somewhat protected here. You can make decisions, but the real test comes when you put your decisions into actions. That part is not so easy. We have some good news for you, though, if you're interested."

"What's that," I asked puzzled.

"Dr. "D" and I would like to continue seeing you. You have an interesting case, and we would like to continue to learn with you. We would help you in the process. The good part is that it won't cost you anything, as long as you are willing to continue to see us for as long as we feel it is necessary. What do you think about it?"

I was elated. "Arielle, that's wonderful. I didn't know you could do that. Of course, I am willing. I feel I have much more to learn, and the thought of never being able to talk to either one of you again is scary. You both have helped me so much. Thank you. You don't know how grateful I am".

She looked very serious as she said, "We're not just talking about a few weeks or months. It may take a great deal longer."

"How long?" I asked.

"Maybe years", she responded.

"Years?" I asked with great surprise.

"Yes. We have some people who have been in therapy for four or five years. Remember, you didn't get confused or feeling like you are in just a few weeks or months, it's been most of your lifetime. It takes some time to undo some things, and for you to change habits and patterns that you have developed all these years."

What she said made sense. I just never thought of it in that way.

She went on. "I'll continue to see you about once or twice a week. You may come as an outpatient. Also, you may attend group if you would like to. It seems you have done very well in there. You have indeed made a lot of progress. Dr. "D" will see if we think it is necessary. We would like for you to attend Group every day if possible, but realize you have a ways to travel, so if you could get there, at least twice a week, that would be good", she said.

"Yes, I will. Thank you both so much," I said to her smiling. Now I felt better about going home, knowing that I could still come here and talk about things that I may be having a problem with.

Arielle always seems to know what to say to make me feel better about myself and other things. I knew I couldn't always depend on her, that I had to learn to have self-confidence and depend on myself, but for now, I felt more secure with her. It was all still new to me.

Most of us were all planning on going home. Dr. "D" and Arielle were to take their vacation soon, and would be gone for several weeks. It was kind of scary to me, the idea of them being gone. We all talked about it in Group, as we all were feeling pretty much the same way.

"It's normal for you all to be feeling this way", Dr. Lee told us. "You all have learned to depend on them for guidance and understanding. This will be a good test for each of you to see how well you can do on your own." Somehow the words 'on your own' stood out. It was frightening.

A few days later when I saw Arielle she said, "I have some more news for you, and I am anxious to find out how you are going to feel about it."

I looked at her without saying anything. I didn't know what to expect.

"Dr. "D" and I are going to be married."

My instant response was, "Arielle that's wonderful. I'm so happy for you."

"Are you sure?" she asked.

"Of course, why wouldn't I be?" I said puzzled.

"Well, Dr. "D" is your doctor, and I am your therapist," she said.

"Why should that matter?" I asked.

"In some cases, it does matter with the patient. They develop an anxiety about it for several reasons. I'm glad you're not, if what you say is true."

I was surprised. "Of course it's true. I'm really happy for you, and I'm really not surprised. I wondered if you two cared about each other," I said with a smile. How can you ask me such a thing, if it's true?"

She smiled and said, "Well, you have been known to put on fronts before and say what you felt would get approval."

"Not this time," I said. "Not with you. I have always been honest with you in everything I say. I trust you."

"Well then, I'm glad," she said. "Now, about your going home. Have you told your husband yet?" Arielle asked.

"No, I'll call him today. I know he'll be glad. I just wish he had a job. I'll be with him all day long. I'm not looking forward to that. I'll just have to handle it the best I can".

"Not like before, I hope," Arielle said.

I smiled and said "No, not like before. I feel different. I feel stronger. Thanks to your and Dr. "D's help and those in group."

"You still have a ways to go though. Coming here weekly will help you get through it," she said. "We will be gone for several weeks in England, but you will be coming to group. If you have any problems, you can talk about them in there, so you won't be terribly alone."

"I'm glad for that. It kind of scares me with you both being so far away. I won't be able to call you or anything. I'm not looking forward to it."

"You'll be fine. I know you will," Arielle said.

I called my husband that night and told him I would be coming home for good, and also the news about being able to continue seeing Arielle and Dr. "D". He was glad I was coming home, but his response was cool in regards to my continuing my therapy.

"I don't see why you have to do that. You're off the medicine, aren't you? That's why you went there, in the first place. Your headaches have stopped."

I didn't tell him one of the reasons my headaches stopped was because I didn't have to be around him all the time pretending everything was all right. It would have just started a big argument, and I didn't want that. I don't know why I was expecting him to be glad for me. I should have known better.

"I had hoped you'd be happy for me," I told him. "I feel so much better already."

"You should, you've been there ten weeks. What about us?"

He was trying to make me feel guilty again. "I told you I was coming home. I'll just be driving back and forth. I want to continue to go there, I like talking to Arielle", I said.

"You can talk to me. I didn't think you needed to stay there, as long as you have, but I went along with what you wanted." He sounded angry.

"I just called you to tell you the good news. I should have known better than to expect you to be happy about anything that mattered to me. You always have had to try to spoil everything." I added, "I don't even want to come home now."

That got to him.

"Now, Veronica don't go feeling that way. We just miss you. I wish you were finished with all of that stuff there. You know I didn't feel like you need it. But if you want to continue to go, go on. Whatever makes you happy."

I hated hearing him say, "what ever makes you happy." He always sounded a bit sarcastic when he said it. It was one of his favorite sayings. I only wished it were true. What would make me happy would be to have him out of my life. He didn't want to hear that and I wasn't ready to tell him.

Knowing that I was going to continue to see Arielle made it so much easier in planning to go home. I wouldn't be saying goodbye. What a relief that was to me. I had come to depend on her very much. I knew I couldn't always feel that way, but right then, I needed her and Dr. "D". I felt good about attending group too. Now all I had to do was have my last visit with Dr. "D".

At that time, for some reason I still didn't fully understand, it made me nervous when I had to see him, only I wasn't quite as afraid as I had been in the past. I remember in the beginning commenting that I felt like I was waiting to go to the gas chamber, waiting for Arielle to come and tell me Dr. "D" would not see me. How I remember sitting before him with perspiration actually dripping from my elbows. My whole body would be visibly trembling. That's how nervous I had been. Now sitting before him, I felt somewhat calmer, but still a bit nervous.

He has all the answers to help me. He knows what's wrong. I wish he could just tell me. I would be so much easier," I thought looking at him behind his desk, and waiting for him to look up from the papers and speak.

"Well, Mrs. Knight, you're going home. How do you feel about that?" He looked up at me.

"I have mixed feelings about it. I dread it in a way, but I know I have to go sooner or later," I said, thinking all last conversations must go this way. I wish I could say something different. Damn, there, I go again, wanting to be different. Well, at least I'm aware of it. Arielle says that's good, when I say something and am aware of why I'm saying it. I have made progress.

D "D"'s' gruff voice broke through my thoughts. "Is there anything in particular you want to talk to me about before you go home?"

I looked at him and thought, God, there's everything, but how do I say it all in just a few minutes. My time with him is so valuable, and I always had to feel like I was taking up too much time. I wish I could get over this feeling. "Dr. "D", do you know what is wrong with me? Do you know what mainly is my problem? Why I feel like I do?"

"Yes", was his reply. "I'd say I have a pretty good idea, by now." He smiled.

"Why can't you just tell me," I said a bit frustrated. "It would make it so much easier for me."

He said seriously, "Therapy isn't meant to be easy. It doesn't work quite that way. It's not that simple. It would be nice if it were, but it's not. The answers are for you to find out. It's our job to guide you along."

I looked at him, wanting to let him know what he's meant to me, and how grateful I was that he and Arielle would continue to help me. "Dr. "D", you have been very important to me. I want to tell you about a poem I wrote, What My Doctor Means to Me. It's how I feel about you." Then I quoted my poem to him.

> *"My doctor to me is like an island. A solid piece of something I can hold onto and feel safe. I swim around this island, venturing out further each time, looking for that solid piece of something I can hold on to and be happy with. When I leave this island, I know each time about how long I can swim on my own, then to return. I have found little islands and pleasures, some larger, in my ventures; but each one was only temporary, and it soon started to sink, so I returned to the island."*

I was very nervous as I recited it to him. There was so much for him to understand. As soon as I finished, I said, "Do you understand? The little islands are people, relationships that are disappointing."

He was nodding his head slightly up and down to let me know he understood, but then he said. "You have it all wrong. *You swim to the mainland. You reach for the mainland.*"

How can one short sentence mean so much? It was profound. I cannot explain the excitement I felt. It was such that I could not hide it. "Of course," I said happily. "I never thought of that. I just thought of islands. Not a mainland. Thank you Dr. "D"!"

He was smiling. I wanted to hug him, but didn't quite have that much nerve yet. Maybe someday I will, I thought. All the way back to my room I kept repeating, *"Reach for the Mainland. Reach for the*

Mainland." I didn't know exactly where the mainland, or what was on it, but it didn't matter. He gave me a clue, a direction. It must be all right there or he wouldn't have told me. Why didn't I think of a mainland? It was the answer and some day I would be there. I will find that something solid that I can hold on to and feel secure with. I will be happy and safe. I will! I will, I vowed to myself, catching myself laughing out loud and hugging myself. All of a sudden, the trees seemed greener and the birds' chirps were louder and sweeter. I loved the outdoor walk back to my room. I wanted to keep this good feeling for as long as I could. I liked it.

Chapter 23

FINDING THE MAINLAND

IT WOULD BE a happy ending to my story if I could say that once I arrived home, things went smoothly in my asking for a divorce and receiving it, however as in real life, things did not go quite that well. My worst fears of what might happen with the children were seriously underestimated, as well as how my husband was capable of reacting. What followed was a nightmare, but the important thing about it all was that I was able to finally come to a decision about what I had to do, and carry it through without the help of medication. I did it on my own, and it was worth it in spite of all the anguish I had to go through to free myself of a life that was destroying me. My only regret is that my children had to suffer the pains of the divorce of their parents. Under the circumstances, it was unavoidable. What followed that subsequent year in my trying to break away from my husband and going through a divorce is another story in itself, but I will attempt to summarize it the best I can.

I was very nervous and scared going back home. The children were glad to see me, and fitted right back into the routine they were used to when I was at home. I wish I could have adjusted easily. It was difficult being there with my husband all the time. I had no escape from him and I could no longer rely on my once precious pills. I had to experience my feelings and they were uncomfortable. I kept reminding myself that it was normal for me to feel like I did and that I was going to continue to feel uncomfortable until I made a change.

How I dreaded talking to my husband, but I knew I couldn't keep putting it off. I finally was able to tell him.

"Please try to understand. I just can't live with you any longer. I don't want to hurt you, but I'm hurting. I can't be the other or person I want to be. I can't be the wife you want."

"Now Veronica, you don't know how you feel. You love me. You're just confused. They have messed up your thinking at the hospital. You know how much I love you and will do anything for you," Ronald said.

I knew he wasn't taking me seriously, or didn't want to. "No, I mean it. I can't go on like this. We can still be friends. You can see the boys whenever you want.

He just smiled and looked away. "You don't mean it. Give us some time. You'll see how much you need me. You don't want to hurt the children, do you?"

My voice rose. "I want a divorce. Why can't you believe me? I don't want to get like I was before going to the hospital. I can't let it happen again."

He said very quietly and patiently. "You were fine before going to the hospital. You're worse now. All you had were some headaches. We're going to be fine. You'll see. It's just going to take some time. You're just confused now. You don't know what you mean. How about a movie tonight?" He smiled and changed the subject.

I felt I had gotten nowhere. Ron said I was confused. I had to keep remembering Arielle said he couldn't tell me how I felt. Only I knew my feelings. How I wished I could talk to her, but she was in England with Dr." D". I felt alone.

My headaches started to return only I didn't have the strong medicine to ease the pain, just something mild. I had to suffer through them. I had been laying in bed a couple of days, when my husband said, "Lets go for a drive, it might make you feel better."

I felt helpless and didn't feel like an argument. I got up and went with him. We were passing the house of a fortuneteller when all of a sudden he said, "Why don't you have your fortune told"

I was surprised as this was not like him. I didn't think he believed in them. I protested saying I thought she was a phony since I had seen a write-up on her in the paper recently.

"Oh, come on. It will be fun. Go just out of curiosity. Here's the money," he said, as we pulled up in the driveway.

Again I didn't feel like an argument. I went in. The lady greeted me at the door and told me to go into the back room and sit down, that she would be right there. I looked around the dark musty-smelling room. There were a lot of religious articles and pictures. I felt uncomfortable. She came into the room and asked for my hand.

After studying my hand, she told me she was very concerned for me. She saw a woman who had great influence on me, negative influence.

"You must not listen to her," she said.

I looked at her puzzled now knowing whom she could mean. "This woman is associated with a hospital."

She's talking about Arielle, I thought. How could she know? "These people are experimenting with you. They do much damage. I see you have a good husband who loves you very much. There, is much outside influence in your life, which affects your marriage. Concentrate on you husband and children. You are a lucky woman to have a man who loves you so much. Hold onto him."

What she had to say frightened me. It did not fit into my plans. I left feeling confused and bewildered. Was I wrong about my husband? I couldn't talk when my husband questioned me. I needed to talk to Arielle but couldn't because she was gone. What was I going to do? What I had learned about myself at the hospital was so important to me. It was my whole life. How could it be so wrong, when I felt so good about it? How can I throw it all away? How did this woman know so much, if she was a phony?

Several days had gone by when my husband suggested that I visit her again.

"Why should I go again?" I asked.

"She might have something else to tell you," he answered.

"I don't want to, besides, she won't be there. She said she was going on vacation. She's already left."

He answered quickly, too quickly, "No she's not leaving until tomorrow."

I looked at him startled. How do you know?"

He looked away and said, "Don't you remember? You told me when you came out from seeing her."

"No, I didn't. Why would I ask her when she was going on vacation? I didn't care," I said with my voice rising. What I was thinking was horrible to me. I screamed at him, "Did you go see her before me and pay her to say what she said to me?"

He said with that patient tone of his, "Of course not Veronica. Don't be silly. You just forgot you told me."

It was no use. I knew he'd never admit it. I let it drop, but I was so upset. He would rather keep me confused for his own wellbeing. How I hated him at that moment. I started talking about divorce again, with always the same response. A week later, he brought up the topic about me seeing the fortune-telling woman again.

"No I don't want to see her. I believe she is a fake."

"I don't agree," he said. "You can tell by all the religious articles that she believes in God and is religious."

"I was getting angry but didn't want to show it yet. I wanted to see what else I could get out of him. I wanted to verify what I though about the whole situation. "I believe she just uses God to make money. I believe it is all a front." He was getting more frustrated. "No, it's not," he said.

"Yes, it is. She's a phony", I added.

"If she's a phony why would she spend….." He stopped speaking.

I jumped on it. "Why would she what?"

"Don't you remember? You told me she was going to spend her vacation at a retreat, some church," he said.

I blew up. I did not. How could I? I didn't even know myself. I know now for sure you saw her before I did. How could you do such a thing?

"Now honey, calm down. You just don't remember. You're still confused. I love you. I wouldn't do that," he said very quietly.

How could I have been so dumb to have even believed him or her. I felt so foolish and ashamed for even doubting Arielle or all the treatment I had, for even a second.

I pressed him again for a divorce. He was beginning to believe me and would cry and beg me not to leave. I stood firm and would not change my mind. One day while he was taking money out of his billfold, I noticed a letter folded up. It came partly out, and he pushed it back inside like he didn't want me to see it. Later that night, I took it out and read it. It was a suicide note from him. I couldn't believe it. He was actually thinking of taking his life. He was serious. When did he plan this? I woke up and asked him about the note.

"Oh honey, I just wrote it one night when I was feeling down. I can't bear the thought of you leaving me. I need you and the children. I can't live without you. I didn't want you to find it now," he said, looking ashamed.

I was horrified. I was angry. "How could you?"

He wanted to dismiss it, like it never happened. He had often said he couldn't live without me. I heard it often when I was just sixteen years old. I felt sorry for him then. Did I feel sorry enough for him now to continue to stay? No, I didn't, but I didn't know what to do. What if he did shoot himself? Then I would be to blame. No, I wouldn't.

I reminded myself. I am not responsible for him. I have to keep remembering that.

I kept saying to myself, I will get away, I will get away. It will just take time. My headaches were getting worse, more persistent. How much longer can I endure them? They were a constant reminder of my situation.

As the months went by, I found out more and more about our financial situation. Bills that I thought were taken care of, were not. The phone was always ringing from bill collectors. I found out that my husband had borrowed money from so many people, including my sister. She let it slip one day when I was at her home. When I pressed her further, letting her believe that I knew about it, I found out that the loan was never repaid. I was so upset. Ron and I had a really big blowup about it, with my ending the argument by running out of the house. I was hysterical. How many other things had he lied to me about – even to others? He had told my sister he borrowed the money because he had spent what he had on me. Did she believe him? Did others believe him?

All the ugliness was just starting. I drove to my mothers. She was not at home, but I knew where the key was and let myself in. I called my sister's house to see if mother was there. She was and – unbelievably – so was my husband.

I don't know what he had told them, but they were saying he was sorry and for me to forgive him and give him another chance. How could they say this? I hadn't even left him yet, and already they were taking his side. This was one of my fears that I had lived with for so long. I had done such a good job of trying to convince them how hard he was trying that my family believed we were fine. I guess I wanted to believe it myself. I hung up the phone crying so hard. I ran to where I knew my mother kept the liquor. I turned up the bottle of bourbon and drank most of it. I can't even remember tasting it as I drank it straight. In the past I could not stand the taste of bourbon, but now it didn't matter. I wanted to numb the pain I was feeling.

"What am I going to do? There's no place to go," I cried out loud. I couldn't go home. My mother and sister felt sorry for my husband. I felt so alone. I ran out to the car and drove down the street sobbing as hard as I could ever remember. I was surprised to hear my voice saying and crying the words, "Daddy, Daddy, I need you. I need somebody." I noticed some children were looking at me and realized what I must look like to them. I drove away from the stop sign fast and went to the interstate, where no one could see me. I didn't know where I was going. I just drove. I don't know how far I went when I realized I was starting to really feel the effects of the liquor. I had to fight to stay awake.

All of a sudden my senses came to me, and I realized it was dark and raining, that I could have a serious accident and that I was endangering other lives.

I didn't even know where I was. I prayed to God to please help me find my way back to a friend's house where I knew I could spend the night. I could barely see as my vision blurred from the alcohol. I managed to find my way back to the interstate and to the road I thought I should turn off on to get to my friend's home. After several wrong turns, I finally saw through the rain a mailbox that looked familiar. It was hers. I turned into the drive, feeling as if I was going to pass out at any moment. When I reached her home, all I could do was blow the car horn. I had tried to get out of the car, but could hardly function. She came out, and with the help of one of her friends, got me out of the car. I was very dizzy and threw up before reaching the house. I asked her to please call my mother and tell her I was at her home and all right, and for my mother to call my husband, so the children wouldn't worry. There was no telling what he was going to tell them.

The next morning, everything looked very clear to me. I walked out to see the horses. Beverly lived on a farm and I loved the peacefulness of it. I thought about what I had done the night before. How foolish it was, yet at the time I felt I had no control over it. I couldn't let it happen again. I was going to be right back where I started before going to the hospital, only in even worse shape if I continued to do such things. I knew I could prolong it no longer. I was leaving.

It had been over a year since my stay at Hospital hospital, and I was still with Ron. I didn't mean to stay that long. It seemed the longer I stayed the more damage was done. One positive thing I had done was to get an office job at a real estate company, so I could support myself as well as the children with my husband's help. I finally had the courage to leave.

The day I left was a very emotional one for the children and my husband. I was surprised that I had the strength that I did. My husband was openly crying in front of the children, begging me to stay. I hated this as it upset the children, and they were upset enough already just knowing their mother and father were breaking up. I felt so sorry for them. The two oldest took it the hardest. Josh, the oldest was sixteen, a tender age. He ran from the house crying the day I told him. My middle son, twelve-year-old Tony, was angry but I knew it was a cover for the hurt he was feeling. The youngest, ten-year-old Roy, didn't seem to be affected as much. I took half of the furniture and left half for Ronald. I told him as I left, that he could see the boys any time he wanted to.

I was surprised that the four of us got along as well as we did. The children seemed to be adjusting to the separation. I was surprised though that their father didn't come to visit or take them anywhere. I had thought Ronald would have missed them. Later I found out he was meeting them sometimes at the school-bus stop and talking to them about us all coming back to him. It started to affect the oldest and the middle child as they wanted us to be together, but they only let me know in a quiet way. I didn't think I had a real problem. How little I knew.

My job was going well. I was even able to go to night school twice a week and take a real-estate course. I was so excited and pleased when I received a notice in the mail that I had passed my state examination. I had come a long way since getting off the medicine. Things were really starting to look good to me. I had known my boss for many years before I went to work for him, but only casually. Since working for him, I had grown very fond of him. He was much older than I. He and my father were the same age, and in some ways, he reminded me of my father. He was very much involved in his business and very orderly. He was a solid man and I admired him for what he had accomplished on his own. I was surprised the day he told me he loved me and wanted to marry me. I felt flattered and pleased. He was some one I could count on. This was new to me. I told him I would marry him, but he had to keep our relationship a secret for a while. I wanted to wait until after my divorce was final to tell my sons, and they needed this time to adjust. I told one person, my mother. She said she was happy for me and would keep our secret.

I few weeks after I left my husband, my mother called me at home. "Veronica, Ronald called me. He was crying. He's really having a bad time."

"I'm sorry to hear that Mom, but why would he call you?"

"He just needed someone to talk to. You know he's still out of work and can't find a job. He didn't have the money to pay the power bill, so it was cut off. He was without heat. I told him he could stay here until he gets it turned back on." She waited for my response.

"I hate to think of him without heat too mom, but it's his fault," I said, feeling a little guilty and hating myself for it.

She went on, "I hope you understand. I just felt so sorry for him. He's so hurt over your leaving him. I know what it's like to be left. Your father left me."

What did that have to do with it? I thought and wished I could say, but didn't have the nerve. I couldn't understand her reasoning.

Several days passed and he was still at her house. This caused me to be uncomfortable. Didn't she realize she was making it easier on him? Living with her, he didn't have to pay house payments and the other bills. She was cooking for him and he was even driving her car. I was very hurt that my mother would do all that. She talked to me like she wasn't doing anything wrong. She was taking his side more and more.

One day I was at her home, when she said, "Veronica you shouldn't talk against Ronald to the boys. He is their father." I was surprised.

"I would never do that mom." My next statement surprised me more. "Because I know what it's like. I've lived all these years hearing you talking against Dad and I would never do the same thing to my own children.

This was the first time I had had the courage to say something like that to her since the time I was sixteen and she last slapped me for back talking her. I guess my anger was finally coming out. What happened next I wasn't expecting. She slapped me.

I don't know what happened to me, but something snapped. I couldn't take it, not on top of all the years I had had with her. What I had done for her. Without thinking I slapped her back. Mom looked stunned for a moment, then I saw a change in her face. She flew at me hitting me over and over. "You god-dam bitch, I'll show you."

There, it was, the intense anger I had feared all these years. Is this what I saw when just a child, that day on the back porch? Is this why I always felt dizzy and 'far away' whenever I tried to remember what happened? I felt sure it was. We both were physically hitting each other. I couldn't believe I was hitting her back. It was like a scene out of the movies. Things like this don't happen in real life, I told myself even while it was happening. It was all so unreal, but real.

My husband ran into the room and broke us apart. I ran out the door to my car. The last thing I saw was my mother standing at her front door screaming, "You bitch. I'll make you pay for this. You'll be sorry."

The words seared my brain like a hot iron. I knew what she meant. I drove home sobbing all the way. What happened to the concerned mother I had known the past few years? I called my sister and aunt. I was scared. Neither believed that Mom would do that. Hadn't I been the sick one? I must have taken it wrong. Everything was going to be all right. Only I knew better. I waited, not knowing for sure what to expect when Mom told my husband what I had been keeping secret. I knew she would tell him. That is what she meant when she said, "You'll be sorry."

The next day was Monday. I went to work as usual, expecting the phone to ring all day. It didn't. When I arrived home, everything was so quiet. I called to the boys. No response. I didn't like the feeling I had. Then I noticed a note. It was in my husband's handwriting. All I could see was the one sentence. "You can have your new life with your new husband, but not with my children." Oh God, no, I thought, as I ran to the telephone calling my mother's number. My husband answered, "I'll see you in court," was all he said before hanging up. I frantically called the police, only to hear, "I'm sorry miss, if you don't have legal custody of your children, there's nothing we can do. I suggest you phone an attorney." I thanked him and numbly hung up.

An attorney, I never thought of an attorney. I didn't think I needed one. I didn't know what the law was. All I knew was that I had to be separated a year and then I could get a divorce. My husband never mentioned wanting any of the boys. He hardly expressed an interest in spending any time with them. What was I going to do? All of these thoughts ran through my mind. The house was too quiet. I couldn't even call an attorney at the time. The offices would be closed.

I called my sister and my aunt. They were sorry to hear it, but acted like they didn't want to get involved. I felt so alone. I called Cliff, the man I was to marry. He came over right away. I felt better having him there, with me. He had some more bad news. My husband had called Cliff's wife and told her of our plans to marry. Cliff and his wife were separated and living apart, and planning a divorce, but with his additional information, she was going to use it in her divorce proceedings. Cliff had spoken to her over the telephone, just before I called.

"Veronica, I'm afraid we're in for a rough road ahead." Cliff said as he put his arms around me. Did Mom realize what she had started when she told Ronald I was going to marry Cliff? How could she do this to me? I was her daughter.

The next morning I woke to a quiet house, reminding me that my sons were no longer there. I called work and said that I would not be in, that I had to see an attorney. I didn't know where to begin looking for one. I chose a woman's name listed in the telephone book, hoping I was making the right selection. I felt perhaps she too was a mother and would understand how I felt. I was disappointed to find out that she was not, but she seemed competent.

"You will have to go to court to obtain legal custody," she told me. "I will have my secretary start typing the necessary forms."

I told her about my husband calling Cliff's wife.

"I'm afraid this could become very ugly for you," she said very seriously. I didn't quite understand what that had to do with me obtaining custody of my children. She explained to me what my husband might and could say. "Just the manner in which he took the children tells me something about him." What she implied scared me. The fact that the children didn't know about Cliff meant nothing. My husband could claim whatever he wanted. "I'll let you know when the court date is scheduled when I hear," she said.

A few days later, Cliff was served papers while he was at the office. My husband was suing him for $100,000 for Alienation of Affection," claiming he and I were happily married until Cliff came into our lives. He further stated he believed that Cliff intentionally alienated my affections from him. I couldn't believe he would have the nerve to claim that. I called my attorney, who only verified that, not only could be claim this, but he was legally within his rights to do so. The state in which we lived recognized it, although it was unusual. She told me I would have to go to court on two different cases. The custody case and the "Alienation of Affection" case, and not to be surprised if I was also summoned to appear in court in Cliff's divorce case as the 'other woman', which later did happen. I hung up the phone, and slid down in the chair beside it, thinking all this was happening because I trusted my mother and told her of my plans. How I wished I had kept quiet, but in my happiness, I had wanted to share it with her. I had trusted her, and all I wanted was a divorce. Why did it al have to be so ugly?

The next few months seemed to all run together. It started with my attempting to see the children at school, several weeks after my husband took them. I had called the school each day. I knew they were tired of having me call so much, but I had no other way of knowing. Finally the day came when I was happily told they were there,. It's funny how I just took the children for granted, never dreaming I would have to go so long without seeing or talking to them. I went to te middle school first to seen Tony, who was 12 years old. I was told to wait in the lobby. After waiting a very long time, growing more and more anxious and uncomfortable as the moments passed, the secretary at the school came into the office and told me, "Tony doesn't want to see you."

I can't describe the pain I felt shoot through my body at the shock of hearing this. I looked at her for what seemed a long time and then said "But I'm his mother. I need to see him. He was taken from me."

I started crying and telling her what all happened. I don't know if I even made any sense. She stood firm and said, "I'm sorry, we have a note from his father saying that he has custody and that you are not to see Tony and upset him, unless Tony says he wants to see you, and he says he doesn't."

"His father told him to say that. I know it. Tony and I are very close. I won't take him. I just want to see him. Please let me. You can trust me." I cried, realizing I was begging.

"I'm sorry," was all she said.

I left in a state of shock, feeling helpless and hurt. I didn't even try to see my oldest. I knew if Tony said this, I didn't stand a chance with my oldest, Josh. The thought of probably hearing he didn't want to see me either, was too much to bear. I couldn't take it again.

After leaving the middle school, I want to my youngest son's school and try to see him but I couldn't help but wonder if I would I face the same resistance as I did at the other school. My heart was pounding as I drove over to Roy's school, parked the car and walked inside and down the hall until I came to Roy's class. I peeked in the window and saw him at his desk. When he saw me he smiled really big and looked at the teacher and then back to where I was. His teacher looked over at the door where I was standing, smiled and came over and said it was ok for Roy to leave with me.

He gave me a big hug and said, "Mommy I missed you so much. I wanted to see you but I couldn't".

I said, "it's ok honey, don't worry about it. Let's go get in the car and go home." I will never forget his teacher's kindness. I didn't have to explain anything to her.

Roy and I got in the car and I was adjusting the rearview mirror when I saw a terrible sight. In the mirror I saw a ball of red dust racing towards us. I knew it was Ronald and that he was furious. He knew I had tried to see my older sons and suspected I would try to see Roy also. I didn't know what to expect, but I quickly locked the doors to the car and before I knew it he was upon us banging on the windows shouting and hollering for us to open the doors, for Roy to open his door.

Roy said, "Mommy, I'm scared. I don't know what to do." "Honey, don't do anything. I'll handle it" I said.

After a moment or two of all this, I slowly backed up the car even though he was still shouting and banging on the car and went on down that long dirt road. He came barreling up behind me very quickly and I thought he was going to ram me or run me off the road. He didn't. He just kept right on my bumper for several miles on that lonely country road. That continued most of the way back to my apartment, then he pulled off.

I was scared to death. I didn't know what to do but I knew his violence was escalating. I couldn't stay there much longer. I planned to see the court counselor the very next day and tell her what happened. I felt so sorry for my son to experience this. I never wanted to expose him to any kind of violence and today he had seen violence.

It's amazing how someone can declare they love you and then when you don't return it or give them what they want, they can turn violent. They don't give the consideration to you that you gave to them being a parent. Ronald was acting like a crazy person. He was out of control.

My youngest son stayed with me. I clung to him perhaps too much. He was all I had left. I loved him so. I loved them all, but felt like I had lost my other two sons. After several weeks, I was able, with the attorney's help, to have my other two boys every other weekend, with their father seeing them on alternate weekends. They had changed drastically. My once happy, carefree and open children were now silent, angry and withdrawn. It seemed I could not reach them, but I kept trying. I was still going to try to obtain custody of the two youngest. I felt they still needed me. Josh was much older and because of this, I felt he was better off with his father, since he wanted to stay with him. My middle son stated he wanted to stay with his father, also, but I felt he was too young to make up his own mind, and believed he felt sorry for his father.

The day finally came when I had to go to court to seek legal custody. Later a court counselor was called in. My husband was claiming I was unfit and incompetent; that I took medications that altered my behavior, that I was irrational. Suddenly he had a job. Our home was sold without either of us making a profit since the payments were so far behind. But he claimed he had a nice large apartment with new furniture. He had a comfortable home that he could offer his sons. My mother stood by him and testified that I had misused medications for many years. I wanted to scream out loud in the court room, "Yes, but you gave me my first pill and drink and that was a long time ago. I'm okay now." But any time I wanted to say something, my attorney told me to keep silent. I didn't understand why my attorney didn't object to many of the questions, or use some of the information that I had given her in my behalf.

I was scared going to court. I had never been in a courtroom before. I had called my sister Dawn, and asked her if she would be one of my witnesses, never doubting for a minute that she would testify on my behalf. I was startled and surprised by her response.

"Oh Veronica I don't think I could handle it," she said.

"What do you mean?' I asked feeling my heart jump as I took a deep breath.

"Well, you know how you have been." She said.

I said suddenly with panic, "Yes Dawn, I know I have had problems in my personal life, but I have been a good mother. I love the children.

The problems I had were before I went to the hospital. I am off the medicine now, and even back then I took care of the boys. I don't want to lose them," I sobbed.

I was defending myself and wondered why I had to. She knew all of this.

"You did drink that bottle that night and stayed away," she said hesitantly.

"I know I did but that was unusual, I was terribly upset. The children didn't see me. They have never seen me drunk or indecent." Now I was really crying.

Dawn went on to say, "Mom says, Ronald says".... I broke into her sentence.

"You know Mom is mad at me. Ronald tells her only what he wants to. He has told her so many untruths. I can't believe you are not going to help me."

"I just don't want to get in the middle," she said.

"All I wanted is a divorce," I cried. "Is that so bad? People get divorces everyday. Now look what has happened! My whole family is in it, and none of them are standing by me." I sobbed as I hung up the phone.

I called my aunt Ginger, my mother's only sister. We had always been close. I idolized her from the time I was a child. She was just ten years older than I. She didn't want to get involved either. To my family, going to court over something was a disgrace and an embarrassment. I can't help but believe, or rather knew my mother was behind all of this. For them to stand by me was not being loyal to her and no one wanted mom mad at them. Also, remember mom was married to Ronald's uncle and knew the whole family. Of course she was going to stand by Ronald. It didn't matter that I was her daughter.

A few days later, I received a long distance call from my sister Betty. I was both shocked and surprised. Shocked that she had my unlisted phone number and surprised, as I had not heard from her in years. The last time I could remember us talking and getting along was when our grandmother passed away and she and I went together to the funeral home to do Gram's hair and makeup. We did well then and it was a special time. I thought we would be close after that, but still I never heard from her. Betty said she called me to tell me she thought I should start the New Year off right by apologizing to Mom for our fight. I couldn't believe by ears that she would have the nerve to call me and say that. She must have been drinking. She continued to say how pampered she thought I had always been. Pampered? That is the last thing I ever was! I told her she had not been around in years and did not know what I had been going through. For that matter, she didn't know what was going on now in my life. I tried to tell her how difficult it had been and what I was going through.

Her reply was, "bullshit."

When she said that, just blowing off what I was trying to tell her and not listening, I let feelings out I didn't even know I had. I then told her Mom was soon going to move up there near her and far as I cared they both could go to hell. I hung up the phone shaking, I was so angry. I had all I was ever going to take from her. I wasn't about to listen to what she thought I should do. I really felt isolated. There was no family left.

Years later when we were on better terms, I asked Betty about this incident. She remembers nothing. Absolutely nothing! As far as she was concerned, it never happened. What hurt the most was I found out later that my sister Dawn was there when Betty called me. Dawn had to have given my phone number to Betty. Dawn had to have told Betty about Mom and my fight and that is what prompted Betty to call me. Whatever Dawn told her had to be what my mother said. It certainly wasn't in my favor. Dawn never asked me what happened. She just believed Mom. This really did hurt me. I wish she had given me a chance to say what happened, but she and my aunt were avoiding me.

I was totally alone in this town going to court. I had no family support at all. I am grateful for my friends that stood by me and came with me, as I was frightened. My Dad and stepmother kept in touch with me as did my brother, but they were in Florida. I was on my own.

I went to court every week for six months. I didn't realize why it was taking so long. It was always postponed, or I didn't have a chance to testify. Even my friends who took off from work just sat and waited for nothing. They were never called to testify in my behalf. I sat sometimes for a day waiting to be called only to find out the hearing was to be continued for some reason or another. Finally, my friends could not come to court with me as it was taking too much time off of work or in their personal lives. I certainly understood. There was just my attorney and I there. She wasn't much help and never gave a real explanation as to what was happening. My attorney advised me it was best Cliff did not come with me and I understood that. I never felt so along.

At all of the hearings, Cliff's wife and her relatives were there. They filled half the courtroom. I was the 'other woman' and everyone wanted to see what I looked like. I felt even more uncomfortable knowing Cliff's in-laws were connected with law enforcement. One of her brothers was the chief of police, and another brother was a lieutenant in the sheriff's office. The clerk of court was her first cousin, and I was told the judge presiding over the hearing was an old friend of Cliff's wife and family. They all were there every day dressed in their uniforms. I felt intimidated by them and stayed in my chair even during recess. The one time I did leave to go to the restroom, I was in one of the bathroom stalls, when Cliff's wife and relatives came in. Of course they were all talking about me in a very negative manner, not knowing I was in the bathroom. I hated having to come out and face them. I didn't know what to expect. They just stopped talking when I came out, and I hurriedly went back to my seat. After that one time, I was careful not to leave during recess again to avoid any further confrontations.

Because of Ronald's accusations against me, Dr. "D" wrote a letter stating that I was under his care and that I was well and competent as a person and as a mother. It was never mentioned in the courtroom. The court counselor's report, in my favor was missing. No one could find it. Finally after much delay, it was presented, but dismissed by my husband's attorney stating she was prejudiced being a mother herself. In it she had stated we were both fit as parents, but she felt that in questioning the children, they were being used by my husband as instruments, in an effort to reach me and get me back at his wife. He had been sending notes to me by the children, opened so that they could read them, letting them know he wanted me back so we could be a family again. He would send clippings on love and marriage to me with my sons when they came to visit. My oldest children were getting more and more angry with me. "Mommy, why won't you go back to Daddy," my middle son would ask me? How could I explain to him? He was just a child. Of course he wanted us to be a family. I was losing him. My son rejected any attempts of love that I showed him. I was hurt and bewildered. I had no fight in me. I didn't know how to handle it at all. I just felt helpless and went to the hearings every week in a daze. My father, Dr. "D" and Arielle were supportive. Cliff was in a state of shock himself.

Finally, one day after court, the court counselor called me aside. "Veronica, I can't watch this go on any longer and not say something." I looked at her. What was she talking about?

"Can't you see what is happening? Can't you see what they are doing? Can't you get mad?" she asked frustrated.

"What are you talking about?" I asked her. "I could lose my job for telling you this, but I have to. Promise me you'll never tell what I'm going to tell you," she said.

"I promise." I was still confused and in my usual daze of so many months of this.

"Don't you wonder why all this is taking so long? Why it is always postponed for one reason or another? All this, the custody suit and it being postponed is your husband's insurance of keeping you here, in the state for the 'biggie', she told me angrily.

"What do you mean? I asked.

"The Alienation of Affection suit. That is what they're all waiting for. They want to take Cliff for all he's worth," she said.

"Who are they?" I asked.

"Your husband, Cliff's wife and their attorneys. They're all in it together," she said. As she said this I was reminded of a few days before, when I accidentally opened a wrong door and inside I saw all of the people she had mentioned and the judge had been laughing and talking with them. They looked embarrassed when I opened the door on them. I apologized and left, dismissing it from my mind. Now what she said made sense. Of course they all had something to gain by it, but it never occurred to me that was why these court proceedings had dragged out so long.

"The report was never lost, and all the other reasons you heard why it was postponed. It was just to buy time," she said.

I felt great terror. "What am I going to do? How can I fight the?" If I were you, I'd take my youngest son and leave town, while you can. Try to get Tony too if that is possible. I feel he belongs with you."

I looked at her feeling so grateful. This was the first time she actually said how she felt to me.

That night, Cliff, my youngest and I left town for good. I called my friends and they said they would take care of my furniture and things I left behind. I was so grateful to them.

The drive away from that town was so painful. I had always tried not to cry in front of the children, but this day I could not help it. I was leaving behind two sons I loved very much. I reminded myself that they wanted to stay with their father, but it didn't help what I was feeling inside.

"Cliff asked, "What's wrong Honey?" I couldn't answer.

Roy said, "I know. It's just everything."

How can one so young say something so profound? I turned around and kissed him and told him I was sorry he had to go through so much, and that I loved him very much. I was so concerned for him. I knew he would miss his brothers. They had been so close.

At first Cliff, and I went to PA. and stayed with Cliff's aunt who had a lovely historic home with lots of property. She was a widow and needed help with all the property. We stayed and helped her for about 6 weeks. When we left we went to stay with my father for awhile until we decided where to live.

We moved three thousand miles away and eight weeks later, Cliff and I were able to obtain a divorce and marry. My little son gave me away at the wedding. He seemed happy and liked his stepfather, but I wasn't sure. I was hoping he wasn't just trying to please me. He seemed so grown up for ten years old. In the months that followed, I spent many nights crying myself to sleep over my children left behind. I had to keep reminding myself it couldn't have been any different under the circumstances, and that I was very fortunate to have my youngest son with me.

In the next few years, we became involved with the community affairs, with church work and made new friends, but the past continued to hang over our heads, as I was told by friends back East that my ex-husband had not given up on trying to find me and getting our youngest son back. We constantly moved and changed our names. From time to time I would ask my son if he wanted to live with his father and that I would understand knowing that he missed his brothers. I worried constantly about his emotional wellbeing.

"No Mommy, I want to stay with you and Cliff," he would assure me.

I lived with the fear that something terrible would happen to one of my sons left behind. The feeling would not leave me. One fall, my father and Beth were visiting us. Dad received a call.

"Veronica, I have something to tell you," his voice sounded very grave. I knew immediately something tragic had happened."

"Is it Josh?" I asked, my heart in my throat.

"No, it's Tony," he said. The next words would barely come out. "Is he alive?"

"Yes. There's been an accident. It seems he and a friend were playing near the railroad tracks."

"I heard his words, but somehow they weren't connecting. This moment seemed unreal.

Dad continued. "He tried to jump a train. He fell and was hurt. He's in the hospital. It's serious."

I was trying to hold on. "How serious?" I didn't really want to know and wanted to know everything. I can't explain how I felt.

"They're operating on him now," he said very sadly.

"My God"! The terror filled me. "I have to go," I said panicky.

My stepmother came to me with tears in her eyes and held me. I started pacing the floor, fighting what I was feeling.

"No, this can't be happening, not to Tony. Oh God, please no," I cried.

"Veronica, you can't go," Dad said. I thought about it and looked at him.

"There's nothing you can do. They're doing all they can. He wouldn't even know that you're there. Try to get hold of yourself," my father said, adding, Roy needs you."

It sounded so logical. Everyone agreed with him. I tried to go through with our plans that day, telling myself Tony's accident wasn't true. We went sightseeing. Every time the reality tried to push its way into my head, I'd push it away. The reality of it was too terrifying, and far more than I felt I could take in.

As the days passed, and every time I would start to go, people from the church, Arielle, Dr. "D", everyone said don't go. I would be dealing with much more than just Tony's accident. I thought of my mother, ex-husband, my other son, my sisters and my aunt. There, was no one there to comfort me. I was afraid to see them. Who would I go to? Cliff couldn't go with me. There were warrants out for him in contempt of court. I was told I might upset Tony. I hadn't thought of that, but it was true. Would it upset him to see me? I was told he might die. How could I not be there? I loved him so. I wanted to take him into my arms as I did when he was a child and he would run to me with a hurt. I called the hospital every day, sometimes twice a day, checking on him. Sometimes the nurses and doctors were informative, and sometimes they were cool to me. I knew they must probably wonder why I wasn't there with my son. I told them to please call me if my son ever asked for me and I would be there. I was never told he asked.

I didn't understand why no family member called me. Didn't they think I would want to be there?

A friend of mine called me and told me not to even think of coming. She was told that my ex-husband was overheard saying, "I told the nursing staff if she comes to the hospital to notify me right away. I'll have the authorities there, to greet her with papers. I didn't understand. What papers? Later it was explained to me that he was going to try to put a restraining order on me keeping me in the state, until he was able to get my youngest son, forcing me to go back into court. I was so naïve about the law. I believed anything I was told. At this point so much had happened, I would have believed anything I was told what my ex-husband might do. I couldn't trust him, but it was hard for me to believe he would do a thing like that at a time when I wanted to be with my injured son, but I knew deep down, he WOULD do it.

Cliff and I tried to go on as best we could, but it caused a great strain on us. We encountered many problems with his own family, because of all the ugliness; he didn't know how to help me. I kept on working and trying to be the best mother I could under the circumstances. The one son that I was able to bring close to me, caused me to worry even more, because I was still afraid of him being taken from me by his father.

I was at work one day when Cliff called me on my phone. "Veronica, now don't get upset."

Just hearing those words I knew something terrible had happened. It wasn't like Cliff to talk that way.

"Roy has been gone for several hours and we don't know where he is."

I didn't want to believe anything bad.

"Oh, Cliff, he's probably at a friend's house and forgot about the time. I'll talk to him about it when I get home. You don't know how involved he gets in his play. Roy was 12 years old at the time.

Cliff said, "No Veronica. I'm afraid it's more serious than that. He was seen by a friend getting into a car, after a man talked to him for several minutes."

Now I was very concerned. That wasn't like Roy. We had often talked about being careful of strangers. I knew he wouldn't get into a stranger's car.

"A friend said he got in the car reluctantly and the last thing Roy said to his friend was, "I'm going just down the street to the store. I'll be back in a minute.

Concern began to fill my very being. I thought, no not again. When was it all going to end? It seemed one bad thing happened after another. This doesn't happen. This can't be real! I ran out of the store where I was working without even saying that I was going. The things that I imagined were terrible. What was my son going through? Where was he? Was he alive? Please God, I prayed, don't let him suffer.

I called the police immediately. They came out to talk to me and asked questions of Roy's friend, Alex, who was playing with him and saw him get into that car. Alex said there, was a man over the fence with his hood of the car open, asking Roy to come over and hold something for him, that he was having car trouble. Roy climbed over the fence and spoke with the man for a while. Alex said when the man asked Roy to get into the car, Roy was shaking his head no, but then after a while, reluctantly got into the car. The last thing that Roy said to Alex was, "I'm going down the street to 711 and will be right back." Roy never came back.

The police asked for a description of Roy, and all the details from his friend Alex. The information was put on the news later that night about him being a missing child.

It is the most devastating, painful, terrifying ordeal a mother could ever go through, to know her child is out there somewhere and not knowing where or who he is with. I wondered if he was alive, if he was being tortured, if he was crying out for me. Those were the most helpless feelings in this world.

Many hours later the phone rang.

"Hello." I said in a whisper, hoping it was my son.

"Veronica, this is Ronald."

The familiar voice came through over the line. I knew instantly what it was about. I was not surprised. 'Roy is with me, where he wants to be,' he said.

I responded, "If he wanted to be you, he could have called you at any time. You didn't have to take him this way, but this is one time I'm glad to hear from you. At least I know he's safe," I said.

"Well this is where he wants to be," Ronald said, he told me so. I replied, "He'll tell you anything you want to hear."

I understood the position he was in.

He went on further to say, "we are here at the hospital with Tony where Roy belongs, with his brother."

I told him I was not going to argue with him. I knew he was saying this for the benefit of whoever was nearby.

All I could say was, "Well Ronald you wanted the boys. Now you have them all. You stopped at nothing to get them. Now let's see what kind of job you do raising them."

I did not want him to know how much what he did worried and hurt me. He would have had much satisfaction in that. I was so emotionally and physically tired, but relieved that my son Roy was safe.

Before we hung up, Ronald said one more thing. "Roy told me you have become a Mormon. I can't believe you became a Mormon."

I replied to him, "You don't know what you're talking about. You are so wrong about what you've always believed. Becoming a Mormon has brought much happiness into our lives. I have nothing else to say to you." And I hung up.

A couple of months later I flew back East in order to try to see my three sons, and to write on my book again. I felt I was not totally alone, that others must be going through things like this too, and I felt the great need to write. Hopefully it will let others know they are not alone, and maybe what I learned could help them.

I wanted to make sure that Roy was all right. I wanted to know he was happy and I had to take my chances to see Tony at the hospital. He had been there a year now. Too much time had passed. I couldn't put it off any longer.

I stayed several weeks in my hotel room writing and visiting with Dr. "D" and Arielle every day, discussing what I had written. Just before going back home, I called my son Roy at his home and was fortunate enough to have him answer. Roy met me a couple of blocks from where he lived, at my friend's house. I was so happy to see him. It had been two months since I last saw him, but it seemed he had grown so much.

The first thing he said was, "Mom, I'm sorry I left like I did. I didn't want to go but Daddy said the plane was waiting and Tony needed me. Besides Cliff was in the house and I was afraid he might come out and see Daddy."

"I understand," was all I could say. I was so sorry to put him in that position, but there was nothing I could do about that then.

Roy started talking about Tony and how well he was doing. "I'm helping him mom," he said with great pride.

I told him I waned to see Tony. He told me the best time to go to the hospital was while his father was at work.

"Mom," he said very hesitantly and slowly, looking at the door. I knew what was coming next.

"Can I stay here with Tony for awhile? He needs me." He knew in his little mind how to phrase the question just right.

I hugged him as I said, "Of course you can, if that's what you want to do."

I had talked to Tony's doctors and was told he had made excellent progress. Tony was not as depressed since his brother was with him.

"I'll write every week mom, and I'll call you too. I promise," he said hurriedly, probably not wanting to hurt me.

I smiled at him and ruffled his hair letting him know it was all right. I knew he meant what he said, but I also knew from now on I would be hearing very little if at all. I knew the influence his father would have on him. My heart ached, as I understood I was losing him too.

"I will miss you so much honey, but I understand why you want to stay. My comfort is knowing you're helping your brother," I said with tears in my eyes.

I hugged him goodbye, not knowing how long it would be before I would be able to see him again.

I called my oldest boy, Josh, and told him I was in town, but leaving the next day, and I'd like to see him. He was cool and surprised but agreed to see me. I went over to his house right away knowing his father wasn't there. Our visit was strange. He was stiff as I hugged him. He seemed afraid of me. I realized he must have been told a lot of negative details regarding his mother. Josh's girlfriend was there, and I was able to visit with her when Josh excused himself to answer the phone. She was nice. I liked her immediately. After just a few moments, I said goodbye. I had to hurry to see Tony before it was too late.

As I was getting in my car to leave, Josh ran out of the house and came to the car saying, "Come back again mother."

I was happy to receive this response from him, although I thought his girlfriend told him to say something to me, as he had been so cool. Nevertheless, I was grateful for it. I left crying. I had to be my strongest. I was on my way to see my son who lay crippled in the hospital.

I had kept in touch with the hospital from time to time with various doctors to have a sense of progress over the year. Tony had been through so many operations to repair the damage that happened. It was a miracle he had lived through the tragedy. Not only was his body broken, he had a fractured skull and severed spinal cord, leaving him paralyzed from the chest down. Tony could use his arms, but not his fingers. I was informed that even though Tony was told he would never walk again, he was determined to do so and had much fight in him. I felt reminded of how he was when he was a baby and young toddler. Tony never complained. The doctors always marveled at how he never cried when given a shot. He was such a good baby, and my pride and joy. I was worried about him more than his brothers because Tony never did let me know something was bothering him physically. He was the quietest of my children and the best behaved. Now, I wondered how much he was really suffering and keeping it to himself. I was told he would not speak of me and avoided any questions regarding me. I had called him, but he would not speak to me. In my heart I felt it was because of his father, and also perhaps he was still angry with me for leaving his father and for me leaving him home. He took the divorce so hard. I was glad to hear not only had he been undergoing physical therapy but also psychotherapy as well. I was so concerned as to his emotional well being in addition to his physical condition. I felt helpless in so far as his physical condition, but I felt perhaps I might be able to help him emotionally as no one knew his feelings. I had to tell him how much he meant to me, and how much I loved him.

I prayed my visit would not upset him and that I was doing the right thing. My mother's instincts now said now to take that chance. I couldn't believe he no longer loved me after all the years we spent together as mother and son. They had been happy years. I prayed that he would remember.

Because of my personal experience with my own parents and their divorce, it helped me understand a little better the position my children were in. I believe that feelings of children of divorced parents have to be loyal to whichever parent has them at the time, to prevent losing them or their love. They don't feel free to express themselves about how they really feel. I don't say this applies to all cases but I do feel this applied to me and to my children. I knew within my heart, even if they did love and miss me, they would not feel free to say so. I felt many times Roy did not feel free to say he missed his father, if he did. This is truly a sad thing and it shouldn't be this way. It's not fair to the children, but many divorced parents are not aware of their children's feelings.

Something happened earlier that was to prepare me for seeing my son, and I knew I wouldn't be horrified to see him in his disabled condition. I could never reject him no matter how serious his impairments. He was my child and I could never love him any less no matter what happened.

I had just gotten through a session with Arielle, and was waiting outside the hospital for a bus. I wanted to do some shopping. I noticed several attendants helping a young man in a wheelchair, when suddenly it occurred to me he looked like Tony. I can't explain the excitement I felt. I was perhaps 50 to 100 yards away. I ran closer, letting the bus pass me by, to get a better look. The nurses were helping him adjust himself in the wheelchair to enter a van. I looked at the van. It had the rehabilitation center's name on it where Tony was staying. I ran closer, my heart beating loudly, to get a better look. The boy was smiling at something the nurses said. He was taller than Tony and thinner. Then I reminded myself that it had been a long time since I had seen him. I ran behind a car trying to hide myself and hoping to get closer. The boy smiled again. It was Tony! I recognized the dimpling of his cheek. I was filled with great joy. I had the impulse to run to him. I was so happy to see him. I caught myself and stopped.

It seemed I heard a voice deep inside me saying, No, you can't, you will scare him. He hasn't seen you in over two years. Think of Tony. I stopped and stayed behind the car watching them help my son into the van, not caring if anyone noticed me. I watched until I saw the van pull away with Tony inside. I ran back into the hospital, past all the patients, doctors and nurses seeing no one. I burst into Arielle's office thankful she had no patients.

"I saw Tony. I saw Tony." I was laughing and crying. Dr. "D" heard the commotion and came out of his office into Arielle's.

"Look at you," he bellowed. That's exactly why your son most probably doesn't want to see you. Look how you are acting. Do you think he could handle this?"

"No, Dr. "D", you don't understand. I didn't let him see me. I could have, but I didn't. I'm crying because I'm happy I saw him," I said through my tears.

He then patted me on the shoulder gently and left so Arielle and I could be alone. I sat down in the chair and cried and cried.

It felt good to cry to let it out. Arielle didn't say anything. She let me have my time. When I finished crying, I looked at her and said, "Arielle, I was so happy to see him. I hated to see him in that condition, but being near him overcame anything else. I have missed him so."

"What are you going to do now?" she asked. I composed myself, outwardly appearing very strong.

"I was proud of myself for letting my own better judgment take charge and not my emotions when I saw Tony outside. I'm going shopping and in a few days, I'm going to see him," I said, feeling very strong. She smiled as I got up to leave.

The day arrived and I was going to see my son. I called the hospital and said, "This is Tony's mother. I am in town and I want to see him. I know you have been told to notify his father should I try to see him, but think of how it would make Tony feel to have his father stand in the way for just trying to visit with me. I have a right to see him as his mother." It all came out at one time. I don't know where I received all the newfound courage, but I welcomed it.

The social worker on the other end of the line responded, "Don't worry Mrs. Knight. We will not call Tony's father. I think it would be good for Tony to see you." I was so happy I was having their cooperation because I didn't know what to expect.

I was very nervous as I walked down the sidewalk to the hospital. When I approached the door, a woman spoke to me. She seemed to know who I was and introduced herself as Tony's caseworker.

"I'll show you to Tony's room," she said.

"Does he know I'm coming"?

"Yes, I told him, but he didn't believe me. "What did he say," I asked nervously. He just said, "She will not come here."

We approached Tony's room and the caseworker said, "Tony, there's someone here to see you.

I looked around the door inside and the bed was propped up a little. Tony smiled, I felt the tears start to sting my eyes but held them back as I walked over to him. I tried to be light, as I wanted to make him feel comfortable.

"Honey, it is so good to see you. You just don't know how good." I'm sure my happiness showed through as I said this to him.

He was still smiling. That was positive. Then he looked more serious.

"Mommy, you didn't come to see me when I had my accident." There, it was, the ultimate question. Why wasn't I there? Of course, he wanted to know. I couldn't tell him his father prevented me. All I could say was, Oh, Tony honey. If I had only known you wanted me to be there, I would have been. I do know how you felt and I didn't want to upset you. You were angry with me, remember?" He smiled and nodded yes. I didn't want him to be uncomfortable. I said, "I understood your anger and I'm sorry I hurt you, Tony. I know you were upset over the divorce but just because I didn't love your daddy anymore, didn't mean I stopped loving you."

It was so hard to talk. It was so important for him to understand that I loved him.

"I've been in touch with all the doctors and nurses to see how you're doing. I call often," I told him.

How could he know what agony I had been through. Would he ever really forgive me for not being there? I could never tell him what part his father played in keeping me away, by threatening me with a restraining order and jail to get Roy from me. How does a mother choose between two sons? It is impossible. Tony didn't know my predicament. It was true, if I had known he wanted to see me, somehow I would have tried to sneak in, but my mother, sister, aunt and Ronald were there. I felt I was in enemy camp. Not one of them called me. Not one family member called to see how I was doing.

My thoughts came back to Tony. I can't be thinking this now. He must not know. He looked at me with those dark brooding eyes of his and said, "You look the same."

I let out a little laugh and said, "so do you," without thinking. Immediately he looked down his thin, crippled body, with a look of puzzlement on his face and kind of a smile. I remember what Dr. D" had told me just a few days before that many times someone in Tony's condition feels extremely self-conscious, and they may not want someone they love to see them in their condition for fear of being rejected. I wondered if this was what he was thinking. I wanted to let him know somehow that I did not love him less because of his condition.

I quickly said to him, "Well, you are much taller and skinnier, and you're staring to grow a beard."

I spoke lightly as I touched his beard with my finger. He laughed a little. I was glad the moment of uncertainty passed. How I wanted to gather him up in my arms and hold him as I did when he was just a baby, but I knew I could not do this. He was a young man now and wanted to be treated as such.

"Tony you are so special to me and you always have been. I miss you so much."

I thought I should keep it lighter although I wanted him to know how very much he meant to me. I told him that I had seem him the other day outside the hospital and that I found it best not to just run up to him unexpectedly. He seemed surprised and wanted to know all about it. I told him how I felt when I realized it was him and how very happy I was to see him after all this time. He didn't say anything.

After a while when I could see he was getting a little uncomfortable, I felt it was time for me to leave. I got up and kissed him on the forehead, telling him I had to go, but I would continue to call about him and would like to talk to him from time to time if he wanted to talk to me. He started shivering. He told me he was cold. I felt tears stinging my eyes again and turned my head a little so he wouldn't notice. I felt such pain that I had to leave him in this condition. I told him I would tell the nurse on my way out and that I would call him soon. I couldn't say goodbye. I hurried from the room feeling myself fill with a great sadness and so many more emotions that I cannot even describe. I went to the nurses' station to tell them my son needed a blanket. I wanted so much to take it to him and cover him as I did so many times in the past when he was just a child. I didn't trust myself to go back. I was afraid I would break down. The pain had been so great having to leave his room. I felt so helpless. I wanted to help but there was nothing more I could do. Having to leave Tony in that hospital and having to go back out West was one of the hardest things I've ever done in my life.

I called Tony several times after that. He always seemed distant and uncomfortable, then finally the day came that he didn't want to talk to me.

I wasn't really surprised when the nurse came back to the phone and said, "Tony said he didn't want to talk to you, and to tell you it was his decision to live with his father."

The last statement did surprise me. I thought that Tony knew I had accepted that decision a long time ago. I didn't realize he was still living with it. This saddened me.

All I could say was, "Tell Tony I just called to see how he was. It is okay that he didn't talk to me. Please tell I understand and that I love him."

I didn't want him to feel guilty for not talking to me, if he felt he had to say that. I stopped calling Roy also as he sounded so nervous when talking to me. I told him to call me whenever he felt free to. My only consolation is that I was told he seemed happy and was doing very well in school and other activities. I hadn't heard from him in over two years, but I really did understand the situation with his father. I knew the day would come when they would feel free to contact me. I realized their father had a big influence on them and made them feel guilty to have anything to do with me. Until then, I would continue to remember them on special occasions such as birthdays and Christmas. I felt I must have some contact, even if it was one-sided, just to let them know I love them.

I feel very sad in writing my marriage to Cliff did not last. It certainly was not his fault. He was a good husband in every way. It was me. Even with all the help I got at Hospital Medical Center, and throughout the years, I could not be comforted in the loss of my three of my sons. Cliff, Roy and I had joined the Mormon Church and were doing quite well. All three of us were active and I was even speaking in church to others on how important faith was and how Heavenly Father will never forsake us when we need Him.

After Roy was taken, I felt beaten. I can't quite describe it. Cliff didn't know what to do to comfort me. I tried to be strong and keep my faith. I even shared my conversion story with a man at work thinking he would be inspired by it. I didn't know this man well. I just saw him pass by my store from time to time, but I was attracted in a way I didn't understand. He was a small- framed man with intense eyes and he was older than my father. He was a strong man and seemed to have a lot of power, which I can't explain.

He read my story, but it had a more adverse effect on him than I expected. He was attracted to me, and I understood much later, that I was a major challenge to him. Not only was I someone else's wife, but also I was a devoted member of the church to which I belonged. I was a Sunday School teacher. He was ladies man, who always got what he wanted. He got me.

He said to me, "Marry me, you won't have to work anymore. I will take care of everything. You won't even have time to cry or worry about your children."

I felt beaten down. It was as if I was taken over by something I didn't understand. I went to Cliff and asked him for a divorce. Just like that. Can you believe he was so kind? We both were crying. I told him I didn't want anything materially. I didn't deserve it. I left everything behind but my clothes. Cliff didn't fight me over the divorce. Maybe he was tired of everything. We stayed friends until he passed many years later.

This new mystery man in my life did take charge of everything. I mean everything. His name was Al. Al was retired Air Force Officer and was a fighter pilot in WW11. I wanted a father figure. Well, I got one for sure now. The first few weeks he proved how much a man he was even for his age, but after that, he assumed the father figure and I the daughter. He planned everything. He chose everything – even the clothes I wore, what we did and whom I was to be friends with. No one. I was his arm candy, even though I did not know back then what arm candy was. He was very proud of me and liked to show me off. He signed me up at the college for many classes. He chose them all. At the time, I didn't care. He kept me busy and we traveled every weekend. I had everything, but I wasn't happy. It seemed I couldn't please him, no matter how hard I tried. He wasn't abusive, not physically anyway. He did say things that were very hurtful and I took it hard at first. I felt very rejected. I had trusted him and I had hurt a good man over him. I left everything behind.

At first I took it hard and started drinking wine during the day and doing a strange thing. I would get in my sleeping bag. Yes, you heard me right. We camped often with a college group and we belonged to the Sierra Club, so we camped outdoors often. But here I was in broad daylight feeling better if I drank wine when he was at work and get in my sleeping bag. Weird, huh? Of course, he did not know. When he got home, I was all perky and beautiful like he wanted. I knew I was getting in trouble again.

I called Arielle and told her what was going on. I didn't understand why I would do such a thing. She knew. "Veronica you are returning back to the womb, where you felt safe. You need to take control of your life."

Holy cow, I never thought of that. Is that what I was doing? The drinking part worried me and it did her also. I told her something else I started doing I didn't understand. I started stealing. I had the greatest desire to steal. I didn't need to steal. I had money and anything I wanted materially. I would steal pretty under things. I wanted to feel desired and did not. I felt rejected. Somehow, I got satisfaction out of this. Again, I didn't understand it. I spoke to Arielle about it. Again, she helped me. I knew I had to leave and gain some independence and a life. I realized I didn't need a father anymore and I wanted to have my own life and control over it.

I went back to church and got active. Al did not like this and pulled away from me. I suspected he was seeing other women and he was. After two years, I didn't care so much.

I knew I had to leave. I started planning it. I was able to go to the Air Force Base commissary, so I started stocking up on K-rations, and putting them under the bed. I saved for a year. We went backpacking and camping often, so Al didn't think anything of it. When I did leave, I had food for a long time. I sold my expensive jewelry he gave me to pay for my rent for several months. I got a job right away, selling large plants to businesses and private homes. I rode my bike to work everyday, as I did not have a car. I was 40 years old and looked my very best ever. I kept in touch with Arielle during this time as I had over the years. She was a great support to me and helped keep me on track.

It was dear Cliff that helped me move from Al's home the day I left. Later Al apologized and asked me if I would remarry him, but by then I had gained my independence and I didn't trust him anymore. We did stay in touch until his death. He remarried and mellowed in his later years I was told by his widow.

My mother did call me when I was married to Al. It had been 5 years since we had spoken. I was resting one day, and Al came into the room and said, "Veronica, your mother is on the phone, do you want to talk with her?" I was hesitant, but knew I had to talk with her.

I went to the phone and hesitantly said, "Hello."

"Veronica, this Mom. I want to say I'm sorry for the way I treated you. I was wrong and I hope you find it in your heart to forgive me one day."

She sounded so meek and humble. I felt she was sincere. I couldn't say anything at first. I was so stunned. So much had happened. So much damage and pain had been done. This was my children's grandmother. They won't forget how their grandmother had Daddy and them live with her, against Mommy. How does one just wipe it all away with "I'm sorry?" She said she acted out of anger, hurt and confusion.

I reminded myself, she was my mother and I know it wasn't easy for her to call me. I had to give her that. I told her thank you for calling me and I would try to put it in the past. After about a year, she and a friend of hers came out for a visit. It all went well. We didn't talk of the past. Mom's husband Dean, who had moved in after Dad, died a few years before. I am told he became kinder as he got older. I never saw that side of him.

My mother remarried again after Dean died. They were married for a long time until they both passed. I know Mom loved Dad and was devastated when he left, but I also know there was not one more to blame than the other. They were both so young when they married and four children one right after another at a young age. They did try for our sake until they just couldn't anymore.

My sisters and I were with our mother when she passed. It was very tender. My sisters never crossed Mom. I did and paid the price. We all stayed loyal to her and loved her as much as we could. We understood Mom had problems too. We had expectations of what we wanted her to be and she could not be that person. Our mother was more of a sister than a maternal person. I don't think she knew how. It's all ok now. With maturity comes knowledge and understanding. We all try to do the best we can with the knowledge we have at the time. I think Mom tried her best. She just didn't have the maternal instincts.

Our dear father passed with Alzheimer's and strokes at the age of 74. I had the privilege to be with him and care for him not long before he passed. I treasure that time with him. His brother, Uncle Jim, and I went to be with him while his wife went on a trip. Dad could not talk then, but knew I was there with him. When he fell out of the bed, I prayed for help in lifting him and I received it. He was as light as a feather. I felt his guardian angel helped. Maybe mine too.

Dad had become very successful after leaving Mom. He had a good job as an engineer and had started a small company outside the home in the garage when he was with us, but it was still a struggle. Dad was a very positive person and had high ideals and dreams that he made into a reality. Dad was a self-made successful man. I was proud of him and he was proud of all of us. It was obvious whenever we all would visit. He loved to show us around Florida and show us off. He would fly us in his plane to an island just to hve lunch! I know he felt bad for leaving us. He told me so. My stepmother once told me that Dad cried about it after leaving. He missed us. I admire him for never talking against our mother. That is something Dad never did.

I felt I knew my stepmother and had come to love her, always giving her the benefit of the doubt, but as soon as the funeral was over, that was the end of our relationship with her. She just dropped all of us as though we didn't exist. We didn't expect that. She remarried 6 months later. She changed Dad's Will after he got Alzheimer's, and we were left out of it. That is not what Dad wanted. My sisters and I did not care for anything materially, but we were very concerned for my brother as he had worked in Dad's business and that was his livelihood. My brother was left without a job and received nothing. We also felt bad as we had a half-sister who we loved and she only heard what her mother said. This was a big surprise to us, that she dropped us like she did, We loved her and considered her family. You feel like you know someone and really you don't at all. When things happen, you have to remind yourself what is really important. You can't put your faith and trust in human kind, as that is just the problem – they are human and fallible. A great reminder how important to know Heavenly Father never changes. Put your faith and trust in Him only.

Readers, I am now going to "fast-forward" 43 years to the present. When I was on my own after leaving Al, riding my bike and living on K-rations, I met a kind and wonderful man. Can you believe, this time five years younger than me? No more father figures for me!

I went with a friend to a dance and a handsome man came up to me and asked me to dance. I was pleasantly surprised, as I had hid in a corner table not wanting to be seen. I had not dressed up and had no makeup on. I was not trying to attract anyone. When he approached me and asked me to dance, I found I liked him very much as he had a wonderful sense of humor and was making me laugh. I also liked the way he danced. We continued to stay on the dance floor for several dances. I really liked him. After awhile we went to the table to talk. He was suddenly serious about when he could see me again. In a few days, however, he called to say we should wait awhile to see each other again as he didn't understand what was happening. I agreed. Two days later he called saying, it wasn't working and he wanted to see me again. I was thrilled, as I liked him very much too. He was so different from everyone else I knew. He was serious, a planner, solid, humorous and kind. He had graduated from the U.S. Air Force Academy, served in Viet Nam and received a Masters Degree. He was working on his doctorate when he went through a divorce after one year (no children), and he went home to help his mother after his father had a stroke. He went into law enforcement with the government and retired after 30 years.

I want to mention that, my Dad came out for our wedding. Dad liked him very much and this was the first of my weddings that Dad ever attended. Just before going down the isle to say my wedding vows, I looked at the man that held my hand. My Dad! My father was to give me away for the first time.

Dad looked at me tenderly, with those blue eyes of his and said, "Make this one work."

This is the one that counts, Dad." I said. He knew what I meant as he securely put my arm through his to walk down the isle. This was one of the happiest days of my life.

I am happy to say we have been happily married 38 years. I have no doubt Heavenly Father put him in my life for which I am eternally grateful.

Now I would like to give an update on my dear sons.

My oldest, Josh is happily married and is the stepdad to two great teenage stepchildren who are in college. Unfortunately, his wife has serious health problems but Josh has been taking care of her in addition to his job, doing both quite successfully. I am proud of him. I do not hear from Josh often, as he is still pretty much a loner, but when we do talk they are long conversations, very loving and respectful. I wish Josh stayed in touch with family more often, but that is not him. His aunts and cousins don't hear from him much either. Josh lived with my husband and I on two occasions when he was going through a hard time. We are good.

Tony is well known at a major Hospital. I am also so proud of him. Not only did he graduate from college there, he is dedicating his life to helping others in need after traumatic injuries. He practically lives at the hospital I am told by others giving all of his time and energy to others. Tony is still in a wheel chair at the age of 54. His injuries were permanent. He is fiercely independent, as independent as is possible for a person who is paralyzed. He lives alone in an apartment, but has help come in to help him get ready for the day. After Tony is in his wheel chair, he gets a bus to the hospital where he spends the day. I am told the hospital and the patients are his family. Tony doesn't keep in touch with any family at all. I don't understand that except what Dr. "D" told me years ago that a person with a traumatic injury doesn't want to be a burden to their family, so they pull away. His brothers, aunts and cousins do not ever hear from him. If we do go see him, he is polite but quiet. He doesn't share his feelings.

I saw him in the hospital when he was a patient several times, but he was always reserved.

There was one time, however, when no words were spoken, but I knew he was happy to see me. We were alone in the room. He hadn't expected me. It was late at night. He was in critical care. I wasn't buzzed in as someone was coming out, and I just walked in. I just had to see him. I was there visiting my sister who was a patient and was told my son was just down the hall. I could not believe it. It was too good to be true. I prayed for help and courage to see him and I got it. After I walked through the door that someone was coming out, I walked right past the nurses' station like I was invisible, put on a gown to protect Tony and just walked into his room. He looked up and when our eyes met he was my little boy and I was his Mom. It was as though time stood still. Nothing else mattered. There were no words spoken. He gave me a smile. How I had waited for that smile and that look. I knew my being there mattered. The moment didn't last long but it was enough for me and I was grateful.

No one knows how Tony feels, as he doesn't talk to any family. I have learned to accept this and just be proud that he is my son and all the good he is doing. In spite of all his challenges, he gives back to others. Tony has a wonderful caregiver, for whom I am so grateful. She messages me and keeps me posted on his welfare. She is such a blessing to me.

Life has not been good for my youngest, Roy, the one who was kidnapped from me. I took him with me to protect him from any further damage, but he was taken right back into that environment. He always tried to do what was right. He has been loving and sensitive to others' feelings always and it has gotten him into trouble. I was horrified when I was just 15 and learned my boyfriend, the children's father had family members who served time in prison. I understand now what my Dad meant when he said to me before he left that I was too young to go steady and his people were not our kind of people. I did not understand then. My poor children paid the price for my mistake. I chose him to be their father, not understanding what I was doing. I, too, was trying to help someone else better his life. I hope some young women read this and realize there are some things you cannot change in a person.

I hear from Roy every week and we are close. He has suffered much in trying to do the right thing in his marriage and for his children. He did divorce, but is doing well now and intends on remarrying his first wife who he never stopped loving. They have a beautiful 34-year old daughter together and two grandchildren.

The boys' father is still alive. His health has been bad and I hear he is not a happy man. He has a good wife who has stood by him in much difficulty throughout the years, but has recently left him. I had hoped he would have some regrets, but I hear he does not. It's ok though as I don't live with bad feelings. I don't believe he realized the damage he was doing to the children or me. He was thinking and acting out of desperation.

I want to mention something that is really big for me. For 30 years I had nightmares of Ronald finding me and doing me harm. I had that fear for so long and would wake up screaming. I had bad dreams regarding my Mother and sisters also. Arielle helped me throughout the many years with this problem. I no longer have those nightmares and I am so grateful.

My family was one of my life's biggest challenges. I now know they, too, were going through their own problems, and could not or did not, understand what I was going through. I needed them and they could not be there for me, as my mother would not have approved. This made it hard for them. They could not choose. I have been fiercely loyal to those I love, but others cannot always do that, or are not allowed to. I could never understand this until now. I expected people to act in the manner I did or would. That hardly ever happened. I felt unloved by my family because I expected them to stand by me. They did not. I didn't know what they were going through. We had no communication then.

It is different now. I have a nice surprise for my readers. Betty who was my enemy for so long is not only my sister, but also my friend. She moved just down the street from me a few years ago. We have gotten to know each other as time has passed, and now she is a gift to me in my life.

I have had to let the past go. Sometimes you cannot get resolve. It's all o.k. The bad feelings are completely gone. Again, God knew exactly what he was doing by having my sisters move close to me.

It is the same with my other sister, Dawn. I know she cares and shows me in her actions and words. We all grow with time. We all have our needs as we are maturing whether right or wrong. I have learned to let that go also with Arielle's help. Dawn and her husband bought a second home not too far from us, and visits a few times a year. We are good.

Arielle kindly reminds me they have not had counseling to open up and express their feelings. It really scared my family when I started expressing how I felt, as no one ever did in my family. We were not ever taught to express our feelings as we had them, and then if we held them in so long, and something triggered us, we would overreact. That is so sad, because no one is listening then. It is vital to express how you feel to your loved ones and keep the lines of communication open. One's perception is their reality.

My dear brother Bob left Dads home and joined the Navy at a young age. He married and had one son. After Dads passing, he didn't have a job, but he had many friends with airplanes. They wanted Bob to fly for them as many did not know how. He was also a great instructor. He stayed very busy until he was recently killed in an airplane crash. He died doing what he loved best, flying. Throughout all the years we stayed in touch often and stayed close. Bob loved family. He is missed terribly but we know we'll see him again, and that is comforting.

Since starting this manuscript many years ago, I am much older and have started having serious health issues. I had kidney failure and I now go to dialysis three times a week for four hours each day and recently was diagnosed with lung cancer. Neuropathy is taking over my body. I have accepted this and I keep trying. I believe I have lived a full life. After all, I will be eighty this year. I am grateful to have lived this long and to finally get this book out. I know without a doubt, I had help from above.

A Bridge to the Mainland

At the time Dr. "D" told me to reach for the mainland, it was enough for me. It was a direction. It was many years later before I fully realized where the mainland was. *It was within myself.* I have now found that peace and contentment that I searched for, for so many years. I always thought I would receive it from other individuals, love, security, acceptance, approval, happiness and so forth. I didn't realize that I had to first give it to myself. I had to accept myself with understanding and patience and love. I had to realize that I was worth something and have respect for myself as a person who cannot be perfect as I always thought I had to be. Without realizing the above, it was impossible for me to be content. Once I realized these things, I knew I was worthy of others' love and I could feel more secure in it. I found out that it was most important to have one's self-approval.

Life is experiencing all kinds of emotions. Happiness is not always there. It comes and goes. Contentment is important. Sadness is something we all have to experience and depression too. What's important is to know how to deal with emotions and to understand them. I work with myself every day and do not take anything for granted. I realize "I" was a lot of my problems. I was truly messed up. My hope is by sharing my story with all of you that perhaps you can find yourself within these pages and maybe get some answers to some of your life's questions. I truly believe it was no accident that I went to the hospital so long ago. I feel it was a gift from Heavenly Father to help me better my life and most importantly to share with others to help them in their life. I was so fortunate to receive this help and I truly want to share with all of you the good, the bad and the ugly letting everything be known in an effort that you can apply it in a positive way in your life.

I wrote this book 43 years ago, when everything was fresh in my mind. The doctors at the hospital suggested I write this and share it with others. I did, but it sat on the shelf all these years collecting dust because I didn't have a good ending. I knew the time would come when it was meant for me to take it off the shelf, blow off the dust and finish it. The time is now with the opioid crisis. I lived it, I conquered it, and I need to share it.

I am no longer that fragile tree on the edge of the high cliff, afraid of falling off, as I was 45 years ago. I picked up my roots, swam across the river and into the mountains to a new life and a new me. The change was scary and the swim was long and tiring. There, were times I thought that the current would pull me away and the riptides would pull me under, but I kept stroking.

Yes, Dr. "D" I am finally at that place of which you spoke to me so many years ago. *I have reached the mainland.*

www.ingramcontent.com/pod-product-compliance
Lightning Source LLC
Chambersburg PA
CBHW030316100526
44592CB00010B/452